*Cultural Memory*
*in*
*the*
*Present*

*Mieke Bal and Hent de Vries, Editors*

# THE AESTHETIC PATHS
# OF PHILOSOPHY

*Presentation in Kant, Heidegger, Lacoue-Labarthe,*
*and Nancy*

Alison Ross

STANFORD UNIVERSITY PRESS

STANFORD, CALIFORNIA

2007

Stanford University Press
Stanford, California

Printed in the United States of America on acid-free, archival-quality paper

Library of Congress Cataloging-in-Publication Data

Ross, Alison
      The aesthetic paths of philosophy : presentation in Kant, Heidegger,
   Lacoue-Labarthe, and Nancy / Alison Ross.
            p. cm.—(Cultural memory in the present)
      Includes bibliographical references and index.
      ISBN-13: 978-0-8047-5487-3 (cloth : alk. paper)
      ISBN-13: 978-0-8047-5488-0 (pbk : alk. paper)
      1. Aesthetics.   I.  Title.
BH39.R672 2007
111'.85—dc22                                                              2006028408

Typeset by Westchester Book Group in 11/13.5 Garamond

*Dedicated to the memory of my mother, Helen M. Ross*

# Contents

Acknowledgments     xi

Abbreviations     xiii

Introduction: The Aesthetic Paths of Philosophy     1

1. The Formulation of the Problem of Presentation
   in Kant's Doctrine of Taste     15

2. Pragmatic Anthropology in the Third *Critique*'s Project
   of Aesthetic Presentation     38

3. Heidegger's Reading of Kant and His Historicisation
   of Relations of Presentation     61

4. 'Technology' and 'Art' as Relations of Presentation
   in Heidegger's Thought     90

5. Lacoue-Labarthe: Aesthetic Presentation and the
   Figuring of the Political     109

6. Nancy: Touching the Limits of Presentation     134

Conclusion: The Path of Presentation     165

Notes     169

Bibliography     217

Index     227

# Acknowledgments

The Arts Faculty at Monash University generously provided a grant to aid in the final preparation of this manuscript. Jeff Davies provided efficient and reliable bibliographic assistance. Amir Ahmadi compiled the index.

An earlier version of Chapter 4 appeared as 'The Work of the Art-Work: Art After Heidegger's "Origin of the Work of Art"' in the *Journal of the British Society for Phenomenology* 37, no. 2, May 2006. I would like to thank Dr. Ullrich Haase for his permission to use this material here. Krzysztof Ziarek kindly invited me to participate in a panel on 'Heidegger's Materialities' held as part of the annual IAPL conference at Syracuse University, USA, in May 2004. This panel was the first opportunity I had to present the reading of Heidegger defended in this book.

My greatest debt is to Amir Ahmadi. His comments on an earlier version of this project helped me to sharpen and refine the position that I argue for here.

# Abbreviations

WORKS BY IMMANUEL KANT

CJ     *Critique of Judgment,* trans. Werner S. Pluhar (Indianapolis: Hackett, 1987).

CPrR     *Critique of Practical Reason,* 3rd ed., trans. Lewis White Beck (New York: Macmillan, 1993).

IUH     'Idea for a Universal History with a Cosmopolitan Intent,' in *Perpetual Peace and Other Essays on Politics, History and Morals,* trans. Ted Humphrey (Indianapolis: Hackett, 1983), 291–41.

WORKS BY MARTIN HEIDEGGER

AWP     'The Age of the World Picture' in *The Question Concerning Technology and Other Essays,* trans. W. Lovitt (New York: Harper and Row, 1977), 115–55.

FCM     *The Fundamental Concepts of Metaphysics: World, Finitude, Solitude,* trans. W. McNeill and N. Walker (Bloomington and Indianapolis: Indiana University Press, 1995).

IM     *An Introduction to Metaphysics,* trans. R. Manheim (New Haven: Yale University Press, 1959).

KB     *Kant and the Problem of Metaphysics,* trans. Richard Taft (Bloomington and Indianapolis: Indiana University Press, 1997).

OT&B     *On Time and Being,* trans. J. Stambaugh (New York: Harper and Row, 1972).

OWA     'The Origin of the Work of Art' in *Poetry, Language, Thought,* trans. A. Hofstadter (New York: Harper and Row, 1971), 17–78.

PI     'The Principle of Identity' in *Identity and Difference,* trans. J. Stambaugh (New York: Harper and Row, 1969).

QCT 'The Question Concerning Technology' in *The Question Concerning Technology and Other Essays,* trans. W. Lovitt (New York: Harper and Row, 1977), 3–35.

SB *Schelling's Treatise on the Essence of Human Freedom,* trans. J. Stambaugh (Athens: Ohio University Press, 1985).

WIT *What Is Called Thinking?,* trans. J. Glenn Gray (New York: Harper and Row, 1968).

WORKS BY PHILIPPE LACOUE-LABARTHE

PEX *Poetry as Experience,* trans. Andrea Tarnowski (Stanford, CA: Stanford University Press, 1999).

TYP 'Typography,' in *Typography: Mimesis, Philosophy, Politics,* ed. Christopher Fynsk (Stanford, CA: Stanford University Press, 1998), 43–139.

WORKS BY JEAN-LUC NANCY

BSP 'Of Being Singular Plural,' in *Being Singular Plural,* trans. Robert D. Richardson and Anne E. O'Byrne (Stanford, CA: Stanford University Press, 2000), 1–101.

EF *The Experience of Freedom,* trans. Bridget McDonald (Stanford, CA: Stanford University Press, 1993).

G *The Gravity of Thought,* trans. François Raffoul and Gregory Recco (Atlantic Highlands, NJ: Humanities Press, 1997).

SW *Sense of the World,* trans. Jeffrey S. Librett (Minneapolis: University of Minnesota Press, 1997).

TM *The Muses,* trans. Peggy Kamuf (Stanford, CA: Stanford University Press, 1996).

WORKS BY PHILIPPE LACOUE-LABARTHE AND JEAN-LUC NANCY

LA *The Literary Absolute: The Theory of Literature in German Romanticism,* trans. Phillip Barnard and Cheryl Lester (Albany: State University of New York Press, 1988).

THE AESTHETIC PATHS OF PHILOSOPHY

# Introduction: The Aesthetic Paths
# of Philosophy

Reading Heidegger, Lacoue-Labarthe, or Nancy with a view to understanding what it is that drives or structures their thought, one is struck by the fact that their writing steers philosophy in an aesthetic direction. In each of these thinkers one can find the aesthetic attitude that one also finds in Kant's third *Critique*. This aesthetic attitude, which in Kant is determined by the exigency of his search for a satisfactory mode of relation between the forms of material nature and human freedom, becomes the framework that these thinkers rely on in order to philosophise. In this regard, we can cite the aesthetic use which is made of language to phrase philosophical problems, such as Heidegger's understanding of language as a 'showing' in his attempt to articulate the experience of being in his late writing; or the way that in Lacoue-Labarthe's writing the kind of intelligibility that one finds in aesthetic experience is given a foundational status as a resource for the definition of philosophical concepts; or Nancy's use of terms like 'art' and 'artwork,' in the manner that they are defined and developed in the context of the topic of aesthetic reflection, in order to forge a vocabulary able to capture the general features of the genesis of sense and meaning and thus to deal with fundamental ontological questions.

The main point I want to make in this study is that this aesthetic steering of philosophy is best understood as an adaptation of the specific and technical employment of the notion of 'presentation' [*Darstellung*] in Kant's *Critique of Judgment*.[1] In Kant 'presentation' is the name he gives to the problem of how to define a mode of relation able to reconcile human freedom with the constraints of materiality. The exigency of this relation follows from the need of finite beings to render in aesthetic or sensible forms what would otherwise be impotent, errant ideas. If we step back for a moment from the specifications Kant gives to this notion and define its scope in more general or schematic terms, we could say that it outlines the terms of a problem that philosophers have been concerned with since the Greeks.

As a heuristic exercise we can classify the different versions of the schema of presentation in philosophy in terms of the mode and exigency of the relation it shapes in different fields and epochs of philosophical thought. In his commentary on Plato's *eidos* in the essay 'Plato's Doctrine of Truth,' Heidegger writes:

the things that are visible in the daylight outside the cave, where sight is free to look at everything, are a concrete illustration of the 'ideas.' According to Plato, if people did not have these 'ideas' in view, that is to say, the respective 'appearance' of things—living beings, humans, numbers, gods—they would never be able to perceive this or that as a house, as a tree, as a god. Usually they think they see this house and that tree directly, and the same with every being. Generally they never suspect that it is always and only in the light of the 'ideas' that they see everything that passes so easily and familiarly for the 'real.' According to Plato, what they presume to be exclusively and properly the real—what they can immediately see, hear, grasp, compute—always remains a mere adumbration of the idea, and consequently a shadow.[2]

In this account Heidegger defines the mode of the relation between 'ideas' and material entities in Plato as visual semblance. The exigency of this relation is answered in Plato by the Idea's 'call' or 'index,' which it carries in itself and by which it demands and refers to its appearance, its 'copy,' in the sensible world. The perceptible presentation is thus justified by the Idea's ontological demand, but at the same time it exhausts that justificatory ground, undermining the claims of art as merely secondary copies. The lesser claims of art can be put in the vocabulary of representation: as they do not respond to the Idea's call, they are also detached from the participatory relation to ideas that perceptible presentations claim.

In Christian theology, the problems that were raised under the topic of Christology, which adopted many of the features of neo-Platonic metaphysics, may also be approached in terms of the notion of presentation.

In each of these traditions, the question was asked: why and how was the intelligible or the divine related to or embodied in the sensible? What was the exigency, what was the mode of this relation? In the case of Christology, the divine takes the form of visual semblance, but this semblance is restricted to the mode of embodiment in human form.[3] Further, the question of the exigency of this relation is taken up in the frame of the history of redemption: it is because human resources are unequal to the task and goal of salvation that the divine is compelled to be presented in the world.

From this schematic outline we can draw out some of the distinctive features of Kant's approach to this topic and also see why it is that 'presentation' is not an active problem in Cartesian thought. Heidegger understands the term 'representation' as it takes shape in modern philosophy with Descartes as the reduction of 'what is' to the terms of its representability as an 'object' by and for a 'subject.'[4] The distinction between presentation [*Darstellung*] and representation [*Vorstellung*] in Kant provides an important perspective on this definition. Kant defines representation in terms of the schematising powers of the subject. This definition places in view the fact that the theme of 'presentation' in the third *Critique* identifies and treats, retrospectively as it were, 'representation' as itself a problem in its inability to provide a comprehensive orientation for the self. To simplify, representation, which we might say is reducible to the subject's formal powers of apperception, contrasts with Kant's definition of 'presentation,' which explicitly suspends the claims of the subject's powers over material forms and inquires instead about the 'favours' that the subject enjoys and that are extended to it by the material forms of nature. In this respect, the reflection on presentation extends to material forms the possibility of a relation to a comprehensive orientation of meaning. Finally, the account of presentation that, in Kant, describes the extension to the subject of nature's 'favours,' and thereby attempts to embed the self in a comprehensive meaning-context, elucidates the different emphasis in his approach to the question of the mode of relation to the intelligible and distinguishes it from the relation of semblance/participation (Plato) and semblance/incarnation (Christology) in ancient and Christian thought. In Kant the mode of relation to ideas is analogical, but the fact that the work that presentation performs is analogical should not obscure the significance of the terms of his approach to this problem and its difference from that of the doctrine of ideal forms in Plato. In Kant what is important is not just that the accent is on the sensibilisation [*Versinnlichung*] rather than the idea, but also that he describes this sensibilisation of ideas as *aesthetic*. The exigency of presentation in Kant is the dependence of finite beings for worldly meaning and in fact worldlihood on aesthetic forms, but he adds to this the claim that the specific field of experience in which this mode of sensibilisation occurs is neither cognitive nor practical, but aesthetic.

I would now like to explain the specific thesis of this work. My thesis is the simple idea that the thinking of Heidegger, Lacoue-Labarthe, and Nancy can (and perhaps in a significant sense must) be understood as ways of addressing the *problem of presentation* as framed by and inherited from Kant's *Critique of Judgment*. To put this thesis somewhat crudely and in terms that will require qualification: these thinkers alter the defining characteristics that Kant's third *Critique* had given to the aesthetic as a specific mode of experience within a typology of different spheres of experience. In their hands the elements of this specific mode of experience are generalised: the aesthetic attitude and the vocabulary used by Kant to describe it are brought to bear on things in general. The impetus for this ontological status is, in each case, a specific understanding of the topic of presentation as it comes from Kant. In these introductory remarks I would like to explain why I think that the alteration to the terms of Kant's conception of the aesthetic in these thinkers is itself based on an understanding of the Kantian problem of presentation, and thus must be assessed in light of this problem.

Let me briefly recall the context of this issue in Kant: the problem of an aesthetic presentation of ideas of reason is the Kantian formulation of the modern philosophy's problematic of dualism. This problem receives a technical solution in Kant's *Critique of Judgment*, in the sense that Kant understands it as a matter of coordination of self-same terms (even if, it is true, one of these is a morally required postulate) and a definite typology of their relations of coordination. In the peculiar metaphysics that structures his final *Critique* Kant needs to find a principle able to mediate the necessity of the natural world and the freedom that defines the domain of practical reason. There are two aspects to the third *Critique* that facilitate this goal: on the side of the subject, Kant expands the conception of the faculty of judgment from its role as a faculty of determination in the first *Critique* to account for its ability to follow the exemplary: those instances which precede the rule governed the procedure that determines objects of cognition. On the side of nature, it is the 'free beauties' of the natural world, what is also described by Kant under the category of 'form' and thereby differentiated from the materiality of sensuous nature, that provide the occasion for such 'reflective' uses of judgment. Here Kant provides a nascent phenomenology where the centrality of a cognitive relation to nature is suspended at the same time that an insight into the subject's powers is won through that suspension. It is precisely nature's independence from human purposes that provides the opportunity to make of it an articulate vehicle for the presentation, by analogy, of reason's ideas. This impulse receives its most extensive treatment in the second part of the *Critique of Judgment:* the 'Critique of Teleological Judgment.' It is here that Kant considers the possibilities for the speculative use of reason when it treats nature under the idea of 'art.' Without the speculative use of the idea of purposive unity—borrowed from art in its broad sense of purposive construction—the cognitive interest in nature would falter. Mechanistic precepts, Kant argues, would be unable to explain how even a blade of grass were possible without the use of a concept of purposiveness (CJ, §75, 282–83). Under the threat of this obstacle to cognition the concept of purposiveness is admitted into the lexicon of theoretical reason although cognitive aims do not prescribe its limits. Rather, the concept of purposiveness is used for a reflection on human ends in nature as well as our status as the ultimate end [*der letzte Zweck*] of nature. The metaphysical claims attached to the progressive realisation of human culture as nature's end in the 'Teleology' has its condition, in the first part of the *Critique,* in the notion of the cultivation needed to train the mind for the reception of the beautiful in the forms of nature. Kant uses these themes to carry out his intention of bridging the gap between ideas of reason and their meaningfulness for a finite being. This problematic can be described as one of 'aesthetic presentation' under which the links between the two parts of his third *Critique* can be gathered together. Kant's *Critique of Judgment* does not simply offer the first formulation of the core problem of aesthetic presentation, but it makes this problem more fundamental than any ontological issue. Indeed one can go further and argue that under the pressure of providing systematic unity for his philosophy, Kant substitutes for traditional metaphysical terms, such as freedom, the existence of God, and the nature of the soul, the technical question of how to provide an orientation and analogous form for these ideas in an aesthetic presentation. In provisional terms it is possible to say that Kant's category of 'form' opens up the possibility for this project in so far as it intensifies the aesthetic field and allows, thereby, singular forms of beauty to model or 'present,' albeit analogically, more than merely sensuous or material representations.

The aesthetic features of experience first described by Kant in the third *Critique* underpin a number of diverse theoretical positions within modern philosophy. In particular, critical thinkers have used the features identified by Kant as elements of the aesthetic field for projects of social criticism. In these thinkers, the type of 'ideal' reference given by Kant's category of form to material representations is turned into a binding claim on one's mode of existence, individual or social. Such an inflection of the Kantian tradition can be found, for instance, in Adorno's conception of the negativity of aesthetic experience, where the critical capacity of art follows from the paradoxical features of its autonomy in the modern epoch. The historical emergence of an art market frees artists from their preautonomous dependence on patronage as it places art within the circuit of economic exchange. In Adorno's writing political interests are annexed to this paradoxically autonomous domain because art as a nonfunctional production engages critically with a society won over to the values of utility.[5] Adorno thus models the view that the material forms of art can exercise a critical effect precisely because he assumes, along with Kant, that such forms carry more than mere material representations. Lyotard's use of the Kantian category of the sublime can also be cited in this regard: the painting of Barnett Newman exercises a critical function because, for Lyotard, its technique of abstraction retreats from the logic of realisable forms that define the operation of 'techno-scientific capital.' In this way it does not just differentiate itself from the latter logic, but does so by singularly rendering the idea of indeterminacy: an idea that makes painting more than its mere material form.[6]

This idea of abundance and unruliness through indeterminacy is also common in theoretical discussions of the essence of modern literature. In these discussions the view that the indeterminacy of meaning carries critical effects is treated as a topic for critical reflection, but the structure that attributes an ideal reference to material representations remains intact. For Derrida, the indeterminacy of literary meaning corrodes its critical function: at once the literary is critical on account of its excess to a single meaning or purpose, but this very excess also hollows out its critical capacity precisely because this excess is only 'fiction.'[7] The logical consequence of this ambiguity is prominent in the writing of Böhrer. Böhrer is sceptical of the ability of art to contribute to historical utopian projects, but he still hopes to save a place for literary avant-gardism. In effect, satisfaction is to be had in literary moments, but these moments, which are unable to sustain a critical posture beyond the moment, also model in their quality of 'suddenness' a departure from the quotidian that cannot be had elsewhere.[8]

The major political ideas of modern philosophy also keep in play these aesthetic features of experience first described by Kant. The central theme of Schiller's early use of Kantian aesthetics for the nineteenth-century anthropological project of an 'aesthetic education' of 'man,' the promise that aesthetic experience could mould political institutions or behaviours, remains strong in contemporary thought. Marxist and post-Marxist theory depend on the aesthetic dimension of experience in order to discharge the function of criticism as well as to model an alternative anthropology and the social arrangements that could support it. This is the case with Marx, who, in the words of Jauss, 'evidently interprets the practical creation of an objective world according to the paradigm of the production of works of art.'[9] Further, Marx's criticism of division of labor and specialisation of productive roles is based on an aesthetic conception of personality.[10] Even in Habermas, who is otherwise scrupulous in following Kant's intended separation of spheres, there is evidence that the aesthetic still claims, as it does in Kant, a function in excess of its field: against the 'culture without thorns' easily 'absorbed by mere needs for compensation' '[a]nother kind of transcendence is preserved in the unfulfilled promise disclosed by the critical appropriation of identity-forming religious traditions, and *still another* in the negativity of modern art.' The exceptional place of religious traditions and modern art follows from their capacity to open up 'the trivial and everyday . . . to the shock of what is absolutely strange, cryptic, or uncanny. Though these no longer provide a cover for privileges, they refuse to be assimilated by pregiven categories.'[11] Like Böhrer, even though and precisely because its promise is unfulfilled, for Habermas modern art still has an exceptional position since it offers satisfactions and a power of critique beyond the register of bare material needs.

I do not mention these recent uses of the features of Kant's approach to the question of presentation, in which aesthetic experience is credited with critical capacity, in order to document the breadth of the relationship

between Kant's question and subsequent philosophy, and still less to re-
hearse once more the well-known influential status of the third *Critique* in
post-Kantian philosophy. Rather, I would like to mark out the crucial difference between these cases of influence and those figures of twentieth-century
thought for whom Kant's question in this *Critique* becomes the core problem for philosophical thinking. In Heidegger, Lacoue-Labarthe, and Nancy,
the assumptions in play in the critical-theoretical uses of the aesthetic are in
the foreground and, on occasion, subjected to scrutiny just because aesthetic
forms and their supposed critical capacity are considered in the context of a
thoroughgoing questioning of the topic of presentation.

Heidegger is a thinker of particular significance for this project. Not
only can his own thought be read in terms of this problem of presentation
(the problem of how to present the relation between human being and being will be read in this study as the problem of thinking, as such in Heidegger), but the itinerary of his path of thinking, I will argue, is determined
by his reading of Kant and his view that Kant retreats from the consequences of the problem of presentation. Kant occupies a singular position
in Heidegger's analysis of modern philosophy on account of the way he
formulates the problem of presentation. In Descartes, and the rationalists
who followed him, including Spinoza, the question of presentation as a
relation of thought and matter is raised downstream from the problem of
defining these elements in their essence and is resolved theologically. German Idealism, generally speaking, tries to resolve this problem by pressing
the presentative relation from a limited, say, analogical relation in the direction of perfect embodiment. This is especially true of the so-called Jena
Romantics. Heidegger criticises German Idealism and Romanticism for
suppressing the problem of presentation entirely in the interest of the
representation of the theologically inspired 'absolute.' But Heidegger is
also critical of Kant, who, with his faith in reason, suppresses the difficult
consequences of this problem and retreats from his insight in the A version
of the first *Critique* into the primacy of the presentation over the terms it
'presents.' In Heidegger's thought, presentation is taken to precede the
problem of the representation of the 'absolute,' which is itself corroded by
the concomitant historicisation of the relations of presentation. Thus, in
Heidegger, the problem of presentation becomes the focus of thinking, as
he defined it in his later work: namely, a reflection on the epochal relations
under which things appear as such. In this respect Heidegger sets the frame

for the conception of presentation in Nancy and other post-Heideggerian thinkers who consider the question of presentation the proper task of critical thought. Nancy and Lacoue-Labarthe reposition traditional political and philosophical themes as matters of presentation. The technical approach taken by Kant thus gives way to a questioning of the stakes of the core metaphysical question of his philosophy: rather than relating the independently defined terms of sensible nature and the idea of freedom in, say, an analogous sensible presentation able to give form to an otherwise empty idea, relations of presentation are conceived of historically, and these relations become the object of critical reflection.

Heidegger, along with the prominent writers of French deconstruction, sustains and extends the Kantian formulation of presentation qua a problem as the matter for thinking. On this basis alone, this thinking may be differentiated from other traditions of thought which one way or another approach this topic not just from the perspective of a burden to be removed but in terms of the absolute that grounds historical relations and precedes and sculpts any sensible presentation. In Heidegger and French deconstruction what breaks down, more generally, is the coherence of the dualism of ideas and sensible form, or of meaning and sensuous matter.[12]

In Lacoue-Labarthe and Nancy the topic of presentation retains the status it has in Heidegger as the core problem for thinking. Nonetheless, in contrast to Heidegger, these thinkers recall that Kant's approach to this problem was developed in the context of his aesthetics. In their return to the original thematics of this problem, each of these French thinkers directs the question of presentation in such a way that literature and the arts become the privileged ground for a critique of philosophical concepts and styles. At the same time as this topic can provide a shared lineage for their work, it acts as a fault-line by which the substantial differences between these thinkers may be marked. In other words, the critique of Heidegger's destinal thinking and the dependence of this on a quasi-transcendent meaning supports in each case a distinctive project. Lacoue-Labarthe's work is focussed on the topic of the mimetic sources of identity, and the prominent themes in his work are the literary, theatrical, and musical devices that render identity as the secondary product of a primary technique. In his work the topic of presentation becomes a reflection on the primacy of the literary and rhetorical dimensions of thinking such that ideas owe their power to convince or make sense to their literary formation. The nineteenth-century approach to anthropology, still current today, is thus criticised by Lacoue-Labarthe, who tries to show that 'man' is the product of, rather than the term behind, 'literary' forms of presentation.

Nancy, while sharing the emphasis in Lacoue-Labarthe's work on the arts and the themes that arise from philosophical aesthetics as the privileged context for the posing of the problem of presentation, develops an ontology that gives an operational force to Heidegger's conception of artwork. 'Art' is used in Lacoue-Labarthe's writing to convey the plastic sense of a formation that is without any originating model or idea; his work tries to chart the effects of this primary plasticity of expressive form in poetry and philosophy. In contrast, Nancy's ontological project identifies in the arts the occasion of a 'presentation' of meaning. It is in the arts, Nancy believes, that this presentation is staged because it is here that the genesis of meaning as a 'coming-to-presence' rather than as a relation to a 'present thing' is presented. For Nancy rigorous attention to the question of presentation makes it necessary to think the world of sense and appearance without any prior point of orientation. Hence the significance of art as that which shows sense in the process of *emerging* from the senses. It is this showing of sense as emerging from the senses and thus as a process rather than a stable form that Nancy believes is the forgotten dimension of sense and meaning. This dimension of sense, he contends, is addressed in a singular way in art's presentation *of* presentation. The view that the arts phrase the general question of sense in a genetic way distinguishes Nancy's project from Lacoue-Labarthe's deconstructive approach to the figural forms that first sculpt and present the identity of the human as a 'type.'[13] Nancy argues that Lacoue-Labarthe's critique of figural forms seems to suggest a 'beyond' to figuration. In contrast, Nancy's approach to the topic of presentation as it is raised in the arts holds to the 'exigency' of figuration as the very point at which presentation can be raised and sustained as a question.[14]

The fact that the topic of presentation is sustained in a prominent way in some of the most significant strains of contemporary European thought raised, for me, a number of questions that the existing literature on the influence and internal form of Kant's third *Critique* did not address. Despite the enormous interest in the category of the aesthetic as the distinctive frame for important themes in modern political philosophy as well as movements such as hermeneutics, deconstruction, and phenomenology, this interest is seldom connected to the project of presentation in Kant's work or, when it is, to the substantial amendments made to this project in recent European philosophy. This connection is important because the understanding of the artwork or the aesthetic domain as 'an exception' to instrumental or cognitive paradigms is itself historically based on a particular understanding of the question of (aesthetic) presentation in post-Kantian German Idealism and Romanticism.

This gap in the literature seemed to me in the process of writing this book to be intimately connected to another: studies on Heidegger and French deconstruction tended to assume that Kant was a mainly negative figure in the itinerary of their concerns. Despite the fact that it has become something of a commonplace to mention the points of connection between Heidegger and French deconstruction, the precise terms of this relationship remained either vague or phrased in terms internal to the French tradition. It was, then, partly my curiosity about how this relationship might be explained by way of an operative use of concepts from the philosophical tradition that motivated this project. In turn, it was my dissatisfaction with the conclusions reached by those approaches from the 'history of ideas' that viewed Kant through the lens of the 'resolution' of the critical system in German Idealism, or considered the category of the aesthetic in isolation from the project of presentation which, in Kant, shapes it, that led me to question more closely the precise terms of the relation between the core metaphysical problem of Kantian thought and the central concerns of some of the major figures of contemporary thought.

This book argues for the general claim that the Kantian topic of presentation is an enduring topic within contemporary European thought. Beyond this general point I hope to show how attention to this topic can place the work of some of the significant figures of recent European philosophy and some of the problems treated in their work in a new light. Accounting for the impact on Heidegger and some of the prominent figures of recent French thought of the chief problem of Kant's *Critique of Judgment* allows us to supplement the Nietzschean frame in which these figures are generally considered. The perspective adopted, then, frees a space for us to question the complex role of Kant and the pivotal position of his conception of aesthetic presentation within twentieth- and twenty-first-century post-aesthetic thought.

In particular, the analysis of the contemporary inflection of the originally Kantian question of presentation will, I hope, help to illuminate the motive force that structures and guides these authors' reflections on diverse topics, such as the significance of aesthetics in modern Western philosophy, as well as important contemporary political themes, including technology, capital, and the problem of social criticism. At the same time, I want to elucidate the more fundamental philosophical trajectory that brings art to the position of exception from which it claims a uniquely potent critical voice in recent European philosophy. Although this position is the heritage of the Romantic and Idealist reinterpretations of Kantian thought, which the authors treated in this study revise, nonetheless in each, the use of the defining elements of Kant's conception of aesthetic presentation maintains 'art' in a position of unique significance.

My argument proceeds in three parts. The first part examines the stakes of the problem of presentation for the aspiration to system of the Kantian philosophy. The two chapters of this part focus, respectively, on the two parts of Kant's *Critique of Judgment*. My analysis of the 'Critique of Aesthetic Judgment' focuses on the different types of presentative relation outlined in this part of the *Critique* by Kant. I argue that Kant's approach to the problem of presentation finally falters because his inquiry into aesthetic presentation is subordinated to what may be called a doctrine of anthropological reason. In the case of the 'Critique of Teleological Judgment' this doctrine takes the form of a melding of nature itself into the project of the presentation of 'man's' final ends [*Endzweck*] as nature's ultimate end [*der letzte Zweck*]. Kant's *Critique* undoes its aim of presenting moral subjectivity by casting this subjectivity in the form of an aesthetic object.

The second part presses for a reconsideration of Heidegger's thinking in terms of the question of presentation. Here I argue that this question is far more than a theme. It is in fact the reflective impulse that drives and structures Heidegger's thinking. This discussion falls into two chapters: first, I interpret Heidegger's 'turn' as a consequence of his discovery of presentation as a core philosophical problem in Kant's critical philosophy; second, I examine the consequences of this reading of Heidegger's 'path of thinking' as a reflection on relations of presentation for his conception, respectively, of the artwork and technology. Despite Heidegger's own use of the artwork as a contrastive value to illuminate technological relations,

I argue that such a contrast is not licensed in his thinking and that it is the status of the problem of presentation in his thought that shows this to be the case. Indeed, rigorously pursued, the question of presentation opens up the distinction between Heidegger's use of Kant's conception of disinterest for his own understanding of truth as a 'letting-be' and the historical approach to the question of being in which precisely this understanding of truth is itself no longer able to sustain a contrast with calculative relations.

This issue of the contrast between the artwork and technology in Heidegger sets up the terms for my treatment of the topic of presentation in Lacoue-Labarthe and Nancy in the third and final section. In Chapter 5, my discussion of Lacoue-Labarthe interprets the topic of presentation as the general orientation for his critique of philosophy in literary and artistic terms and examines how this topic influences his famous critique of Heidegger's thought as an 'originary mimesis' that commits him, among other things, to his notorious engagement with National Socialism. The chief consequence of Heidegger's inadequate analysis of the topic of presentation is, for Lacoue-Labarthe, his implicit conception of the political as the project for the founding of an identity able to precede and guide its 'presentation.' In Lacoue-Labarthe's writing, the task of analysing 'presentation' opens up the issue of the political not as an 'aesthetic' question, but as a question disclosed by reflecting on literary and artistic techniques and practices.

Next, and following once again the thread of Heidegger's influence on the contemporary interpretation of the question of presentation, Chapter 6 shows how Nancy's ontology can be understood as a radicalisation of Heidegger's core theses on the artwork. Although Nancy's thought is generally described as a reworking of the category of *Mitsein* in Heidegger's *Being and Time*, Nancy, I argue, uses the staging of presentation as a question in Heidegger's artwork essay as a type of genetic accounting for the general ontology his thinking describes. However, unlike the substantial ambiguity on the critical potential of art cultivated in Heidegger's late work, Nancy's view that sense is not given but a 'praxis' tries to twist free of the metaphysical dualism that gives the arts a place exceptional to the prevailing schematisation of experience in the contemporary conditions of techno-capital. In this respect, the rethinking of presentation in Nancy's thought, even despite its aesthetic orientation, offers the first outlines of a critique of the doctrine of art's exceptionalism that Heidegger's rethinking of the topic of aesthetic presentation had hinted at but failed to deliver.

# 1

## The Formulation of the Problem of Presentation in Kant's Doctrine of Taste

In Kant's *Critique of Judgment* there are two different intellectual patterns of treatment of topics associated with aesthetic presentation. The first operates through a type of structural dislocation. Here the detachment of aesthetic judgment from practical and cognitive fields gives it a special connection to ideas. This pattern of structural dislocation is distinguished by the fact that through it a path is opened for material things to be seen to have a capacity to present ideas otherwise not accessible to forms of sensual experience. This pattern of treatment has been influential for thinkers like Adorno, who use it to identify in art's dislocation from functional contexts a capacity to present unique perspectives on social relations.[1]

The second pattern of treatment is the relational structure proposed by the analogical mechanism of aesthetic presentation. In this pattern too the theme of access to ideas not otherwise accessible in the experience of a material thing is treated. Here Kant distinguishes the presentation of a material *content* from the presentation of the *relation* taken to this content.[2] It is through the relation to a material form that ideas not otherwise cognitively or practically determinable can be established, determined, and qualified. In this pattern it is in fact a certain perspective on relation to objects that aesthetic judgment establishes. From this perspective, these objects are seen to be significant in special ways. This pattern of treatment forges the possibility of relating to material forms in nature as if they were made for us and, correlatively, of presenting in the form of this relation the ideas of an ultimate purpose to nature and of a cause behind nature's forms.

The general feature of this pattern that is important is that in the relations taken to objects, significant features of these objects that would not otherwise be apparent are captured. The material forms of animal and plant life do not on their own carry the idea of a cause to nature or of nature as a system of ends. Rather, through the relation taken towards nature's forms these ideas are given an analogical presentation. Put in these terms, it is possible to see the similarities between this pattern of treatment of material forms and the core problematic in Heidegger's thinking. In Kant the relation to the object in the mode of its being aesthetically presented *is* the source of the qualities that bear significance or meaning. Heidegger's thinking can also be characterised in these terms; he tries to draw our attention to the fact that it is the way we *relate* to objects that determines how these objects *are*.

Together these two patterns of treatment of material forms in Kant's third *Critique* develop an optics in which material things are seen to have a capacity to present more than their constituent materiality and, in fact on this basis, are able to authorise moral feeling. I want to elaborate here on those themes in Kant's 'Critique of Aesthetic Judgment' that support this contention. My thesis is the following: the structure of aesthetic presentation in each of these patterns of treatment pulls Kant in opposite directions. On one side, the ideal reference Kant gives to material forms depends on the separation of the fields of nature and art; beauty and charm; and history and taste. On the other, the independence of beauty from charm is *because* beauty models the moral idea; nature's forms are contingent *because* they confirm the moral vocation of 'man'; and taste is not an historical artefact *because* it is an analogical indication of moral autonomy. These different directions in argumentation are indicative of the way that nothing binds material forms in relation to moral ideas; rather, the structure of argumentation is necessary in order to find in material forms a register of ultimate meaning which is not there.

This way of approaching the *Critique of Judgment* is clearly different to the two main branches of interpretation regarding this work. In the Anglo-American approach to the *Critique of Judgment* Kant's division between aesthetic and teleological judgments is frequently used as a frame for its reception.[3] This scholarship often foregrounds the significant interpretative difficulty posed by the division between aesthetic and logical judgments in the *Critique* but deals with it by restricting itself to a discussion of one of its parts.[4] There are inevitable costs in this type of approach. For instance, the fascination with the topic of the validity of judgments of taste in the 'Critique of Aesthetic Judgment' leads critics to ignore the section on the sublime with its obvious links to the anthropology of historical and religious culture raised in the 'Critique of Teleological Judgment' and thereby look past the problem of system to examine the *Critique of Judgment* as if it were a treatise on beauty.[5] In the context of this project, such styles of interpretation of the place of taste in Kant's text are not adequate because they block from view the distinctive feature of this work: its treatment of taste in the context of the problem of an aesthetic presentation of reason's ideas.

Nineteenth-century German Idealism and Romanticism, which locate their conceptual origins in this *Critique,* focus in contrast on the interrelation between the two parts of the *Critique of Judgment.* However, because they argue that Kant's aspirations to construct a philosophical system end in failure and aim themselves to bring Kant's intended project to completion, the tenor of this school of interpretation also sidesteps the problems I wish to raise here.[6] The *Critique of Judgment,* I believe, needs to be read as a whole; but, equally, the productive tension in this work between the contingent forms of nature and the ideas of reason should not be seen in the terms of nineteenth-century German Idealism and Romanticism as a failure or crisis that needs to be remedied.[7] It is a consequence of having placed the chief categories of metaphysics outside of direct intuition that Kant's final *Critique* is able to put forward as a question how sensible forms can be more than their constituent materiality. From this perspective, and despite Kant's clear intentions, the technical approach taken to the question of presentation in this *Critique* can be seen to replace classical metaphysical categories and even, I will argue, erode the assumptions that support them. Once the presentation is given primacy in this way the metaphysical privilege of a presentable idea that is 'behind' it begins to lose force. Instead of a secondary term called forth by a prior idea, the presentation becomes or 'is' the originary form of the idea, and this occurs as a consequence of Kant's approach precisely because presentation is, for him, the only legitimate access to pure ideas. It is this conclusion which I think Heidegger, Lacoue-Labarthe, and Nancy each draw from their studies of the theme of presentation in German Idealism and Romanticism. For each thinker the significance of the topic of presentation is both its corrosive effect on the metaphysics of ideal entities and the way it opens up a new path to reflect on elementary or constitutive states of affairs.

The erosion of metaphysical categories, which forges the link between Kant's final *Critique* and some of the most significant movements of twentieth-century philosophy, is, despite Kant's intentions, a consequence of his foregrounding of the question of presentation.[8] With this question he replaces faith in the category of 'God' with a chain of purposive relations in nature that is supposed to yield this category by other means. Similarly the supposition of 'man's' moral vocation and the pragmatic anthropology of the 'Teleology' are both already given not by means of the analogical presentation of the idea of freedom, and thus not by a relation to a prior idea, but by the presentations of acts of discipline and resistance to sensuous temptation, which *are the forms* of Kant's moral anthropology. The next chapter will show how Kant's pragmatic anthropology thus installs the figure of 'moral man' as an aesthetic object. In this chapter I will focus on the points of connection in the treatment of the topic of aesthetic presentation between Kant's doctrine of taste and his teleology.

My discussion will follow the two patterns of treatment that Kant takes in his approach to the topic of aesthetic presentation: in the first two sections, the structural dislocation that establishes the independence of taste will be juxtaposed with the thematic and argumentative connections made by Kant between judgments of taste and teleological judgments. These connections will show how taste's independence and the conception of aesthetic autonomy that it supports are necessarily compromised within the 'Critique of Aesthetic Judgment' on account of the connection to moral ideas that the thesis of taste's dislocation from 'interests' establishes. The final two sections will examine the elements and motives of Kant's structural dislocation of interests in light of his use of 'symbol' and 'analogy' as forms of aesthetic relation. The structural dislocation of interests is played out in Kant's treatment of all the major themes of the 'Critique of Aesthetic Judgment': form rather than charm, pleasure rather than gratification, pure taste rather than historical taste, and nature rather than art. The aesthetic relations of symbol and analogy are the means by which, I will argue, the privilege of form, pleasure, pure taste, and nature are secured. These relations school a certain perspective on our relation to objects that infuse these objects with a moral significance they would not otherwise have. Cultivating this perspective is crucial for Kant's agenda in this *Critique* because it institutes contexts of meaning that allow our relation to material forms to be at least interpretable in light of moral ideas and hence to motivate and give orientation to action.

## Kant's Formulation of Taste's Independence

There are two striking features in Kant's formulation of taste. First, the way Kant articulates taste's independence follows the defining elements of his conception of universal validity in cognition.[9] Second, the importance he gives to the independence of taste from practical and cognitive fields is motivated by the connection that pure taste, on the basis of its independence, forges to reason's ideas. In this regard, Kant's formulation of pure taste in relation to his conception of universal validity in cognition is notable because this framework of comparison introduces criteria able to distinguish 'pure taste' from crude 'appetite.' These criteria can be summarised in three terms: communicability (*sensus communis*), freedom (reflective judgment), and form (representation).

In both taste and cognition Kant describes how a finite subject can expect its representations [*Vorstellung*] to be universally valid. The relation between concepts and intuitions outlined in Kant's conception of schematic judgments ensures the intersubjective communicability of knowledge that is generated by the representational faculties of a subject. For Kant, the subject of representation is a finite, empirical consciousness, which concretises general concepts by particularising them in time.

*Schematism* is the term Kant uses to describe the mediation between concepts and sensible intuitions. The doctrine of the schematism aims to resolve the empiricist objections to the Cartesian understanding of the representability of general concepts. Kant recognises the empiricist claim that innate ideas and general concepts are devoid of meaning in their nonrepresentability for a finite subject. In thinking of a triangle it is not the abstract notion that we represent to ourselves but the image of a particular triangle. Nonetheless, whereas empiricism concludes that general concepts in their nonrepresentability are necessarily empty, Kant allows the existence of necessary and a priori universal concepts, or what he calls the categories of understanding.

He does this through the doctrine of schematism. The pivot of this doctrine is the dependence of an empirical consciousness on the particularisation of concepts. Through it concepts are redeemed from their status as universal 'empty images' to gain a content meaningful for an empirical consciousness. Schemata are universal methods, valid for every time and place, for the construction of objects. In this respect Kant's break with Cartesianism consists in transforming concepts from 'general images' to an activity and thereby from a passive representation to a work.[10] The finite subject needs to match its concepts to sensible intuitions. These concepts retain their universal validity while as *schemata* they gain a cognisable content for the subject. The subject particularises universal concepts through constructing them as objects in time. This sensible content, because it is produced through a universal *rule* of construction, has a universal validity. The schemata thus imply a conception of intersubjectivity that joins subjects through the shared content of their representations. Further, in their incorporation of rules for intuitions that make them law-governed and thus *shared,* formal concepts themselves gain a content that is cognisable.[11]

In the case of taste the claim in cognition to universal validity is retained in a modified form. Kant argues that our taste makes a claim to 'serve as a universal rule.' This claim rests on two features of judgment that are analogous to the argument for universal validity in cognition where the schemata describe both the shared operation of the categories amongst subjects and the representational nature of knowledge. The doctrine of taste's independence lies in its modelling of these aspects of the schemata *without rules.* Taste is a specific operation 'that in reflecting takes account (a priori), in our thought, of everyone else's way of representing [*Vorstellung*] [something]'[12]; but it does so, second, by comparing 'our judgment not so much with the actual as rather with the merely possible judgments of others, . . . merely by abstracting from the limitations that [may] happen to attach to our own judging; and this . . . we accomplish by leaving out as much as possible whatever is matter, i.e., sensation, in the representational state, and by paying attention solely to the formal features of our representation or of our representational state' (CJ, 160). As a representation [*Vorstellung*] of a mere form by the cognitive faculties, taste, like cognition, presupposes a common accord amongst subjects. Unlike cognition, the accord claimed by taste is free rather than regulated by rules. In the *Critique of Judgment* Kant uses the Latin *sensus communis* to distinguish it from the 'vulgar' conception of a common sense that is merely a 'sound' but 'not yet cultivated' understanding. In Kant's view taste can be called *sensus communis* more legitimately than sound understanding since it involves 'our ability to judge a priori the communicability of the feelings that (without mediation by a concept) are connected with a given representation' (CJ, 162).

The specific value of this free accord is elaborated in the *Critique of Judgment* by way of a distinction between reflective and determinative judgment. This distinction aims to separate aesthetic judgment from the determinative operation of judgment described in the first *Critique*.[13] Whereas a determinative judgment places its particular object under a *given* universal and thereby identifies it as an instance of a general rule, in a reflective judgment only the form of an object is given and the universal needs to be found. In part, this conception of reflective judgment aims to sustain the idea of a relation between our faculties and the natural world not constrained by the purpose of a cognitive determination. Aesthetic judgment is in this sense the best exemplar of reflective judgment as it suspends cognitive aims in its exercise. In contrast, the logical reflective judgment described in Kant's 'Teleology' entertains a cognitive purpose but maintains its status as a *reflective* judgment by using only a regulative rather than determinative principle for the judgment of phenomena.

In general terms, it is the absence of conceptual determination that defines the relation between reflective judgment and freedom. But this 'freedom' pertains both to the undetermined play of our faculties in the contemplation of nature's particular forms (this freedom is specific to aesthetic judgment) and the freedom particular objects enjoy in the absence of a conceptual determination. The quality of this freedom differs between the two parts of the *Critique,* but in each part reflective judgment offers a mechanism for the analogical presentation of the ideas of reason which determinative judgment is unable to provide. As we will see, it is the nondeterminative, free quality of aesthetic reflective judgment that makes of it a mechanism for the analogical presentation of ideas.

Kant uses these points of differentiation from cognition to describe the doctrine of taste's independence. The feeling of pleasure that follows from the subject's representation of a singular form of beauty in nature constitutes the judgment of taste.[14] A pure judgment of taste judges a mere form (the organisation of parts into a whole) that is detached from any determinate purpose. The feeling of pleasure that constitutes taste is not determined by the form of a singular, beautiful object but by a specific relation between the cognitive faculties, which represent form. It is this particular relation between the faculties that is the ground for Kant's claim of an a priori universality for aesthetic judgment. This claim has its conditions in a judgment that deals not with a sensible form in nature, but the reflection of this form in the faculty of the imagination. Put simply, it is the subject's representation of form rather than the object that determines, for Kant, taste's value. Kant's definition of aesthetic pleasure as a subjective universality (a representation by the faculties) thus retracts it from the field of qualities able to be determined by the understanding in nature as well as from the constraint of rules of cognition. Some of the mechanics of this retraction include the dislocation of aesthetic judgment from determinate claims regarding the object or needs of the subject.

Let me alert the reader to the philosophical context that prompts this dislocation. The Kantian doctrine of taste's independence dislocates 'pure' taste from the interests cultivated in the Wolffian rationalist tradition and the eighteenth-century British theory of taste. In the latter case the subject is linked by a pathological desire for and thus depends on 'the real existence of the object' (CJ, §5). Unlike this case of what Kant terms the liking for the 'agreeable,' the rationalist account of beauty as a confused perception of perfection judges an object in relation to a concept of perfection. In this case, too, Kant discerns an interest in the object of taste as 'good' in relation to a concept, which disqualifies such judgments from the category of taste. Taste's independence from these external points of arbitration or 'interests' is the source of its value as 'free.' Hence 'interest' at its simplest refers to factors that are external to the mere representation of form by the faculties. Such factors detract from the quality of pleasure that constitutes pure taste as a disinterested pleasure in form. Further, without such disinterest the representation of form would have no claim to parallel the schemata in an aesthetic *sensus communis*.

## The Connections between Teleology and Beauty as Forms of Aesthetic Presentation

This emphasis on disinterest jars, however, with the systematic connections Kant tries to establish between beauty and teleology. The connections between beauty and teleological judgment follow from but also undercut the distinct way that beauty qualifies for a symbolic relation to the moral idea. There are two main indications of the opposing directions from which Kant approaches beauty: (1) the special significance that places beauty apart from the other paths to aesthetic presentation in the third *Critique,* and (2) the role beauty plays in the chain that allows nature to be considered as a purposive construction or 'art' in the 'Teleology.'

Within the *Critique of Judgment* there are four fields in which the topic of presentation of reason's ideas is discussed: the beautiful, the sublime, genius, and teleology. Each field takes the specific form of a search for a sensible figure or analogue for an idea of reason. The genius creates in art a second nature, one that is analogous to rather than representative of the principles of order in primary nature.[15] In the case of the sublime, nature proves inadequate in relation to reason's power and the presentation takes the 'form' of a negative image. Amongst these fields the beautiful has a particular quality that separates it from the other paths of solving the problem of the presentation of ideas. Beauty presents in an 'indirect' but, as Deleuze puts it, 'positive' form the intimacy between nature's forms and human freedom.[16] In other words, the significance of beauty is that nature's forms enable a relation to reason's ideas. In this respect beauty is to be differentiated in its relation to nature, not just from the genius and the sublime whose relations to nature are respectively analogous and negative, but also from teleological judgment. In the case of teleological judgment a concept of finality is applied to nature that aims to meet the question of the possibility of particular organised forms of nature and thence of nature as a system. Teleology is prepared for by the contingent accord of the beautiful with nature's particular forms.

The topic of the preparatory role of beauty for teleological judgments is best comprehended from the perspective of the features of beauty that recommend it as a mediating term for the split in Kantian philosophy. The manner in which the second *Critique* poses the question of freedom introduces a split within Kantian philosophy between the natural necessity of the laws of the sensible world and the noumenal moral faculty through which we posit our own ends independently of sensuous interests.[17] Our freedom is noumenal: no sensible object matches its concept. In the terms of Kantian philosophy, however, noumenal ideas at least need to be presented [*Darstellung*] in experience: first, because without experience the ideas are undermined by the suspicion of impotence, and second, because without a sensible orientation our capacity to reason is unmoored from its sensible limitations and led to the illusions of dogmaticism that Kant attributes to both Spinozism and Platonism.[18] Hence shadowing the division between the sensible world and the ideas of reason is the distinction in the third *Critique* between two distinct modes of presentation: those, respectively, of schematic and symbolic presentation.[19] The former provides a direct presentation for the concepts of understanding which yields knowledge while the latter gives an analogical presentation, a *sensible guide* and *analogical content* to what is otherwise a hopelessly impotent concept of reason.

Particular instances of beauty in nature, what Kant calls the 'cipher language' of beautiful forms, meet this need for a symbolic presentation of ideas. The tulip, which is Kant's preferred example of natural beauty, presents the idea of freedom precisely because, as a product of nature, it is not cultivated for this purpose.[20] There are, however, further conditions to be fulfilled, this time on the side of the subject's own purposes, to qualify the judgment of this form for the role of a symbolic presentation of ideas. The tulip stands as a symbol of morality not when it is cut and placed in a vase for a decorative purpose, but when, without any contrivance for our ends, the mere presentation of its form pleases us.[21] The *contingent* accord struck by a singular instance of natural beauty with our faculties does not gratify any sensible interest of ours nor does it fulfill a cognitive goal, and for Kant this tulip accordingly attunes us to the idea of a purposiveness which is without a purpose: what he calls a formal purposiveness. The flower is able to present the idea of freedom by virtue of a double dislocation: one from concepts (we do not see the flower in terms of its purpose as the botanist does), that is, its beauty does not relate to anything determinate about it as an object; and one from purposiveness; as the flower does not satisfy any end of mine, it is free as well from any determinate end of the subject. Freed from the demands of cognition and, on the side of the tulip, as a product of nature not cultivated for any of our ends, the flower is able to present, albeit analogically, our freedom.

The symbolic relation that beauty establishes to the moral idea is a way of negotiating the bar on access through the experience of sensible forms to the moral idea. However, this symbolic relation of beauty to freedom needs to be distinguished from the status of beauty as the preparatory form for teleology. Although in both cases a relation to reason's ideas is forged, in the case of teleology the organic order and 'design' of the beautiful in nature feed into the speculative interests of reason. In doing so the distinctive feature that underpins the value of form (that it is in 'nature,' not 'art') as a symbolic link to moral ideas is pulled away from 'nature' and into the contrary field of 'art.'

As we saw in the last section, a pure judgment of taste judges mere form (the organisation of parts into a whole) detached from any purpose. This conception of form introduces the main point of contrast between beauty, the sublime, and teleology in this *Critique*. The beautiful is a bounded, discrete, particular form whose accord with our faculties is contingent. In contrast the feeling of pain in the sublime follows from the subject's encounter with a surplus of parts (the formless or deformed in nature) that occasions an idea of reason. This surplus of parts comes to depend on the forming capacity of the subject's faculty of reason in order to be unified into a whole as an *idea* (not a presentation by images). Where the sublime describes a negative presentation that aggravates the split between nature and reason, depicting the shift away from an inadequate sensible nature and towards the subject, the beautiful is a synthetic category. Its synthesising action works in two main senses: it integrates a manifold into a form and prompts the reflection that this integrated form is the product of an art, thus bringing together nature and a rational agency. These synthetic functions further underline the connections between beauty and teleology. In the 'Critique of Teleological Judgment' the reflective judgment that the world is the product of an intention knits the particular, organic forms of nature together into a *system* and licenses the question of the purpose of this system. The synthetic style of 'Teleology' starts by assuming a purpose to natural forms that enables the synthetic judgment of a purpose in relation to nature as such. This train of thought has its condition in the purposeless beauty of a pure object of taste.

In Kant's paradigm of beauty, the form of the natural flower, the organization of parts (petals, stamen, pollen) into an ordered whole conveys an order that is cut off from its purpose as an organ of botanical reproduction.[22] This purposeless organic form is nonetheless connected with a principle of production: nature's singular instances of beauty, indeed, lead to the thought that this particular form is the product of an art and it is this further reflection on form that underlies the privilege beauty enjoys over the sublime. Although Kant's *Critique of Judgment* includes a division of the fine arts and devotes some space to the discussion of genius, the central features of beauty are those of the ordered, organic relation between parts judged without a purpose in nature. If this formalist aesthetic is deliberately cut off from the judgment of a purpose, the 'Critique of Teleological Judgment,' in contrast, gathers together the same integrated manifold of natural forms but places it under the concept of art and thereby judges nature itself reflectively as the product of an intention, or 'art.' Considered in terms of the indices of organic order, aesthetic presentation, and connection to nature, the relations between teleology, genius, the sublime, and beauty can be expressed in the following fashion:

*The Four Modes of Presentation of Ideas in the* Critique of Judgment

|  | Beauty | Sublime | Teleology | Genius |
|---|---|---|---|---|
| Organic Order | Parts organized into a whole | Surplus of parts without a whole | Parts organised into a whole in particular forms of nature also used as a model to organise the particular parts of nature into the systematic whole of Nature | Conception of a whole organises parts in relation to a unifying intention |
| Presentation of Reason's Ideas | Symbolic relation to ideas derived from a singular form of order in nature | Nature's might or size provides the occasion for the negative presentation (i.e., a presentation without a sensible form) of the forming power of reason's ideas | Direct and primary relation between reason's ideas and nature | Secondary and analogous relation to ideas |
| Relation to Nature | Contingent relation to nature | Negative relation to nature | Direct relation to nature | Analogous relation to nature's mode of productivity |

Let me briefly summarise the general points of this section: the connections between the parts of the third *Critique* can be organised into two main categories. First, there are the thematic connections that include the theme of presentation, the relation between nature's forms and aesthetic presentation, as well as the conception of organic form as an art. Second, there are argumentative links between the two parts, and here we can cite the role of beauty as a precursor to teleology in the conception of nature as art. These connections exert a contradictory pull over the conception of taste. This can be seen in the way that beauty prepares for the application of a concept of a final end to nature, but the particular quality that qualifies beauty for this preparatory role is lost under the speculative and practical interests of reason that organise nature's forms and nature itself under the concept of ends in teleology. Teleology introduces 'art' as a concept that allows the unitary organisation of the particular forms of nature. It thereby applies the mode of presentation [*Darstellung*] as a specific type of production (a principle that organises the discussion of genius in the fine arts) to nature and undermines the value of a contingent accord between our faculties and nature's forms in beauty. These connections show that the doctrine of taste's independence cannot be maintained. The impossibility of this doctrine is, further, a direct result of the fact that Kant's overall project within the third *Critique* requires systematic connections between the two parts. In the case of taste the elements of its compromise with the project of aesthetic presentation are symbol and analogy. The elements and motives of the compromise pure taste makes with the project of aesthetic presentation can, I think, be made clearer by analysing the pivotal role played by Kant's treatment of the topic of aesthetic relations to objects in the third *Critique*.

## Natural Beauty as Symbolic and Analogical Relation to Ideas

It is important to keep in view the way that the dislocation of interests in the case of taste is the means by which Kant attaches an ideal reference to a material form. Further, the terms by which beautiful forms qualify for this reference to ideas (the quality of communicability in the *sensus communis*, the 'free' accord with nature's forms in reflective, aesthetic judgment, and the repudiation of charm) sets up pure beauty in a specific relation to moral feeling. The importance of this relation to moral feeling cannot be overstated: it shows how Kant's conception of the specific relation to material forms in taste authorises, in fact, his conception of moral feeling. This authorisation, I think, stems not just from the aesthetic relations we take to objects, but from the perspective that inflates such relations to the status of vital indications of moral autonomy.

The theme that is important in Kant's discussion of aesthetic relations is the distinction between the fields of art and nature. The aesthetic relations of symbol and analogy open the possibility that forms of sensible experience can present an idea of reason. However, the manner by which an ideal reference is given to these sensible forms blurs the distinction between the fields of art and nature through which this reference was possible in the first place. Kant's view that beauty gives an analogical presentation of ideas in a positive form means, in fact, that if we can attach moral feeling to a material form it is not because of the *content* of the presentation but the *relation* we have to it. Nonetheless this relation is used by Kant to authorise moral feeling.

The term favoured by Kant to sketch a relation between sensible forms and ideas is analogy as this rhetorical device also, he hopes, preserves their distance. Unlike the direct presentation of concepts by a corresponding intuition in schemata, a symbolic rendering of a concept is indirect or mediate (*What Real Progress Has Metaphysics Made in Germany since the Time of Leibniz and Wolff?*).[23] Kant's explication of the analogical model of presentation in the case of the beautiful underlines the intimacy between his critiques of aesthetic and teleological judgment on the specific issue of nature's particular forms. Explaining the symbolic relation between beauty and morality, Kant argues that symbolisation presents an object in relation to its effects or consequences. As in the 'Teleology' where it will be through an analogy with moral capacity that the concept of God receives a moral determination, in *Progress of Metaphysics* the representation of organised things in nature in relation to their cause draws its presentative force from a symbolic hypotyposis, or analogical presentation, of human production. The relation of causality is present in the case of our production of a watch as well as in the notion of animals and plants as products of an author. What makes this presentative relation symbolic is that 'the subject that has this relation [to its effects] remains unknown to me in its intrinsic character, and hence I cannot present it, but can present only that relation' (CJ, n.31, 226, cited from *Progress of Metaphysics*).

In symbolic hypotyposis there is an idea, which only reason can think, and judgment treats the intuition that gives it reality 'in a way merely analogous to the procedure it follows in schematizing' (CJ, 226). What judgment transfers in this analogy is not the content of the intuition but the rule followed for the form of the reflection. The presentation of the concept is one in which the content of this concept is given as an analogical derivation.[24]

It is precisely here, in the conception of the aesthetic presentation of beauty as a symbolic, reflected form, that one of the central distinctions in Kant's *Critique of Judgment*—the distinction between art and nature—is undermined. The project of aesthetic presentation depends on the elevation of natural beauty over the fabrications of art.[25] Beauty can be used as the vehicle for the mediation between nature and freedom in the 'Critique of Aesthetic Judgment' because of its merely formal purposiveness. Equally, however, it is the preparatory role of beauty for teleological judgments that alters the value of nature's peculiar productivity, ultimately licensing the reflective teleological judgment of nature as an art. To repeat, the path to this teleological judgment is no mere afterthought within the 'Critique of Aesthetic Judgment.' Rather it is implied in the definition of pure taste as a form of aesthetic presentation. According to this definition, the reflective activity of taste has an analogous relation to the moral idea. Kant is explicit that the reflective pleasure (CJ, 158) in purposive form is not just the analogous mode of presentation for but is itself sustained by moral ideas. The independent liking that moral ideas foster differentiates pure taste from the liking for sensory pleasure which 'makes the spirit dull, the object gradually disgusting, and the mind dissatisfied with itself and moody because it is conscious that in reason's judgment its attunement is contrapurposive' (CJ, 196). Now, if the quality of sustained contemplation in pure taste can find a suitable vehicle within the fine arts, it is not the case that a sensitivity to the beautiful in art has any *necessary* connection to a moral disposition. The value of natural beauty over the fine arts is that, for Kant, a direct interest in the beauty of nature 'is always a mark of a good soul' (CJ, 166). To comprehend what is at stake once this central distinction between nature and art is undermined we will need to carefully follow the logic behind the superiority of 'natural beauty' in Kant's discussion of taste. In particular I would like to emphasise the pivotal role this distinction plays in Kant's treatment of aesthetic presentation as an aesthetic relation to material forms.

The symbolic relation to material form in pure taste allows us to see in material forms an ideal reference that would not otherwise be either cognitively or practically determinable there. This relation is in the strict sense of the term an aesthetic relation, since it qualifies an object in terms of its relation to us. This relation is produced through adopting a certain relation to objects: we relate to these objects *as if* they were made for us. Not only is the object considered as the endpoint of this special kind of relation, but also it is the fact that we are able to establish this relationship to nature that is significant. Indeed it is possible to go further and say that, for Kant, the very idea that this object is there for us to have this relation with us *is* the source of aesthetic pleasure.

Seen from this angle, the logic of the instability of the distinction between art and nature in this text can be made clear: there is no moral significance *in* nature's material forms. Such significance can only be attached by reflecting on our relations to objects, and this reflection already presupposes the purposive construction of an object for an end that Kant defines as 'art.'

Reason has an interest in nature showing a 'trace' or 'hint' that 'it contains some basis or other for us to assume in its products a lawful harmony with that liking of ours which is independent of all interest' (CJ, 167). The argumentative structure that tries to attach an ideal reference to material forms frays the very terms of the distinction between 'reason' and 'nature.' Although Kant concedes that the 'cipher' by which 'nature speaks to us figuratively in its beautiful forms' (CJ, 168) may look 'rather too studied,' 'nature's beauty' qualifies for a connection to reason's interest precisely because it is of 'nature.' Our interest in nature's beauties and our expectation that others share this interest rest on the condition that 'it must be nature' (CJ, 169). In §42, 'On Intellectual Interest in the Beautiful,' Kant differentiates art from nature according to the fact that art, having been 'intentionally aimed at our liking,' is of direct interest to us 'by its purpose and never in itself.' Against the objection that the link of nature's beauty to a moral idea becomes the purpose that interests us in nature Kant insists that 'it is not this link that interests us directly, but rather the beauty's own characteristic of qualifying for such a link, which therefore belongs to it intrinsically' (CJ, 168–9). Beauty's qualification for this link is its independence from material interests *and* the moral idea.

Our liking beautiful products in nature 'resembles' the harmony reason seeks between its idea and nature. Let us recall that Kant defines moral action in opposition to an action that is motivated by material interest.

The capacity to like something in the absence of any sensuous or material gratification recalls our moral capacity for action. In each case a feeling is entertained without any material reward. The dislocation of taste from material rewards qualifies it for an analogical relation to moral feeling. It is also crucial that taste be determined independently of moral interests, for it is only in this case that its testimony of our moral calling counts as an 'independent' confirmation of these interests.

The distinction between nature and art subtends the fragile series of distinctions that grants the beautiful a state of independence from the interests of sensuousness, cognition or function-driven activity. This distinction also structures the division in this text between aesthetics and teleology—securing for aesthetics the quality of formal purposiveness. But even in the case of the division between aesthetics and teleology there is a purpose behind nature's significance for our interests. According to Kant nature in its beautiful products displays itself as if it were art, as if it were beautiful *intentionally*, and thus presents a purposiveness without a purpose. Unable to find this purpose outside us, 'we naturally look for it in ourselves, namely, in what constitutes the ultimate purpose of our existence: our moral vocation' (CJ, 168).

To recap the main points of this discussion: the 'Critique of Aesthetic Judgment' at once exploits the fact of nature's contingency for our understanding as it recasts this contingency under the concept of purposiveness to make nature an art with a purpose. It is the thought of nature as an art that Kant uses in the 'Critique of Aesthetic Judgment' that supports the attribution to nature of the systematicity of an intention in the 'Critique of Teleological Judgment.' Aesthetic reflection depends for the quality of its feeling on nature's contingency. Nonetheless, it places itself in the service of an obscure art of moral symbolism and of a teleological reflection, which organises this contingency under the idea of an intentional art. The contingent purposiveness of nature for our judging (aesthetics) prepares the ground for nature to be considered in its totality as a product of an intention (teleology).

The significance of the beautiful—that our judging relies in this case on a relation to a material form outside ourselves and the limitations of our purposive constructions—is precisely what introduces the paradoxical idea of nature as an art able to confirm a purposiveness of nature for us (CJ, 99).

## Compromising Aesthetic Disinterest:
## *Sensus Communis,* Charm, and History

The fact that nothing binds material forms to moral ideas pulls Kant's text in opposing directions: he is committed to both establishing the 'independence' of beauty from the claims of the senses and reason and 'qualifying' it as an intermediary between sensation and reason, on grounds of this same independence.

In this context it is worth carefully considering not just what Kant's account of aesthetic judgment enables in terms of the relations between reason and sensation that would not otherwise be possible, but what the implications are for the Kantian project of aesthetic presentation when the role of beauty as an independent term breaks down.

In the following discussion I will take Kant's category of the aesthetic *sensus communis* as exemplary of the tensions between the doctrine of taste's exceptionalism (whose partners are contingent, particular forms of nature and free, aesthetic pleasure) and the constraints that its role within the project of aesthetic presentation imposes on it.

One of the main objects of the doctrine of taste's independence from charm, discussed in the first section of this chapter, is to provide aesthetic judgments with a claim to a common accord between subjects, what Kant describes as an aesthetic *sensus communis.* This accord can be described in the vocabulary of aesthetic presentation. In the case of the *sensus communis,* an aesthetic presentation suggests an unmotivated agreement between different subjects about forms. In schematism rules give structure and coherence to sensible data. In aesthetic judgment the doctrine of the schematism is amended: whereas the rules of the schemata under which particular forms in nature can be known secure communicability in knowledge, in aesthetic judgment the subject's feeling and the particular sensibility to nature's forms are the contingent conditions under which an undetermined agreement between *different* selves is entertained. This agreement at the level of feeling can be explained both from the perspective of the object of taste (contingent form of beauty) and the subject (detached from calculative interests) who is qualified to judge it.

On the side of the object, Kant's conception of a *sensus communis* as a shared feeling, or unarticulated agreement about forms, could be used to analyse contemporary media production.[26] Contemporary media presuppose a common agreement about what constitutes a pleasing form. The principles of this agreement like the aesthetic *sensus communis* do not need to be brought into a stated, articulated form; the key is the presupposition that a particular form will engender a shared feeling within an audience of diverse subjects. Equally, and this time on the side of the subject, Kant presupposes particular conditions for the possibility of this unarticulated agreement: specifically, the adherence of the formal features of aesthetic presentation to the basis for comparability in cognition. Hence taste's detachment from charm and emotion supports the claim of its presentation of form to communicability. However, here too it is possible to discern a link to the 'Teleology' in the organisation of taste's claim to consensus. The unarticulated nature of the *sensus communis* means that Kant's rationale for this shared sense is only its conformity to the conditions for a *potential* communicability of aesthetic pleasure. What integrates this aspect of taste to the project for culture in the 'Teleology' is the anthropology under which the *actual* exercise of this potential communicability is considered a core element of our human vocation.

It is an integral component of the doctrine of taste's autonomy that it remains independent from the influence of the judgment of others. Accordingly, the principle of aesthetic consensus is not the actual communication of judgment but the subjective purposiveness that considers what we judge to be formally purposive to also hold for others' judgments. In the relations Kant develops between taste, culture, and civility, however, these transcendental conditions become intimately involved with both charm and the 'art' of social observation. Since judging is a priori and claims universal validity in its reflection on the mere form of a representation, this transcendental focus has to eschew not just the material elements of an empirical register but the empirical social interest that would introduce an imitative dimension to the autonomy of judgment.

Charms are extraneous to 'genuine, uncorrupted, social taste —' (CJ, 71). But at the same time, material charms are given the role of prosthetic support for taste: charms can 'supplement' or encourage taste in those whose taste is 'crude and unpracticed' (CJ, 71). In their distance from the formalism of pure beauty such charms, nonetheless, impair taste 'if they draw attention to themselves as [if they were] bases for judging beauty' (CJ, 71). Charms do not contribute to beauty, but are instead tolerated as 'aliens' whose prosthetic function for weak taste must 'not interfere with the beautiful form' (CJ, 71). The role of charm in training the crude, un-refined taste gives a positive, albeit heavily regulated, place to the empirical in taste. It is precisely this empirical supplement of taste that Kant aims to preempt by his location of the aesthetic *sensus communis within* the faculty of judgment.

When taste is determined by the judgments of others, its structure is imitative and its autonomy lapses into heteronomy. On the other hand, this autonomy in our powers rests not simply on a transcendental structure but on our history. Our transcendental powers have as their empirical index a his-tory constituted by exemplary products of taste. This index does not, for Kant, diminish the autonomy of our powers. In an argument whose logic shadows the prosthetic role of sensory elements for the judging of form, Kant observes that our taste develops from historical example. It needs examples so that 'it will not become uncouth again and relapse into the crudeness of its first attempts' (CJ, 147). In this sense, taste, in its transcendental constitution, avoids, yet relies on, empirical interests; and it does so, both in terms of the charm that accompanies judgment and the history that informs it.

The empirical social interest under which taste is communicated comes under the category of civilization. Unlike the intellectual interest that constitutes Kant's conception of culture, civilization is based in an in-clination inherent in human nature. It is only in society that it occurs to man 'to be, not merely a human being, but one who is also refined in his own way (this is the beginning of civilization)' (CJ, 164). For Kant man's sociability is a property of his humanity (CJ, 163) and taste, having its ba-sis in shared feeling, furthers what our natural inclination demands. The communicability of feeling connects taste to the 'vocation' of our 'hu-manity' as sociability (CJ, 163). Our inclination and skill to communicate our pleasure to others increases the refinement proper to our civility. Thus the empirical interest in the beautiful forms an element in what Kant sees as the ever-higher progression of taste from a response to charm to the em-brace of pure beauty, and it manages this transition by transforming an in-dividual sensibility to a *communicable* one (CJ, 164).[27]

In response to the paradoxical dependence on charm, history, and communication within the 'Critique of Aesthetic Judgment,' Derrida has argued that Kant's text 'constantly' presupposes but 'holds back the analy-sis of' the *sensus communis*. This suspension, Derrida suggests, 'ensures the complicity of a moral discourse and an empirical culturalism.'[28] In §22 Kant remarks that he cannot determine whether the *sensus communis* exists as a constitutive principle of the possibility of aesthetic experience or whether it exists in a regulative capacity according to the demands of reason. Having thereby suspended his analysis of this term, we might say with Derrida, Kant has retained the *sensus communis* in the dual roles of a constitutive and a regulative feature of taste. What follows from this dual conception of the *sensus communis* is a close partnership between the empirical, historical domain of the exercise of taste and the noumenal and atemporal morality which, properly speaking, exceeds any empirical form. A noumenal and atemporal morality in this instance recruits the (properly inadmissible) support of the empirical progress of culture.[29] Kant's conception of morality, as we will see in the next chapter, needs the historical reference on which its progressive realisation in civil refinement can be pegged.

The paradox of the relationship between taste as autonomous and history as its external measure emerges clearly in the Kantian conception of culture. This conception is framed by a dual reference to an empirical interest on one side (for which we communicate our pleasure for purposive forms) and moral feeling (which is, like the empirical interest, secondarily attached to taste) on the other. Kant specifically wants to tie culture, as the locus of an ethical sensibility, to the intellectual interest in the beautiful. Hence the role of culture in attuning us to moral ideas is met in the case of taste through its regulation by an intellectual interest. Pure taste emerges from disinterest, and its resulting purposiveness for reason and the intellectual interest it elicits mark it out from the conditioned, contrapurposive pleasure of mere happiness. The distance Kant places between culture and the empirical, conditioned purpose of happiness is embedded in the regulative status of his notion of culture. The end towards which culture, like taste, unfolds is that of a pleasure purposive for reason. The kind of pleasure we take in the beautiful has a reflective quality. We 'linger' in our contemplation of the beautiful, its pleasure is *sustained,* and the contemplation 'reinforces and reproduces itself ' (CJ, 68).

However, the moral discourse of the third *Critique* shifts the order under which taste is a pathway to the interests of reason. The negative relation of charm to taste shows how reason already regulates taste for its need of presentation. Similarly the regulative aspect of the *sensus communis* explains the Kantian conception of culture in terms of a model of progress whereby the pleasure in purposive form cultivated by taste contributes to the historical progress measurable only by an empirical interest towards the ends of reason. Man is the source of value by which culture as free purpose is opposed to happiness as conditioned purpose. The anthropology that justifies the link between the founding disinterest of taste and its necessary relation to reason in culture is primarily, as we shall see, the province of the 'Critique of Teleological Judgment.' It is here that Kant places the discussion of purposiveness in a typology of value in which man is credited with a final purpose [*Endzweck*] and made nature's ultimate purpose [*der letzte Zweck*]. Before turning to examine the perspective on aesthetic presentation raised by the 'Teleology,' let me briefly recapitulate the results of the discussion of this chapter.

The regulative notion of the *sensus communis* and the transitional role in which it casts taste clearly defines the value of nature as contingent in this *Critique*. Nature's contingency for our reason not only frees it from our interests but also makes its confirmation of these interests *significant*. The pleasure that issues from the harmony between nature's forms and our power of judgment is a reflection of the contingency in this relation as well as the unarticulated accord of this judgment with those of others. And yet it is crucial to mark the sleight of hand that allows this relation to be described as 'contingent.' When Kant cites moral feeling in the 'Critique of Aesthetic Judgment' as the appropriate 'propaedeutic' (CJ, 232) to taste, the moral interest in taste exceeds its position as a secondary attachment to become taste's precursor. With this gesture, Kant verges on undermining his use of beauty as the singular, analogical presentation of reason's ideas and the reputation of the *Critique* as giving the sensible world a priority in its singular forms. In effect, reason's interest precedes the 'contingency' of nature's forms and it organises behind the stage, so to say, these forms for taste.

Cast in relation to the systematising aims of the third *Critique* it is easy to see *why* taste is transformed from a point of transition between sensible charm and moral interest to become the 'universal human sense' whose ability consists in judging how 'moral ideas are made sensible' (CJ, 231-32). This transformation leads Kant to make statements that seem to contradict the intent of the doctrine of taste as a vehicle of aesthetic presentation. For if taste is to judge how moral ideas 'are made sensible,' it no longer succeeds as a mechanism of aesthetic presentation whose disinterest in relation to charm and reason qualifies it as their mediary. In the end, the structural disconnection of taste from cognitive and practical fields collapses into a statement of the purpose of material forms as the bearers of moral significance. The circuitous path of argumentation that Kant takes to reach this point is necessary, however, because it is this path of argumentation (and nothing else) that establishes the credible relation between material forms and the moral idea.

## Pragmatic Anthropology in the Third *Critique*'s Project of Aesthetic Presentation

In his book *Kant and the Problem of Metaphysics*,[1] Heidegger refers to Kant's lectures on anthropology and states that these lectures may be used to interpret Kant's critical philosophy as they 'provide us with information concerning the already-laid ground for metaphysics' (KB, 90).[2] The view that Kant's critical works are conducted on the prior ground of a conception of 'man' is not unique to Heidegger, although it is arguably he who opens the path to this style of interpretation.[3] The claim that the critical philosophy has its genesis in empirical studies of man has fuelled the recent investigations into Kant's precritical writing, as well as those treatments of the second *Critique*, which focus on the problem of the ineliminable references to anthropology in Kant's critical conception of the moral law and which argue, on this basis, for a reappraisal of Kantian ethics.[4]

We know that the third *Critique* receives only a cursory mention in Heidegger's Kant book. Derrida, on the other hand, has analysed the pragmatic anthropology that underlies many of its propositions.[5] In *The Truth in Painting*, he maintains that this anthropology, which is developed in the 'Teleology,' is the framework that renders many of the otherwise opaque categories and distinctions in the 'Aesthetics' understandable and that, as a consequence, 'a book like this must be read from the other end.'[6] While the discussion in Kant's 'Teleology' may be used, as Derrida has shown, to illuminate the anthropology that underpins his 'Aesthetics,' it is also important to analyse the ways in which the 'Teleology' extends on and intensifies the anthropology of moral man first raised in Kant's deduction of taste.

This chapter will examine the role Kant's anthropology plays in the 'Critique of Teleological Judgment.' The 'Critique of Teleological Judgment' does not just grapple with the problem of systematising the critical project, but in doing so also extends the problematic of presentation to the major topics and themes addressed elsewhere in Kant's oeuvre, including in his popular essays on politics and history. The presence in this part of the *Critique* of topics and themes from Kant's writings on politics and philosophy of history point to the distinction in the 'Critique of Teleological Judgment,' first outlined in Kant's *Anthropology from a Pragmatic Point of View,* between 'anthropology,' understood as the empirical knowledge of human physiology, and 'pragmatic anthropology,' according to which knowledge of 'man' is directed to his status as a 'freely acting being.' Associated with this latter are the political and historical consequences that bear on man's status, not as in physiological anthropology as an 'object of and in nature,' but 'as a citizen of the world.'[7]

The project of presentation in the 'Critique of Teleological Judgment' can be described in part as an attempt at a resolution of this division within anthropology. Like the account of presentation in Kant's discussion of taste, the 'Critique of Teleological Judgment' raises as a question how the material elements of human existence can be more than their constituent materiality.[8] However, because the 'Teleology,' as in Kant's discussion of the sublime, approaches this problem from the perspective of the concerns drawn from Kant's pragmatic anthropology of historical and religious culture, it foregrounds topics which are only implicitly present in Kant's use of singular forms of natural beauty to 'present' man's moral character in his doctrine of taste.

There are two main indications of the pragmatic anthropology that guide Kant's concerns in the 'Critique of Teleological Judgment' and explain the pivotal role of anthropology in the project of presentation. First, the expansion of the reference to nature from aesthetic cases or instances to the idea of nature as a system of ends under the synthetic category of 'art' is oriented by the conclusion Kant wishes to draw: that nature's system of ends is for man, because man's final purpose [*Endzweck*] is nature's ultimate purpose [*der letzte Zweck*]. Kant understands the conception of 'art' under which nature is systematised in the broad sense of purposive construction; hence the chain of reasoning in the 'Teleology' attempts to arrive at a determinate form to think the idea of God as the 'cause' of this construction, but does so, in a manner I will analyse later in this chapter, through the analogical device of man's practical capacity. Second, the systematisation of natural purposes for the being who is able to submit nature to freely chosen ends complicates Kant's project of an aesthetic presentation of ideas by introducing in addition to the aesthetic and tele-ological avenues of presentation an historical platform for aesthetic pre-sentation.

Kant understands nature and history as contexts in which the question of an ideal reference to the elements of material life can be meaningfully posed and addressed. The 'Critique of Teleological Judgment' contributes to this project of presentation the view that man can mediate the division between the elements of material life and moral ideas. The description of the shift from physico-teleology to ethico-teleology in the 'Critique of Teleological Judgment,' for instance, attaches an ideal reference to nature in linking the concept of nature's order to the idea of the realisation of man's practical ends in nature. Similarly, Kant's moral conception of cul-ture as an exercise of discipline over merely sensuous interests together with his advocacy for the republican constitution as a political manage-ment of human vices provide frameworks in which a moral interpretation of history grounds man's moral disposition in the elements of material life.

My thesis in this chapter is that in his moral readings of nature (ethico-teleology) and history (politics and culture) Kant articulates con-texts able to give a foothold in the elements of material life for man's moral disposition. These contexts are ways of grappling with the problem of characterising an action as moral. This problem arises as a consequence of the fact that there is no certain way, for Kant, of knowing that an act is moral.[9] He defines moral action in formal terms as an act that is motivated by respect for the moral law alone. The difficulty of ever knowing an act from its motive cause, however, fosters a hermeneutics of moral interpreta-tion that is only able to stylise acts as moral.

The condition of possibility for a moral action is the idea of free-dom, defined as the capacity to act against sensuous inclinations. In addi-tion to the idea of freedom the postulates of God and immortality are used by Kant to ensure that freedom itself is neither out of place in the world nor inconsistent in its formal conditions of possibility. The fact that these postulates are, in Kant's terms, necessary conditions for moral action does not, however, make them credible. The only way these postulates make sense is as terms able to rationalise and give substance to a moral universe. Like a fairytale that furnishes the necessary grounds for magic in mythical figures, Kant's postulates do not make, thereby, the moral perspective truer or more credible. What I would like to focus on here, then, is less the internal justifications Kant's system gives to moral action than the fact that in the absence of a way of actually determining the purity of motives and judging actions as moral there is a need for contextual motivations that can shape and defend 'moral' motivation.

In the moral reading of history, for instance, Kant's popular essays raise the question of whether or not it is possible for violence to be integrated into a moral story. The sense the postulates provide for this moral story is what makes them credible. But the ambiguity of the aesthetic presentation of these postulates in historical episodes and dispositions is that such presentations do much more than provide these ideas with secondary clothing. Rather, and I believe this is a point that is emphasised in Kant's own writing, these ideas feed off the sense of progress that the moral interpretation of history shows. Hence in Kant's famous 1793 essay on theory and practice he writes:

the cry over the irresistible growth in human depravity is due to the fact that, when man attains a higher stage of morality, one can see further still and can make more rigorous judgments regarding what man is in comparison with what he ought to be; consequently our self-censure will always be the more rigorous the more stages of morality have been ascended in the known course of the world.[10]

Kant's formal conception of freedom makes it important to interpret the elements of material life so that freedom is not out of place there. As we will see, in his 'Teleology' and popular essays, unlike his discussion of taste, it is the contraindications of this thesis, such as violence in history, that provide the privileged contexts for such interpretations.[11]

The orientating role and driving force for moral ideas that Kant's presentation of the elements of material life has constitute a further theme in his discussion of anthropology. Although Kant does not address this theme in the terms I will use to describe it, these terms are implied by his treatment of the topic of presentation. Material elements and processes from culture, education, and history provide sensibly accessible forms for the presentation of the moral disposition. In this respect we can say that the idea of the moral man is in fact an aesthetic image. Kant alludes to this theme by the way he treats material elements and processes as evidence for the moral idea. After Kant, particularly in the Romantics' reflection on the problematic of aesthetic presentation, this theme is made more explicit. In Romanticism a symbol or a figure might be taken to be a perfect embodiment of an ideal or the absolute. In Kant's case the elements that suggest this theme may be formulated as follows. If a moral being is defined not by an act but by its motive and if practical knowledge of freedom is not sufficient to determine the morality of a motive, the question of how pure morality can be known becomes crucial.[12] What Kant's texts on politics, history, and teleology suggest but do not and cannot state and defend as a thesis is that a moral being can only be known as a presentation. The presentation of this person, for the reasons previously outlined, is not sufficient to present motives. Rather, it can only present someone who resists sensuous inclinations. In other words this moral figure can, in a very important sense, only be known in sensible forms as a paragon, that is, an *aesthetic* figure. This situation, despite Kant's intentions, makes the problem of morals one that is even more in keeping with an historical and educational perspective on culture and cultivation than he had, on the evidence of his popular essays, believed. To put these remarks into a simple thesis: characterising action that resists sensuous inclinations as moral is the problem of pragmatic anthropology. Despite the fact that such a thesis contradicts Kant's conception of moral action, a compelling case can be made that the moral man is understood first and foremost as an aesthetic image presented as an object of inspiration and emulation.

In this respect it is not really a question of whether an aesthetic presentation of an idea comes first or whether a presentation does in fact presuppose the idea it 'presents.' Aside from the fact that the very idea of the moral law and its supporting postulates are handed down in cultural forms, the crucial point is that their functioning or force is aesthetic. The sense for humans of the concepts used in the postulates such as God or immortality is dependent on their aesthetic presentation (so that God, for instance, is understood aesthetically as the maker of freedom through sublime defiance of the sensual). The way the postulates of God and immortality make a moral standpoint possible in the real world (Kant says they are practically necessary although theoretically unknowable) is aesthetic, first of all in the sense that one is reassured that the moral disposition is not out of place in the world and that virtuous conduct will be finally vindicated. Put in this perspective, two difficulties in Kantian moral philosophy are worth noting. The postulates of God and immortality that are supposed to encourage moral attitude and suppress resignation necessarily encourage calculation of results in terms of reward and punishment. On the other hand, respect for the moral law as the sole motive of the moral act is by definition (since one cannot have any knowledge of one's motives) indistinguishable from aesthetic motives. In other words, acting morally cannot be distinguished from acting the moral person, or 'playing' at morality.[13]

My discussion of these themes is divided into two sections. The first section examines the different contexts Kant builds up to interpret a moral disposition in the fields of material existence in his popular essays as well as his discussions of the judgments of the sublime and teleology. The second section analyses the way that Kant's development of a moral interpretation of history and nature provides an aesthetic form for the moral disposition. The idea of the moral man that Kant thereby presents in his moral philosophy, I will argue, is in fact an aesthetic image through which acts that resist sensuous inclinations are characterised as models of moral duty.

## Material Life and the Moral Disposition

There are three main contexts in which Kant uses elements of material life to build up a foothold for the moral disposition: (1) his discussion of nature as an ethico-teleology in the 'Critique of Teleological Judgment,' (2) his treatment of anthropology as the motor for historical progress in the popular essays, and (3) the analysis of contrapurposive forms of nature in the *Critique of Judgment*. In the way he describes these elements of material life, Kant generates a context in material existence for moral feeling.

### Ethico-teleology and the Moral Interpretation of Nature

Unlike aesthetic judgment, which qualifies for a role in the project of aesthetic presentation by detaching itself from the extraneous interests of sensation and cognition, Kant's inquiry into teleological judgment starts with a cognitive problem. This cognitive problem in itself, however, is ultimately of less significance for Kant than the chain of reflection it initiates.

Kant argues that the concept of purposiveness is necessary to 'indicate a basis that makes' forms in nature 'possible' (CJ, §78, 296). Not so much as 'a blade of grass' could be explained without the assistance of the concept of purposiveness. However, the use of this concept introduces a dualism between mechanistic and teleological explanations of nature. Instead of the tulip in nature that organises his discussion of taste, Kant illustrates the problem raised by the involvement of teleological judgments in the cognition of nature through the example of the competing explanations offered by the principles of mechanism and teleology in the case of a maggot:

> if I assume that a maggot should be regarded as a product of the mere mechanism of matter (i.e., of the restructuring that matter does on its own, once its elements are set free by putrefaction), I cannot then go on to derive the same product from the same matter [now regarded] as a causality that acts in terms of purposes. Conversely, if I assume that the maggot is a natural purpose, then I cannot count on there being a mechanical way of producing it and cannot assume this as a constitutive principle for judging how the maggot is possible. (CJ, §78, 296–97)

Production from physical causes (which excludes an explanation of the *possibility* of such production in terms of the organised form of nature's product) and production from final causes (which fails to function as a *constitutive* principle of explanation for nature's forms) are here described as competing principles of explanation for the same natural form. Each are inadequate as sole principles of explanation—reason needs to be guided by sensible forms (mechanism) but also requires the teleological principle to think the possibility of a natural object that is inconceivable through mechanism alone. In the face of this dilemma, Kant argues for the reconciliation of these principles through positing a further principle 'that lies beyond both' (CJ, §78, 297). This principle, the supersensible, allows us to explain the possibility of things in such a way that we can 'subordinate the one type of production (mechanism) to the other (an intentional technic)' (CJ, §78, 299), and thus allows for the possibility that these types of production may be 'reconcilable in one principle' (CJ, §78, 298).[14] As the product of 'intentional technic' or 'art,' nature's forms become able to be thought as the product of an intention. This judgment is a reflective judgment whose hold is regulative, rather than constitutive, of the phenomena it judges.

From the systematising perspective of theoretical reason, such reflective judgments of purposiveness correct the double inadequacy of mechanistic explanation: mechanism is not able to synthesise the parts of a natural organism into a *whole,* nor can it connect the different parts of nature into a *system.* The possibilities for natural science are thus expanded by logical, reflective judgments in so far as science is able to consider natural things in terms of a law-governed order through referring them to a given basis, or purpose, under which their form is determined. In his discussion of the synthesising interests of theoretical reason, Kant emphasises that the reflective use of the principle of purposiveness licenses the consideration of the order of natural things as purposive but does not 'allow us to decide whether any thing we judge . . . is an *intentional* purpose of nature: whether grass is there for cattle or sheep, and these and all other natural things are there for man' (CJ, §67, 259).

Kant argues that the dependence of our understanding of nature's products on the concept of final causes 'entitles' us 'to go further' and judge products as part of a system of purposes and in doing so to consider 'the unity of the supersensible principle . . . valid not merely for certain species of natural beings, but just as much for the whole of nature as a system' (CJ, 261). The introduction of the concept of purposiveness to render nature's products comprehensible thus introduces a chain of reflection that extends in its implications well beyond the specific problem of the cognition of nature's forms. The systematisation of nature for the cognitive ends of theoretical reason enables Kant to go beyond the 'physico-teleology' of nature's design to anchor this design in a purpose that is beyond nature—'ethico-teleology.' Physico-teleology is criticised by Kant as inadequate for satisfying reason's demands because physico-teleology is not strong enough to support the idea, which it suggests, of design in nature. Instead it is the process of reflection physico-teleological judgments set in train that equips them, in a manner that exceeds their genesis in a cognitive problematic, for a role in building up nature as a material context able to support moral ideas. Kant, indeed, goes so far as to state that the circuit of reflection on purposes in nature is *only* significant in that it leads to the thought of an intention behind nature.[15] This is a telling remark: it points to the fact that the cognitive problematic of teleological judgments is treated from the perspective of building a context in nature for the moral disposition.

'Ethico-teleology' draws on this context to license the view that although nature's forms were not produced *for* human utility or decoration nature is able to be made of use *by* man, because he alone is a creature able to submit nature to freely chosen rather than instinctually driven ends. This capacity of men to use nature as means for the choice of their ends is nature's purpose for man. This purpose, called 'culture' by Kant, cultivates, but as an historical project extends beyond, the freedom of particular men. In the 'Critique of Teleological Judgment' the role of history in this project is foregrounded by Kant's distinction between two sorts of culture: the lower culture of skill (which leads to the decadence of a leisure class) and the higher one of discipline (under which the negative relation to sensation necessary for moral conduct takes shape) (CJ, §83).

Despite the fact, then, that the concept of 'art' as purposive construction is introduced to meet the threat of an obstacle to cognition, cognitive aims do not prescribe the territory of its use. Once the concept of purposiveness is used to supplement mechanism in nature, the concept of nature as a system of purposes raises also the associated questions of nature's purpose and of the cause behind this purpose. On the one hand, these questions sustain, after the doctrine of taste, the idea of a value to nature outside of the calculative perspective of cognition; but on the other, they do so through the idea that the world is 'a product of an intelligent cause (a God)' (CJ, 282).[16]

As I argued in the previous chapter, the question of presentation involves the prospect of a technical resolution of dualism and as such may be contrasted with ontological doctrine. Hence the reflective idea of an 'intelligent cause' behind the world is distinguished by Kant from its 'dogmatic' consequence, 'expressed as holding objectively,' that 'There is a God' (CJ, 282). In place of such dogmatism Kant tries to determine the idea of a cause to nature by an analogical relation to the forming power of the subject of practical reason. What is significant here is that Kant's investigation of teleological judgments establishes the idea of nature as a system of ends for man and authorises this chain of ideas by an analogy to man's own practical capacity. A context is thereby built up for pragmatic anthropology in the elements of material existence.

As we saw in the last chapter, the deduction of taste prizes natural beauty in its externality to human interests. The reconceptualisation of nature as the object for the exercise of man's practical vocation places the 'Teleology' in a tense relation to this crucial aspect of Kant's doctrine of taste. This tension is amplified in the discussions of violence in Kant's popular essays on politics and history and his treatment of the topic of contrapurposive forms of nature in the *Critique of Judgment*. In both cases Kant tries to integrate material elements that appear to be recalcitrant to moral ends into a moral narrative.

### Anthropology and the Moral Reading of History

In the case of politics the mechanism of integration is the perspective of history. The chief political problem of Kant's philosophy is also an historical problem: namely, how to institute a constitutionally framed republic.[17] A constitutional republic is seen by Kant as the organised form able to shape 'men' into good citizens. In the famous §59 of the 'Critique of Aesthetic Judgment' 'on beauty as the symbol of morality' Kant uses organicism as the model for formative political organisation. Here Kant inaugurates a technological metaphor of the state contrasting the analogies of government as hand mill (rule by monarchical will) and animate, organic body (constitutional monarchy). The main features of this contrast follow from the distinction between an external principle of causation, which is unable to confer on parts a necessary or causal relation to the whole, and the internal mechanisms that connect parts to one another and to the whole in a causal chain.

A well-fashioned state is described by Kant in the vocabulary of an organised whole that makes of each member a means as well as a purpose. It is this form alone, according to his remarks on the 'complete transformation' wrought by the American Revolution in the 'Critique of Teleological Judgment,' that is able to form a person with bad motives into a good citizen (CJ, §65).[18]

The problem of fashioning or shaping man into a good citizen explains the context in which Kant negotiates the self-interest of finite men with an organisation capable of issuing from and constraining such interests. The use of the settings of this problem for the treatment of morals in the *Critique of Judgment*, however, is motivated by the question of whether violent events and human imperfections can be integrated into a moral reading of history. The very need for the fashioning of man structures the political problem, according to Kant's popular essays, as one that is without a perfect solution. In thesis no. 6 of his 'Idea for a Universal History,' Kant writes that 'man' is an animal who needs a master, but, and here lies the perpetual irresolution of politics, this master is himself a man (IUH, 33). He goes on to state that 'man' is made 'from such warped wood . . . [that] nothing straight can be fashioned' (IUH, 34). This view that nature (by which Kant here means 'destiny') enjoins us only 'to the approximation' of the idea of a just and human guarantor derives from his view of man's constitutive imperfection. Two consequences immediately follow: it is nature's design, rather than man's, that can reach an 'appropriate' solution to the political puzzle; and this design will require history, or the scope of the species, rather than finite men for its realisation. The institutional dimension of this problem, the fashioning device of a constitutional republic able to correct man's imperfections, is thus itself the historical effect of the shortcomings of human nature (anthropology). The violence of war, for instance, is cited by Kant as a key instrument for the formation of international organisations.[19] An absence of violence (either human made or in the form of natural disasters) hampers human progress; seen in this perspective, violence is sanctioned by Kant for its effects of constitutional formation:

> Just as universal violence and its resultant duress must ultimately bring a people to the point of deciding to submit to the coercion of public laws—a coercion that reason itself prescribes to them—and to enter into a civil constitution, so also must the duress of constant wars, in which nations in their turn seek to reduce or subjugate one another, at last bring them to the point of entering into a cosmopolitan constitution, even against their wills.[20]

This approach to politics—for which, as the example of war indicates, the structuring perspective is historical rather than moral—is worth comparing with the shaping role Kant gives to the moral law.[21] A number of similarities frame the two topics: the constitutive imperfections of man in politics as in morals necessitate the shaping role of law over action. Further, just as the corollary of the historico-institutional approach to politics is that man's vices have a forming effect that operate within institutional forms to modify and check his own tendency to self-interest, so too it is human imperfection that shapes the form of the moral law.[22] The moral law, Kant argues, is given to us in the form of an imperative because, as we are not holy beings, we have vices that resist this law.[23] Finally, the indications in Kant's popular essays on history and in the *Critique of Judgment* that the adherence to this law, again on account of human vices, is shaped historically, that is, externally and in time, allows us to ask after the forms of materiality that have this forming effect. This path of inquiry is significant for two reasons. First, it elucidates the historical approach Kant takes towards the problem of aesthetic presentation and shows how the formative role of material elements gives Kant a better prospect of resolving the dualism between the principles of freedom and nature than the analogical (beauty) and negative (sublime) mechanisms of presentation in which the two principles remain separated.[24] Second, it points to the conflict this path of resolution occasions between the critical conception of the moral law and its historico-anthropological shaping.

Kant's reflections on politics and the task of presenting the postulates of practical reason in sensible forms in his 'Teleology' respond to a similar problem. In either case, Kant aims to provide a structural coherence and support for the pursuit of man's practical ends, which also entails paying attention to the mechanisms suitable to shape him for these ends. The sensible particulars of nature are inadequate for the presentation of reason's ideas and this inadequacy is marked in the cases of beauty and the sublime by the analogical or negative paths to presentation. In the field of human action this gap is evidenced historically. Reason's ideas are not able to be realised in particular historical events; at the same time, however, practical action needs to be orientated by the possibility of future progress; that is, presentation of the idea of progress is necessary, given that for Kant practical reason requires some determination of its possibilities (but not of its content) for action to be possible. The idea of historical progress thus, like teleological judgments of nature's forms under the idea of 'art,' has an integrative force, which, in the case of history, organises past, particular, contingent events into a meaningful whole anchored by the hope of future progress.[25] This hope of progress is in a twofold relation to historical events: on one level, it is supported by the evidence of progress in past historical events; but on another, because such proof is not ever fully adequate to this idea, neither then can the evidence of events counter to progress disprove it. Thus Kant diminishes the weight of any counterevidence and looks to the past selectively to ground this hope in the future.

Similarly, in the field of moral action, the causal capacity of man for intended ends that adhere to the moral law is the proof of the idea of freedom, or what Kant refers to as the 'fact' of freedom. In the second *Critique* Kant hypothesises from the pure moral law an infrastructure of postulates that are logically necessary supports of the possibility of adherence to this law. The moral law is a command that does not just regulate our conduct, but makes the 'highest possible good . . . the *object* of all our conduct' (CprR, 136, my emphasis). This 'object,' the *sunum bonum,* combines the three necessary postulates of practical reason: the immortality of the soul (the practically necessary condition of the duration necessary to fulfil the moral law)[26]; freedom (the necessary presupposition of a causality independent from the world of sense that is able to conform to the law of an intelligible world); and the existence of God (the necessary condition of an intelligible world compatible with highest good). These postulates are necessary conditions of possibility for, but are also necessary (as in the idea of progress in politics) to *promote,* the ends of practical reason.[27]

### Anthropology and the Moral Interpretation of Contrapurposive Forms of Nature

In the 'Critique of Teleological Judgment' Kant builds up contexts in nature and history able to sustain and encourage a moral reference because these postulates need a stronger source of support than that they meet logical conditions of possibility for moral action. His integration of the themes of human vice and violence into a moral interpretation of history, like the thesis that emerges from ethico-teleology on culture—that nature's 'ultimate purpose' is to cooperate and make it possible for man to pursue his 'final purpose' through the cultivation of his nature in skill and discipline (CJ, 319)—retracts the key elements of the doctrine of taste. Instead of there being a secondary connection between nature and moral feeling as the deduction of taste suggests, Kant's conception of nature's 'ultimate purpose' means rather that a moral interest is the probable basis for attentiveness to both the beauty (formal purposiveness) and purposes of nature (teleology) (CJ, 350).

This position, which completely alters the moral significance credited to the relations between judgment and natural beauty in the doctrine of taste, is foreshadowed prior to the deduction of taste in the 'Critique of Aesthetic Judgment' in Kant's appendix on the sublime. Like his approach to politics, in this appendix the theme of the historical shaping of moral feeling by material elements is once again in the foreground, as Kant argues that, despite having their 'foundation in human nature' and not being 'produced by culture' (CJ, 125), judgments of the sublime require a 'far more cultivated' aesthetic power of judgment as well as 'the cognitive powers on which it is based' (CJ, 124) than judgments regarding beautiful nature.[28]

According to Kant's definition, the sublime is that which 'by its resistance to the interests of the senses, we like directly' (CJ, 127). In its esteem for what is against our sensory interests, the sublime models the feeling of respect that necessarily accompanies duty determined by the moral law. Indeed, unlike the complicated circuit that connects taste and morals, Kant holds that the sensibility required for the sublime presupposes moral feeling (CJ, 125). As I have already indicated, however, Kant thinks the sublime is less significant in its implications than the beautiful primarily because beauty gives ideas of reason an external, analogical form in nature (CJ, §30). Unlike beauty, the sublime demonstrates nature to be counterpurposive for our faculties and testifies to the absence in nature of anything with the magnitude of an idea of reason.

Despite Kant's comments regarding the 'lesser' significance of the sublime, the points he raises in support of its deficiency are peripheral, I think, neither to the key themes of the third *Critique* nor to the important role that human vices play for the progressive ends of constitutional reform. Rather, the sublime's judgment of nature's forms as contrapurposive actively rescales nature, as does teleological judgment, according to a pragmatic anthropology of moral culture.[29] This rescaling, further, allows Kant to entertain theses that are contrary to the explicit path of reasoning he follows in his deduction of taste, but they are implicitly present in its conclusions: on this basis it is possible for Kant to retract in the 'Teleology' the thesis of the pure judgment of taste and to write that a moral interest already directs the aesthetic appreciation of nature's beautiful forms (CJ, 350).[30]

His comments in the *Critique of Judgment* on the seemingly contrapurposive forms of nature are instructive in this context. In his discussion of the sublime, Kant refers to Saussure's[31] comment on *Bonhomme,* one of the Savoy mountains—that 'A certain insipid sadness reigns there'— and writes: 'Thus clearly he [Saussure] also knew an *interesting* sadness, such as is inspired by a wasteland to which people would gladly transfer themselves so as to hear or find out no more about the world, which shows that such wastelands cannot, after all, be quite so inhospitable as to offer no more to human beings than a most troublesome abode' (CJ, 137, his emphasis).

In the 'Teleology,' Kant elaborates on the implications of and extends the rationale behind this aesthetic account of the 'wasteland' that considers its utility in terms of 'feeling,' writing that even those 'things that we find disagreeable and contrapurposive in particular respects' such as vermin in clothes, hair, or beds or mosquitos in the 'wilderness areas of America' can be considered from man's perspective as beneficial for him. Thus vermin, 'we might say . . . are there by a wise provision of nature, namely, as an incentive to keep clean' and thus as a means to 'preserve . . . our health.' The mosquitos that make 'the wilderness . . . so troublesome for the savages' 'we might say' 'are so many prods to stir these primitive people to action, such as draining the marshes and clearing the dense forests that inhibit the flow of air.' And again the 'benefit' would be the health (not of the people, this time, but) of the place (CJ, 259).

These passages are significant because they show the formative role given by Kant to contrapurposive forms of nature for man's ends. The contrapurposive forms of nature, like the purposive forms of beauty, are formative of freedom. Just as in Kant's essays on politics violence is seen as a necessary prod for human progress, so too what is inhospitable in the natural world is formative of the disposition man has over his material circumstances.[32] The idea of nature as a system of ends in ethico-teleology, like the wasteland that is used to occasion elevated feelings in the sublime, or the incentives to development of contrapurposive forms of nature such as vermin described in the 'Teleology' underpin the practical possibility but also shape and promote the agency of man's forming power in the world. The difficulty for the moral agenda of the Kantian philosophy is that this forming power can only be characterised as moral aesthetically.

## The Aesthetic Image of the Moral Man

There are two axes along which the moral man is constituted as an aesthetic image. First, Kant's opposition between desire and moral action (out of respect for the moral law) falls under the genus of the sacrifice of personal inclinations in fidelity to a cause. Put in these terms, there are compelling indications that Kant thinks of the 'moral' dedication to a cause as based in a self-image and thus the moral man as an aesthetic figure. Second, because the motives for action are inscrutable, they can only be *characterised* as moral. Such characterisation, like Kant's interpretations of nature and history as contexts able to bear moral significance, is an aesthetic exercise.

There are two sources of evidence for these claims: (1) the treatment of the theme of the sacrifice of personal inclinations in Kant's appendix on the sublime, and (2) the pivotal role of examples in stylising acts and persons as moral in the *Critique of Practical Reason*. In both of these contexts Kant implicitly raises as a question whether acting against sensory inclinations makes one a sublime or a moral person. In both cases this question is raised because Kant presents the constituent features of pragmatic anthropology against the sliding scale of sensory 'refusal.'

In his popular essays Kant strongly genders this scale. In the 1786 essay 'The Speculative Beginnings of History,' modesty, in the guise of covering the body, is said to instil in 'man' a capacity to refuse sensory gratification that is, for Kant, also the nascent form of the moral idea.[33] This capacity is one that Kant consistently deems women, whose modesty elicits it, incapable of developing themselves.[34]

Four years later, in his appendix on the sublime, the scale of moral refusal is measured against the 'savage' who fails to have the cultivated mental attunement that connects the sublime to moral feeling.[35] The feeling of the sublime 'degrade[s] as small what is large . . . and so . . . posit[s] the absolutely large . . . only in his [the subject's] own vocation' (CJ, 129).[36] Kant characterises the savage's 'superior esteem for the warrior' as a deficient refusal of sensory inclinations because 'in a fully civilized society' more is demanded of those who resist fear: specifically, 'that he also demonstrate all the virtues of peace—gentleness, sympathy, and even appropriate care for his own person—precisely because they reveal to us that his mind cannot be subdued by danger' (CJ, 121). The esteem for the warrior who does not 'yield to danger' is only a nascent presentation of respect for moral action against personal inclinations because it does not also present the virtues of peace which Kant characterises as the sign of a mind that is firm in the face of danger. In this aesthetic, rather than moral, account of the feeling of respect Kant fuses together the values of the moral vocation and war that he had also attempted to connect in his popular essays on history. Hence he writes, 'no matter how much people may dispute, when they compare the statesman with the general, as to which one deserves the superior respect, an aesthetic judgment decides in favor of the general. Even war has something sublime about it if it is carried on in an orderly way and with respect for the sanctity of the citizens' rights' (CJ, 122). The spectator's respect for the general is not in itself moral, but does train the moral habit in its guiding fidelity to duty over personal inclinations.[37] Moreover, such judgments endorse the moral reading of history in the popular essays according to which the violence of war is integrated into a moral worldview.

His use of the examples of the woman's modesty and the savage's esteem for the warrior as nascent indications of the operation of moral restraint in view of a cause is significant because those examples point to the way the moral vocation is installed in an aesthetic image. This image styles the evidence of the renunciation of sensory interests into the form of moral man (himself, as the negative examples of the savage and woman indicate, heavily coded as a European male).

It is not just in his discussion of the nascent moral category of refusal in judgments of the sublime that Kant's use of examples presents the moral man as an aesthetic image. Examples are an integral part of his understanding of moral education, in which the liking for the moral law is formed.[38] These examples are, however, given the demoted status of educational prostheses for the unpracticed.

In his discussion of the topic of moral religion in the appendix on the sublime, Kant presents resistance to dependence on such prostheses in moral and political terms as fidelity to the idea of freedom. He contrasts the adherence to 'duty' above a 'fawning,' 'grovelling' 'base ingratiation' to God (CJ, 134). Moral duty (unlike the semblance of devotion as in the example of the woman's modesty) is given a political reference by his view that the 'images and childish devices' used by religions based on 'ingratiation and fawning' (CJ, 123) are the mechanisms identified and favoured by political authority to manage its subjects. Against these mechanisms Kant favours the negative presentation in the ban on graven images in the Islamic and Judaic traditions. The sanctioning of this ban and with it the negative mechanism of presentation in judgments of the sublime, however, seems hollow when only a few pages earlier Kant had proclaimed the superiority of the general's conduct of war over the less adequate figures of the statesman and the warrior-savage:

It is indeed a mistake to worry that depriving this presentation [of the moral law] of whatever could commend it to the senses will result in its carrying with it no more than a cold and lifeless approval without any moving force or emotion. It is exactly the other way round. For once the senses no longer see anything before them, while yet the unmistakable and indelible idea of morality remains, one would sooner need to temper the momentum of an unbounded imagination so as to keep it from rising to the level of enthusiasm, than to support these ideas with images and childish devices for fear that they would otherwise be powerless. That is also why governments have gladly permitted religion to be amply furnished with such accessories: they were trying to relieve every subject of the trouble, yet also of the ability, to expand his soul's forces. (CJ, 135)

This passage—in which images are criticised as 'childish devices' linked to the ends of political despotism and the positive aesthetic presentation of the moral idea is chided as a false limit on the resistance in morals to the inclinations of the senses—needs to be read in conjunction with Kant's remarks on the positive role of examples as the prosthetic supports necessary to shape the interest of children in the moral law in the second *Critique*. The path Kant outlines there of 'founding and cultivating genuine moral dispositions' (CPrR, 159) accepts that the way to the moral vocation proceeds by nonmoral inducements:

Certainly it cannot be denied that in order to bring either an as yet uneducated or a degraded mind into the path of the morally good, some preparatory guidance is needed to attract it by a view to its own advantage or to frighten it by fear of harm. As soon as this machinery, these leading strings, have had some effect, the pure moral motive must be brought to mind. (CPrR, 158)

Kant describes these 'leading strings' in the vocabulary of systematic philosophy as 'method.' This method has two steps: (1) 'to make judging according to moral laws . . . a habit' and (2) to 'call . . . to notice the purity of will by a vivid exhibition of the moral disposition in examples' (CPrR,

165–67). He encourages the 'educators of youth' to have 'examples at hand' from 'biographies of ancient and modern times' of moral duty (CPrR, 160). Such examples, introduced as a supplement to the instruction of moral catechism, are to 'first show the distinctive mark of pure virtue' and, unlike the heteronomy encouraged by the accessories used in 'fawning religion,' can be 'put . . . before, say, a ten-year-old boy for his judgment [to] see whether he must necessarily judge so by himself without being guided by the teacher' (CPrR, 161).[39]

What is significant here is not that the moral vocation is the product of a moral education, nor that the morally good is introduced by encouraging the nonmoral calculus of rewards and punishments, but that the pivotal place examples play in forming this vocation are themselves aesthetically styled interpretations of motive. These aesthetic stylisations of motive, like the moral interpretations of history and nature, are ways of giving orientation and motivation for action. The postulates of practical reason are not scientifically determined. Although Kant places morals under the auspices of the question 'What must I do?' in contrast to the problem of historical progress which is catalogued under the question 'What may I hope?' the moral world also falls, I think, under the rubric of 'hope.' Indeed the respect for the moral law as a motive for action defines motive in such a way that an agent has no access to this law. There is no way for the agent of an act to know, for instance, that an action structured by a repudiation of sensory inclinations was not in fact motivated by a sense of sublime tragedy. Kant's texts concede this point in their use of self-image as a path to moral habit. In an example he selects as suited to the task of training moral judgment—'the story of an honest man whom someone wishes to induce to join the calumniators of an innocent but powerless person (say, Anne Boleyn accused by Henry VIII of England)' (CPrR, 161)—Kant lists the suffering this man undergoes in his fidelity to the moral law and comments:

> Thus one can lead the young listener step by step from mere approval to admiration, and from admiration to marvelling, and finally to the greatest veneration and a lively wish that he himself could be such a man (though certainly not in his circumstances). Yet virtue here is worth so much only because it costs so much, not because it brings any advantage. All the admiration and even the endeavor to be like this character rest solely on the purity of the moral principle, which can be clearly shown only by removing from the drive to the action everything which

counts as happiness. Thus morality must have more power over the human heart the more purely it is presented. (CPrR, 162)

It is noteworthy that for this image of a moral man to successfully function as an exemplar and figure of identification for the moral education of the young Kant maintains that his suffering should be highlighted.[40] In order to differentiate such suffering from the fanaticism to a cause that may also result in suffering, Kant notes that sensitivity to his needs and those of others sacrificed in the course of his duty differentiates this as a case of moral duty rather than a mania for suffering.[41] The listener's path to the feeling of veneration and the 'lively wish that he himself could be such a man' is trained not just to the man's suffering but also to the 'man himself, who, though righteous, has feelings which are not insensible or hardened to either sympathy or his own needs, at the moment when he wishes never to have lived to see the day which brings him such unutterable pain' (CPrR, 162). Kant explicitly stylises the figure of this suffering man into an aesthetic image presented as an object of inspiration and emulation.

Two features of Kant's chosen method of stylising the difference between moral and nonmoral acts are important to emphasise. First, the language in which Kant describes nonmoral acts is that of a fairytale: the agent is a 'hero' whose acts are called 'noble, magnanimous, and meritorious' (CPrR, 163). Second, it is these features of the nonmoral act that produce in the listener 'a shallow, high-flown, fantastic way of thinking' (CPrR, 88–89) and corrupt the moral education of the soul, 'speedily making [children] . . . fantastic romancers' (CPrR, 163) when their thinking should be directed instead to esteem for the 'firm and accurately defined principles' of morality (CPrR, 89). In his characterisation of the tales of acts not motivated by esteem for the moral law as shallow romances, Kant suggests by way of an example that it is the true moral stories that have more durable effect on their listeners than the presentation of 'noble and magnanimous' acts:

The action by which someone with the greatest danger to his own life seeks to save others in a shipwreck and at last loses his own life will indeed be counted, on the one hand, as duty, but on the other hand, even more as a meritorious action; but [in the latter case] our esteem for it will be weakened very much by the concept of his duty to himself, which here seems to have been infringed. More

decisive is the magnanimous sacrifice of his life for the preservation of his coun-
try, and yet there still remain some scruples as to whether it is so perfect a duty to
devote oneself spontaneously and unbidden to this purpose, and the action itself
does not have the full force of a model and impulse to imitation. But if it is an in-
exorable duty, transgression against which violates of itself the moral law without
respect to human welfare and, as it were, tramples on its holiness . . . *we give our
most perfect esteem to pursuing it and sacrificing to it everything that ever had value
for our dearest inclinations; and we find our soul strengthened and elevated by such an
example when we convince ourselves, by contemplating it, that human nature is capable of such an elevation above everything that nature can present as a drive in opposition to it.*[42] (CPrR, 164, my emphasis)

This example of moral elevation—in which Kant uses the language
of the sublime 'elevation above . . . nature'—is used to defend the view
(contrary to Kant's aesthetic stylisation of these case studies for moral education) that the true moral motive is the one that presents itself as 'a
model and impulse to imitation.'[43]

These examples of good conduct are more than mere devices of
moral education; they are used to testify to the presence of moral motives
in material life. Indeed it is important to take careful note of the way Kant
uses these examples to respond to the pressing need for mediation between
the elements of material life and moral ideas. The examples he uses provide evidentiary frameworks for morals in two ways: they allow man to
think (1) his action is moral and (2) that the postulates of practical reason
may be credibly looked to when he acts. These examples have a formative
role in the determination of moral ideas, not just because they are cases of
material life able to instantiate criteria from which the spectator may characterise acts as moral or judge them to be deficient in relation to esteem for
the moral law, but also because they encourage his faith in (on Kant's view
they impel him to 'imitate' what is apparently already given) the moral dimension of life.

In this context, contrary to his protestations, the fact that the moral
vocation is aesthetically trained and constituted does not concern Kant.
In fact he identifies the considerable social interest attached to the topic
of debating and imputing motives to agents on the basis of their acts as
a useful platform for moral education.[44] Although the inscrutability of
motive in such arguments needs to be negotiated at one remove through
the aesthetic characterisations of action, it is clear that Kant defends these

aesthetic stylisations of moral character, in part because they provide a social context of evidence that motivates belief in a moral world:

> One can often see the character of the person who judges others revealed in
> his judgments. Some of them appear to be chiefly inclined, as they exercise their
> judicial office especially upon the dead, to defend the good that is related of this or
> that deed against all injurious charges of insincerity, finally protecting the entire
> moral worth of the person against the reproach of dissimulation and secret
> wickedness. Others, on the contrary, incline more to attacking this worth by ac-
> cusations and fault-finding. But we cannot always ascribe to the latter the wish to
> argue away virtue from all human examples in order to reduce it to an empty
> name; often it is a well-meaning strictness in the definition of genuine moral im-
> port according to an uncompromising law, in comparison with which (in contrast
> to comparison with examples) self-conceit in moral matters is very much reduced,
> and humility is not merely taught but is also felt by each in a penetrating self-
> examination. Nevertheless, we can often see, in the defenders of purity of inten-
> tion in given examples, that where there is a presumption of righteousness they
> would gladly remove the least spot; and they do so lest, if all examples be disputed
> and all human virtue be denied its purity, virtue be held to be a mere phantom
> and all effort to attain it be deprecated as vain affectation and delusory conceit.
> (CPrR, 159–60)

In this passage Kant emphasises that those who tend to 'fault-
finding' do not reduce virtue 'to an empty name.' The aesthetic presentation of motive in social arguments, in other words, constitutes another
context in addition to the moral interpretations of nature and history in
which Kant builds up a moral idea that is not there and therefore needs to
be put in place.[45]

According to the evidence of social disputes on the topic of moral
character, an action that shows restraint from personal gratification is not
necessarily a moral action. In sanctioning debates over moral motive not
just as a means of cultivating an interest in the moral law but as testimony
to its reality, Kant is, in part, developing a credible context for the judgment of elements of material life as moral. This context acts as support for
the spectator's judgment as well as for the self-image of the 'moral man.'
This image of a practically sovereign subject able to suppress sensual impulses is, however, only a moral fiction because the shaping relation it has
to circumstances is not ipso facto moral. Rather, Kant puts in place the devices of aesthetic presentation as ways of *characterising* man's practical being

as moral and thereby presenting in a 'moral' form the practical disposition over circumstances.[46]

Aesthetic presentation is the characterisation of man's practical being as moral being. It follows that it only makes sense to look at the person with a moral disposition as an aesthetic object[47] and at the ultimate object of the problematic of aesthetic presentation in Kantian philosophy as a 'moral-aesthetic anthropology.'

# Heidegger's Reading of Kant
# and His Historicisation
# of Relations of Presentation

In his Nietzsche lectures, Heidegger defends the Kantian doctrine of aesthetic disinterest against its 'misinterpretation' by Schopenhauer and Nietzsche as a doctrine of 'aesthetic indifference.'[1] In this defence, Heidegger lends support to the view that Kant's doctrine is a nascent form of the phenomenological comportment towards things in which the suspension of a calculative interest intensifies our relation to 'what is.' The terms of Heidegger's defence of Kant on this topic are instructive because they indicate the scope of his own reinterpretation of the salient features of the aesthetic from its status in modern, Kantian philosophy as a specific sphere of experience to the status of a general comportment towards 'what is.'

My thesis in this chapter is that Heidegger's intensification of aesthetic experience away from its status as a specific domain of experience in the direction of a primary ontological relation to things as such needs to be understood from the perspective of his rethinking of the Kantian topic of (aesthetic) presentation. Heidegger's adaptation of Kant's problem of presentation into the status of ontology ultimately, I will argue, underpins what is meant by 'experience' [*Erfahrung*] in his late writings.

We must note that despite the importance of Kant's problem of presentation for Heidegger, the meaning and stakes of this problem are entirely transformed in Heidegger's thought. Heidegger treats Kant's 'ideas of reason' as an 'adversary to thought' because of the primacy given them over their aesthetic presentation.[2] But beyond its role in this criticism of

Kant, 'presentation' can be used, I will argue, to analyse the broad outlines of the itinerary of Heidegger's path of thinking. With such a task in mind and formulated in provisional terms, 'presentation,' for Heidegger, we may say, names the relations in which, in a given epoch, things 'are' for human beings. In this sense, it is the conceptual tool Heidegger uses to think the historicality of being of things.

This provisional formulation of the meaning of presentation in Heidegger's thinking can be clarified by expanding on his objections to the manner of the deployment of 'presentation' in the Kantian philosophy. The critique of Kant on this topic sets out the approach Heidegger will take in his writing on the history of philosophy to the task of critically reflecting on the structure of philosophical dualism. In the Kant book, published in 1929 just two years after *Being and Time,* Heidegger argues that Kant stabilises the problem of presentation by tying it to ideas of reason and in this way suppresses the abyssal structure of presentation. Heidegger's critique of Kant's treatment of this question is instructive for the central topics and shifting themes of his own thought as well as his position on the important post-Kantian traditions of Jena Romanticism and German Idealism.

From his 1927 work *Being and Time* until the lectures of the 1960s such as *On Time and Being* (1962) and *The End of Philosophy* (1964), Heidegger's thought reflected on what he called 'the question of being.' His thinking can be schematically organised in terms of what I take to be the three main approaches he took to this question: in *Being and Time* this question is posed at the level of an inquiry into the being who asks this question; in the major works of the 1930s and 1940s he approaches the question of being in terms of its determination within the philosophical tradition as the 'ground' of beings; and finally, he becomes interested in the question of the experience of being and how language might 'say' this experience.

At each point in this 'path of thinking,' the focus of Heidegger's questioning falls on the problem of presentation. In *Being and Time* this problem takes the form of asking what it means for something to be: in his approach to this question Heidegger adopts the mode of an inquiry into the questioner. What does it mean, he asks, for such a question to be formulated? What kind of being can ask such a question? What are the practical and worldly contexts (including moods such as anxiety and care) in which things are fundamentally revealed to us? In his work on the history of philosophy the approach to this question no longer proceeds by a cata-loguing of the properties of the questioner. The emphasis instead falls on how the question of what it means for something to be is answered in Hegel, Kant, or Descartes, in medieval theology, or in ancient Greek phi-losophy. In this vein, Heidegger is interested in the ways different philo-sophical systems answer the question 'What is being.' Philosophy does not 'forget' the question of being as does 'man' in his absorption in the proxi-mal in the manner in which Heidegger describes the everyday in *Being and Time,* but rather 'mistakes' beings for being and in this way consigns being to oblivion. As we will see, Heidegger comes to recast this 'mistake,' argu-ing that the oblivion of being in beings does not occur at the level of human error, but as a structural feature of what being 'is.' It is this discovery of being's refusal to calculative inquiry that also redeems the project of *Being and Time* from the status of a failed line of questioning.[3]

Heidegger frequently underlines the distinction between his writing on the history of philosophy and a mere 'historiography of ideas'; instead of a description of intellectual trends, Heidegger's writing on the history of philosophy inquires into 'the very ground' of what it means for some-thing 'to be' in fields such as art or technology.[4] 'Art' and 'technology' are each understood by him in epochal terms as particular relations of presen-tation in which an experience of being is given its texture and significance by the prior understanding of 'what is.' Finally, in his later interest in how language is implicated in being, presentation is no longer the question of what it means for something to be, but becomes a question of experiencing the occurrence of being in a sayable way. This 'saying,' which is a 'show-ing,' is the final mode in which Heidegger understands the problem of presentation where the question of the relation between human being and being can be thoughtfully experienced.[5]

Even from this schematic outline, it is possible to see how in each of these approaches to the question of being, the mode of access to this ques-tion, and the terms in which the problem of presentation is formulated, change. The different aspects that the problem of presentation has in Hei-degger must be placed and understood within the frame of reflective expe-rience. Herein lies the continuity of his thinking. Thus he defends *Being and Time* as one way of approaching the question of being in his Schelling lectures of 1936 and maintains the importance of this early work in later pieces such as his 1946 'Letter on "Humanism,"' stating there that what was at issue in the 'turning' from the framework of *Being and Time* was not 'a change of standpoint' but 'the fundamental experience of the oblivion of being.'[6]

As we have just noted, the oblivion of being is not understood as a human failure, but instead as a structural feature of how being itself is. This insight transforms the way that the question of the relation between being and beings is posed in *Being and Time*. Indeed the analysis of the different ways being 'is' in metaphysics leads to the insight that being 'is' a turning away. In Heidegger's later work, thinking is charged with the task of 'saying' this 'turning,' and this 'saying' is the end of philosophy, because having grasped the turning of being in *experience,* thinking is devoted simply to 'saying' this experience.[7] The shift from *recalling* an understanding of how being 'is' in the systems of the history of philosophy to having an *experience* out of the ground of metaphysics from which a saying of being is possible introduces a more emphatic tone to the earlier frameworks of Heidegger's venture. Here the poet/thinker along with whoever reads the poet/thinker's work is given a mode of access to an experience of being.

Admittedly, for the most influential interpreters of Heidegger the different ways of characterising the main shift in emphasis after *Being and Time* under the vocabulary of the 'turn' [*Kehre*] are highly controversial. Otto Pöggeler, for instance, emphasises that Heidegger's thinking needs to be understood 'as a way,' presumably with the quality of continuity, and that the failure to understand 'the consistency of Heidegger's way' from *Being and Time* until his last works leads inattentive readers 'to ascertain and discuss a change in Heidegger's point of view.'[8] In his study of Heidegger's turn, Jean Grondin also stresses that a 'philosophical interpretation' of the turn needs to understand it 'as the consequence of a problematic which appeared after and because of *Being and Time,* but which permitted a better articulation of this work's first intuitions.'[9] In this sense the distinction often made between an 'early' Heidegger developing the project of fundamental ontology and a 'later' Heidegger who revises this ontology in his concern with art, poetry, and language should not be confused with the turn itself: 'for . . . this turn is not primarily a sudden alteration in the itinerary of a thinker, but rather a *thing* or *cause* (*Sache*) which has to be thought for itself.'[10] The cause that prompts this 'turn' is the failed attempt to think the question of the meaning of being within the frame of *Dasein* as the horizon of intelligibility for this question. However, the *Kehre* does not designate an inability on Heidegger's part to think being in the horizon of *Dasein,* but instead names the idea that 'being itself . . . *refuses* itself to a purely metaphysical understanding.'[11] It is ultimately this refusal of being that explains the continuity of Heidegger's 'path of thinking.'[12] Such readings can call on considerable textual support. Heidegger himself states and endorses the principal framework of these readings in his repeatedly expressed view that *Being and Time* was misunderstood when it was dismissed as a failed experiment, as well as in the emphasis he places on 'paths, not works,' or 'questioning' rather than 'answering,' as the modality in which thinking occurs.[13]

In terms of the intellectual content of his writings, however, it is clear that some of the early ways of approaching the question of being will have to be cast aside. There are, in other words, discontinuities in Heidegger's 'path of thinking,' and these can be described by a careful analysis of the different frameworks that organise his approach to the question of being. Let me briefly draw attention to the salient discontinuities in Heidegger's intellectual itinerary before I turn to the task of defining the different respects in which these are important for assessing the place of the topic of presentation in his thinking.

There are two cluster effects that the theme of the refusal of being to calculative inquiry has on Heidegger's project after *Being and Time.* First of all, being is now to be grasped in terms of its historical manifestations and history in turn grasped as a destining of being itself, that is, as we will see, of its having occurred with the Greeks as a disclosive questioning. Thus among the nuances the theme of the forgetting of being takes in Heidegger's philosophy after *Being and Time* is what he refers to in 'The Origin of the Work of Art' lectures[14] as the 'double concealing': the sense in which the forgetting of being is itself a (historical) working of being in the history of modern metaphysics. The significance of this 'double concealing' is that the historico-cultural epochs, which frame the different understandings of being and induce a forgetting of being, are also the frames in which being destines itself as a forgetting. In the writing on the history of philosophy from the time of the 1930s, the central task is that of recalling being, from this forgetting, as a disclosure in metaphysics. It is this recalling of being in metaphysics that prepares the way for the later 'step back' to 'another beginning' rather than, as *Being and Time* had envisaged, the project of a 'fundamental ontology.'[15]

The second group of effects that follow from the thought of the refusal of being concerns the retraction of *Dasein* as the horizon for the intelligibility of the question of being. In *Being and Time* Heidegger assumes an anthropological core, or however one may care to characterise his catalogue of structural or fundamental traits of human existence as such. After *Being and Time* Heidegger delivers a historicising of human persons. The refusal of being relocates the question of the meaning of being away from the horizon of *Dasein* to an occurrence in the history of philosophy. What follows from this relocation is Heidegger's departure from the premise of any philosophical anthropology and the block, therefore, on any fundamental ontology of human beings. The turn to the occurrence of being in relation to the history of metaphysics is also a turn to the Western philosophico-cultural tradition—even if we might be hesitant to define it exclusively in these terms—which asks about beings and thus to a historicisation of 'human beings' within the particular epochs of this tradition.[16] In this connection, the idea of experiencing beings in so far only as they 'are' moves out of the methodological frame of a phenomenology of practical human comportments that it had in *Being and Time*. This idea, after *Being and Time,* is instead understood in the context of a historical semantics of 'what is.' Of course, this semantics is not like any other; it illuminates the historical opening of whole new sets of relations that define in each case (i.e., 'epoch') how beings are treated. It is the insight into the historical variability of the constitutive relations to things only rudimentarily formulated in *Being and Time* that makes impossible the mode of inquiry into the question of being pursued in that work. Instead of understanding beings as *entities,* ontic or ontological, this semantics puts forward epochal *relations* as constitutive of beings. From this perspective, and despite the contrary indications in some of Heidegger's retrospective assessments of this early work, the increasing emphasis on the relations in which things 'are' marks a departure not just from phenomenology but also from the anthropological leanings of *Being and Time*.[17] One indication of this discontinuity can be seen in the insistence in his late work on the hyphenation of *Da-sein*.[18]

The reading Heidegger gives of Kant in *Kant and the Problem of Metaphysics* is, I will argue, pivotal for the articulation of these points of transition: as we will see, this reading marks the shift to the understanding of 'what is' where 'is,' understood as distinct from any other predicate, opens up the terms for Heidegger's analysis of metaphysics *as* the history of being.[19] In particular, the central place Heidegger gives to the transcendental imagination in Kant's doctrine of the schematism institutes the terms of the shift away from the project of fundamental ontology (understood as a repetition of the laying of the ground of metaphysics) towards the features of a thinking, brought out by the groundlessness of presentation in Kant, which leads through the recalling of this groundlessness in the history of metaphysics to the poetic project of 'saying' the experience of being.

From the perspective of this brief schematisation of the main staging posts in Heidegger's so-called path of thinking and the discontinuities this introduces into his approach to the question of the meaning of being, some important themes in his discussions of technology and art become clear. Art is a significant topic for Heidegger's approach to the treatment of the question of what it means for something 'to be.' In his lectures of the mid-1930s on 'The Origin of the Work of Art' he states that there are 'historical variations' in what it means for something to be and looks to the defining vocabulary of philosophy to understand what an artwork 'is.'[20] The mode of presencing in art works is fundamentally altered in modern philosophical aesthetics, which understands art 'to be' an object for a subject.

Against this aesthetic determination of 'art,' which displaces art from any relation to truth, Heidegger argues that van Gogh's painting of the peasant shoes shows the 'truth' of these shoes as reliability. Heidegger's attempt to retrieve a relation between art and truth that would counter the aesthetic subjectivisation of art and with it the exclusive claims of calculative thinking on truth has led to the interpretation of 'art' in his late writings as a counter-term to the modern technologisation of experience.[21] From the perspective of the itinerary of Heidegger's thought previously outlined, important points of clarification can be made to the interpretative framework used to set 'art' apart from 'technology' in this way. Seen from the vantage point of the problem of saying the experience of being, the important question is not how to 'counter' technology, but rather, how is the articulation of the experience of technology enabling for a saying of being? What is it about technology that allows this 'saying'? Equally, and on the other side of the equation, if 'art,' as some prominent commentators on Heidegger insist, allows the free comportment towards 'what is' that would allow the saying of being in the technological *Gestell,* how is this role of art consistent with Heidegger's understanding of the historical variability of 'what is' in the epoch of technology? Clarifying the status of 'art' within the itinerary of Heidegger's thinking of being is important because the claim that art has an anomalous, critical position in the age of technology is a pervasive assumption not just in recent Heidegger scholarship but in current literary and theoretical debates.

The respective positions of art and technology in the economy of Heidegger's late thought and the stakes of these terms for the prospects of contemporary criticism will be examined in the next chapter and taken up again as a central theme in my later discussions of Lacoue-Labarthe and Nancy. In the rest of this chapter my focus will fall on the task of defining the place of the topic of presentation in Heidegger's writing on the Western philosophical tradition. My discussion of this topic will be divided into three parts. First, I will approach this question from a genetic angle: how does the problem of presentation arise and how and with what effects is it altered in the course of Heidegger's thinking? These questions, I will argue, can usefully be clarified by considering the pivotal place of Heidegger's reading of Kant for the itinerary of his thought. My second line of inquiry will be to define the different respects in which this problem, as it is defined in his reading of Kant, is important for Heidegger's account of the approach of the modern philosophical tradition to the question of being and, in particular, the status of Jena Romanticism and German Idealism within this account. In Heidegger's lectures on Schelling the earlier discussion of presentation in his Kant book is revised in light of the importance of the topic of presentation for the idea of the system, as Kant's *Critique of Judgment* frames it, in post-Kantian philosophy. Finally, I would like to consider the perspective that this consideration of Heidegger's approach to the central topics and themes of modern philosophy has for the later path his thinking takes towards the task of 'saying' the experience of being.

## Heidegger's *Kant and the Problem of Metaphysics*

According to the schematisation of Heidegger's thought outlined previously, his Kant book leads out of the first and into the second phase of his approach to the thinking of the question of being. There are structural reasons to do with the incomplete composition of *Being and Time* as well as reasons to do with the content of the Kant book that could be used to support such a categorisation. In his original plan for *Being and Time,* Heidegger had envisaged two parts, each with three divisions. In the first part of *Being and Time,* only two of the three projected divisions were published. The first two divisions were (1) the preparatory analysis of *Dasein* and (2) the analysis of *Dasein* and temporality. The third division, 'Time and Being,' was composed and published late in Heidegger's career, after it was delivered in 1962 as a lecture.

The second part, guided by the problematic of temporality supposed to have been completed in part one, was to have performed a phenomenological destruction of the history of ontology. Although none of this destruction of ontology was published in *Being and Time* and the methodology of phenomenology was later discarded,[22] the topics of the three projected divisions of this part—Kant's doctrine of schematism and time, the ontological foundation of Descartes' *cogito sum,* and Aristotle's essay on time—are all topics of discussion in later publications and lectures.[23] Two peculiarities in the context and content of Heidegger's treatment of Kant are indicative of Kant's importance for the itinerary of his thinking: not only is the projected division on Kant the only one of the projected second part that is the subject of a book-length study, but despite the fact that the book on Kant is published with the aim of clarifying the incomplete project of *Being and Time,* it becomes the pivotal text, not for the continuation of the project in *Being and Time,* but for setting out the terms of Heidegger's departure from the mooted project of 'destruction of ontology.' It is a notable feature of this book that it makes this departure in relation to the topic of presentation. In this regard, it is not without significance for the trajectory of Heidegger's thinking that the Kant book precedes the lecture 'Time and Being' which was to have been its precursor and the forerunner to the 'destruction of ontology' in the original plan for *Being and Time.*

Heidegger's interpretation of Kant is the hinge for his turn to the historical setting or 'occurrence' of the question of being in the philosophical tradition. Kant's *Critique of Pure Reason* occupies a special position in this tradition, which Heidegger, in his 1973 Preface to the fourth edition of the Kant book, describes as 'a refuge' in which he 'sought . . . an advocate for the question of Being which [he] . . . posed.'[24] This 'refuge' comes not from 'what Kant says' but from the 'abyss' at the ground of metaphysics that 'occurs' in his philosophising.[25] The refusal of being to metaphysical understanding that occurs here and that causes Heidegger to revise his project of fundamental ontology is a consequence, in Heidegger's view, of Kant's subordination of the finitude of the subject to a calculative, metaphysical ground. Heidegger finds the evidence of this subordination in the shift in the role of the power of the transcendental imagination in the passage from the A to the B version of the *Critique of Pure Reason*. The power of the transcendental imagination is significant for Heidegger because as the 'hidden root' of sensible and intelligible knowledge in the A version of the *Critique of Pure Reason* it undoes Kant's attempt to ground metaphysics in the operations of a transcendental subject. Were the transcendental imagination to be at the root of 'knowledge,' the unity of the subject as the ultimate ground of knowledge would be shattered. The demotion suffered by the transcendental imagination, which becomes in the B version of the *Critique of Pure Reason* a subordinate tool for the faculty of understanding, obstructs from view the possibility that the synthesis of intuitions and concepts is beyond the disposition of the subject. For Heidegger, whose repetition of Kant is an assertion of this very possibility, the inability to ground metaphysics in a calculative function is a loosening of the grasp of the faculty of the understanding and the subject who is its agent on the question of being. In his Kant book Heidegger thus finds some general points of compatibility between the role of the transcendental imagination in the A version of the *Critique of Pure Reason* and his own thinking. However, we can be much more precise about the significance of the power of the transcendental imagination in Kant's first *Critique* for Heidegger's approach to the question of being once we set out its role in the problem of presentation.

According to Heidegger's reading of the *Critique of Pure Reason*, what Kant retreats from in the B version is the priority of the problem of presentation, understood here as the question of 'what is,' over the subject who now purports to answer this question in its claim to ground 'what is.' The significance of this priority can be understood in negative terms as the defeat of the subject as the ground for experience of things and, more positively, as an implication of human finitude.[26] Thinking through this implication will, in turn, lead Heidegger after the Kant book to a conception of being as a relation to 'what is' in which the reflective relation to the relation to things is no longer secondary to, but constitutive of, what beings are. In his Schelling lectures of 1936, which adopt this posture towards Kant, the questioning of Kant is concerned with what it means for something to be within the perspective of Kantian philosophy. The Kant book leads to this path because it discovers that the transcendental imagination in Kantian philosophy is the *Ab-grund* for what beings are. Thus the project of recalling the conceptions of how being occurs in the history of philosophy becomes, after the Kant book and because of the questions posed there, the main venue for the reflection on the question of being as such. When Kant retracts the grounding of knowledge in the transcendental imagination in the B version of the *Critique of Pure Reason* and identifies the operations of the subject with the faculty of the understanding, he retracts the thought that intuition might precede the calculative ground he seeks for knowledge.[27] In casting the understanding in a determinative role over the synthesis of intuitions Kant, on Heidegger's reading, turns the subject into a ground through which objects exist in time, and as such a ground its own finitude would be lost and it would become an origin. Hence Heidegger contests not just the cognitive primacy asserted in the epistemological reading of Kant in the neo-Kantian tradition, but also the way in which this primacy awards the subject the status of a ground through which its own finitude is forgotten. What is crucial here is that the problem raised by the priority of the question of presentation over its calculative ordering by the understanding is suppressed *by* the forgetting of the subject's own finitude. This problem, starkly put, is how to comprehend the relation to 'what is.' The orthodox, epistemological reading of Kant makes time the internal sense of the subject. As a result the activity of the subject's faculties *constitutes* the field of objectivity: the imagination constitutes objects in time (synthesised intuition) and supplies objects for determination by the categories of the understanding. Time thus becomes a tool of the cognitive faculties and one that supports the operations of the subject. The rewriting and subordination of the role of the transcendental imagination in the B version cover over what for Heidegger is the central problem raised by the *Critique of Pure Reason:* namely, the question of the constitutive relation of finitude to 'what is.' Neither of the stems of the Kantian schema—intuition and understanding—is adequate to this problem because each already assumes that 'what is' is given and given in relation to the operations of the subject.

It is in phrasing presentation from the perspective of human finitude as a problem to be thought that Heidegger's Kant book rejects the epistemological framework in which the givenness of 'what is' is assumed. His 'repetition' of Kant takes Kant's transcendental imagination in the direction of Heidegger's conception of existence as transcendence beyond beings to being. The transcendental imagination is not tied to beings or to that-which-is, but to what in comparison with beings is a 'nothing.' This no-thing, described in Heidegger's later work as the 'clearing,' is in the terms of his repetition of Kant the transcendental condition through which beings are able to be present *as* beings. Defined by a surmounting of beings (a transcendental nothing) that allows a receiving of beings, the transcendental imagination is essentially time. The origin of presentation in time provides a glimpse of the nothingness, or in the later vocabulary the *Ab-grund,* of the thing. Heidegger thus understands through his repetition of the place of finitude in Kant that before entities are 'present' there is a relation to the entity as such which discloses its taking place with and alongside us, and a relation to this relation that frames how 'we' and 'things' belong together. His repetition of Kant draws attention to presencing over any present thing and in this way restores the question of being as the root of metaphysics.

The consequences of this repetition can be explained in terms of the salient features, previously described, of the 'turn.' Whereas in *Being and Time* finitude has a thematically minor place as one of the existential modalities of *Dasein* (as the authentic setting of being-toward-death), the designation of finitude in the Kant book as the abyssal ground of metaphysics leads Heidegger to a nascent formulation of the refusal of being. The route Heidegger takes to this refusal is crucial for understanding the role of Kant in the 'turn.' For it is not just that finitude, on Heidegger's repetition of Kant, becomes the abyssal nonground for the question of being; more importantly, it moves to unseat the ground-laying of metaphysics through dislodging the grounding status of the subject of representation in Kant's transcendental philosophy. Heidegger treats the theme of the abyssal nonground of the question of being in a number of his essays and lecture courses, but its occurrence in his reading of Kant is significant for the path his thinking takes in these later pieces. Finitude, represented by the transcendental power of imagination in the A version of the first *Critique,* is the term through which the historicisation of human persons is ventured but also 'concealed' in Kant's B version of the first *Critique*. The theme of finitude that is used by Heidegger as a discreet form of access to the originary meaning of metaphysics after the Kant book leads him towards a reading of being as it occurs in the history of metaphysics and commits him also to the path that will 'reveal' the modality of this occurrence as a 'refusal' or 'concealment' of being.[28]

## 'Presentation' and the 'History of Being' in Modern Metaphysics

The turn to the analysis of the question of being as it occurs in the history of philosophy alters the settings for the question of presentation from an inquiry into the being who asks this question to the way that this question is understood in particular epochs of philosophical investigation as the constitutive relations for what being 'is.' When Heidegger turns his attention to the question of how Kantian philosophy answers the question of what being is, he concludes that the way Kant answers this question gives him a distinct position in the history of modern philosophy. In my view, Heidegger understands the exceptional position occupied by Kant in modern philosophy in terms of the way that Kantian philosophy raises the question of presentation.[29]

Although Heidegger's so-called repetition of Kant in *Kant and the Problem of Metaphysics* signals the end of his project of fundamental ontology, the importance of Heidegger's treatment of the topic of presentation in this book has a restricted scope. Neither the insight of the turn into the historical variability of the relations between being and human being nor the occurrence of being as a disclosive questioning in the history of metaphysics is able to be pursued within the stated framework of this work, which investigates the ground-laying aspirations of Kantian philosophy with a view to a more original ground. In this respect there is a gap between Heidegger's intentions and the tools of his analysis; one might say that the aspiration to fundamental ontology cannot sustain itself in the face of the demands on thought that the transcendental imagination makes. But once this question comes into view in the formulation I give here, there is a logic of consistency of stages that push aside the aspiration to fundamental ontology. Moreover, the investigation of this book is conducted within the horizon of the doctrine of the schematism in Kant's *Critique of Pure Reason.* The provenance of presentation as the key question of the critical system is mentioned only in subsequent editions of the Kant book and its status as the driving problem of subsequent German Idealist and Romantic philosophy, which itself depends on the later perspective that being is a disclosive questioning within the history of metaphysics, is only systematically examined in Heidegger's lectures of the mid-1930s.

At first glance there are two possible genealogies for the problem of presentation in Heidegger's thought. First is his reading of Kant's third *Critique* in which presentation is the concept that frames the relation between essence/existence or the ideal/actual (and here it is important to signal Heidegger's careful attention to the development of this concept in his account of the German Idealists and Romantics). Second, the Greeks also provide a genealogy for this problem in their understanding of presencing as a taking place. The Greek conception of being as presencing enjoys an early, defining position for the task of framing the question of being. But being as presencing loses its absolute orientating role and becomes only one system of understanding being when Heidegger turns his attention to the different treatments of being in the history of philosophy.

In this respect, the significance of the topic of presentation as an historical question is made explicit in Heidegger's analysis of the provenance of the Kantian problem of presentation in German Idealism and Romanticism in his Schelling lectures. The lectures on Schelling, delivered in the summer semester of 1936, later published as *Schelling's Treatise on the Essence of Human Freedom,* are a guide for the development of Heidegger's thinking on the points first raised in the Kant book but now thought in terms of the project of recalling the thinking of being in philosophy *as* a disclosive questioning.[30] The Kant book links finitude and time with the abyssal ground of metaphysics. The importance of this link is registered in Heidegger's view that in Kant, like the Greeks, one finds 'authentic philosophizing'[31] and in his assertion that because Kant 'sleepwalks' towards authentic questioning and 'forgets' and even 'suppresses' the question of fundamental ontology, Heidegger himself will need, in his reading, to 'repeat' this question.[32] On the topic of finitude this 'repetition' manifests itself in Heidegger's insistent query as to what precisely is meant by Kant's assertion that all thinking is finite and in his seemingly impatient remark that this assertion is tautological, 'in the fashion of a round circle' (KB, 175). In these respects, (1) his inquiry into the ground of appearance in general and (2) his setting of subsequent thinking in the direction of approaching this ground with time as the guide, Kant occupies a unique position in Heidegger's description of modern metaphysics.[33]

Conversely, the texts of post-Kantian German Idealism and Romanticism represent in their fascination with system the culmination of tendencies already present in Kant but closer in style to the suppression of so-called authentic philosophising in Descartes. The overriding concern with system in Idealism and Romanticism closes off the path that Kant's problem of presentation had opened, although this concern with system is itself taken up on the terrain set by Kant's problem. Even though Heidegger credits Schelling and Nietzsche with escaping the lures of the moderns' path to the systematisation of reason and, for this reason, as standing out against this background, he also describes their thinking as 'stranded' because their manner of questioning was not foundational (as Kant's was). Further, their failure is described by Heidegger as 'the sign of the advent of something completely different, the heat lightning of a new beginning. Whoever really knew the reason for this breakdown and could conquer it intelligently would have to become the founder of the new beginning of Western philosophy' (SB, 3). In his writing of the late 1940s, the call for a 'step back' to 'another beginning' comes out of his rethinking of 'the ground of philosophy' but also, I think, seems to call for an experience of being fundamentally discontinuous with the perspective of the history of being. I will return to this point and the sense in which the call for an experience of being signals an aporia in Heidegger's reflection on the history of being in the following section, but first I want to define more closely the significance of the topic of presentation for his understanding of the landscape of modern philosophy.[34]

For Heidegger modern metaphysics attempts to 'ground' being in a causal, calculable system in which being is assimilated to the operations of a subject. In general, Heidegger understands the conception of being as representation in the moderns against the background of ancient Greek metaphysics. The distinction, introduced by the Greeks, between *what* beings are (essence in Christian theology) and *that* they are or are not (existence in Christian theology) is the 'event' in the history of being that inaugurates metaphysics.[35] This 'event' does not inaugurate a continuous historical progression that preserves as it develops the fundamental constituents of metaphysics. Such a notion of historical continuity is an 'illusion' whose support lies in the 'opinion . . . that the fundamental concepts of metaphysics remain everywhere the same.'[36] The essential constituents of being, in Heidegger's view, change with changes in the state of the language in which the meaning of being is questioned and understood, but also change by the imperatives and questions that the tradition places on thinking. These changes, further, are 'destinings' of being that are impervious to the construal of them in logical or historiographical terms as 'a sequence belonging to a process of history.'[37] The beginning of metaphysics as the history of being establishes the key distinction between 'essence' and 'existence' that sets up being as a 'cause' that is distinct from 'appearance.' But this distinction has an altered stature in modern metaphysics. In modern metaphysics calculative thinking becomes the ground for being. The features of this new ground amount to an 'onto-theology' (SB, 51) which, through the key conception of system, makes possible the grasping of being as 'representation' for a subject.

Three key features of modern metaphysics connect the forgetting of the question of being to the question of presentation. The moderns install being in a false relation between an 'absolute' that is 'exterior' to appearance and this appearance[38]; this split between being and 'appearance' has its origins in Plato's metaphysics but reoccurs in modern metaphysics as the split between ideas and their presentation (QCT, 12);[39] and this Kantian theme of the presentation of ideas undergoes a 'completion' in German Idealism where ideas become 'ostensive' rather than, as they are in Kant, 'heuristic' (SB, 41).[40] With the notion of system, German Idealism resolves the problem of presentation, but in so doing it suppresses the question of being as a question, reducing being to a provocative idea of the history of philosophy in need of an adequate presentation, that is to say, in the perspective of metaphysics, a constitutive self-same intelligible order, on the one hand, and an experientially accessible adequate representation on the other.

It is worth underlining the significance of the fact that the context Heidegger gives to these features of modern metaphysics is, as his comments on historiography and language both indicate, not a straightforward, linear development. In his lecture course on Schelling he foregrounds the role of the idea of system in the epoch of modern metaphysics. The systematic history of philosophy can be written only from the standpoint of the philosophical system. In 'The Age of the World Picture' and 'The Question Concerning Technology' this idea of system resurfaces as an index of the modern age but in each case finds its essential coordinates in Cartesian philosophy. Whether it is in the context of German Idealism or Cartesian thought, system is the modality in which the intelligibility of being is fully grasped in modern metaphysics as a disposition of the subject over being. It is, finally, this positioning of the subject that defines the modern epoch of the 'world picture' as the 'represented-ness of that which is' for a subject (AWP, 132).

Kant's position in this history is significant beyond his discovery and suppression of the question of finitude. His significance lies in the unusual relation he has to the key figures of modern metaphysics: at once Kant's philosophy represents the final major turning point of the threads of the history of *subiectum* in metaphysics since Plato, but it also stands out from the conception of system in German Idealism and the theological motifs of rationalism in posing presentation as a problem.

Heidegger consistently points up the crucial importance of Descartes for the modern 'mathematical system of reason' (IM, 35).[41] He suggests in a number of places that Descartes opens the path for the 'completion' and 'consummation' of modern metaphysics as representation.[42] However, I would like to emphasise not just that Kant is also intimately involved in this process by which the systematisation of reason alters being, but that for Heidegger the Kantian involvement has an epochal stature that distinguishes his contribution to modern metaphysics from that of Descartes. In Heidegger's account, the distinguishing feature of the metaphysics of the moderns is that it splits appearance from being and grounds the essence of things in the certitude of the subject's representations. The core of this representation, as we will see, is a *willing*. In the previous discussion of Kant we saw that Kant used aesthetic presentation as a way of resolving the specific problem in modern philosophy of the dualism between reason's ideas (the subject's representations) and sensible forms (appearance). In Kant's third *Critique* the question of an adequate sensible presentation for reason's ideas becomes a problem in the context of dualism in Western thought. The significance of Kant's text within the Western canon can be seen historically backward and forward: for his successors, this text sets the terms and problems for the German Idealists; but it also departs in a radical way from the guiding assumptions of his precursors in rationalism.

Heidegger understands Kant's unique significance in terms of the double divorce his understanding of the question of presentation effects from these other philosophical movements. Kant starts out from the question of presentation as such and in so doing redefines the terms of the relations which were supposed to be self-standing, such as free will and nature. In contrast, in Descartes and the rationalists who followed him, including Spinoza, the question of presentation as a relation is raised downstream from that of the elements that are related in the presentation and is resolved theologically. Kant's discussion of presentation *as the key problem for metaphysics* thus stands out against this background of rationalist philosophy. But it also stands out, as Heidegger saw, from the German Idealists whose own project rests on Kant's foundation (SB, 35). There are three topics, which I will treat in the following text, that may be used to frame Heidegger's understanding of the significance of the treatment of the question of presentation by German Idealism. These three topics are (1) the status of ideas of reason vis-à-vis the elements of material and historical life, (2) the idea of system in German Idealism as the integration of ideas and the elements of material and historical life, and (3) the place that the will to system plays in German Idealism as the mechanism of this integration. Heidegger's account of the treatment of these topics by German Idealism is important not just because it elucidates the factors involved in the suppression of presentation as a question in modern metaphysics, but also because it shows, from this perspective, why Kant's own treatment of this question culminated in failure.

The German Idealists follow Kant's lead by asking how the absolute can be present in material and historical life. Again the frame for the answers to these questions is set by the third *Critique*. The concept of the literary absolute in early Romanticism and of 'Spirit' as the historical presentation of the idea in Hegel are, like the conception of symbolic presentation in Kant, so many ways of bending presentation to the need of the absolute as the self-same intelligible ground. Kant's peculiar position in modern metaphysics can be summarised in the following terms: Kant calls for the systematisation of reason's ideas and this means the grounding of reason's ideas in a totality. But the place of finitude in his thought also undermines the self-relation that system demands. Heidegger's Kant book can be read in this context as identifying in the transcendental power of the imagination the priority of presentation to the supposed terms that are to be related through it. Kant's 'shrinking back' before his discovery of the transcendental power of imagination is in these terms a 'shrinking back' from the insight that the absolute does not 'precede' or ground 'its' presentation.

Heidegger characterises the 'new reflection' that Kant gives of reason as a consequence of the requirement in modern philosophy for a 'more primordial knowledge about the nature of reason' (SB, 35). In Heidegger's view the failing of Kant's conception of reason and its need for the presentation of its ideas is not so much that the ideas are merely 'heuristic' but that Kant trusts 'in the truth of the basic fact of human reason' (SB, 38). This trust structures the particular form that the problem of system takes in Kant as an attempt to ground the ideas of reason. This uncritical belief in reason is also understood by Heidegger as the motive behind Kant's turn away from the insights of the A version of the *Critique of Pure Reason*. Kant's failing in this respect is indicative of the wider difficulties that, for Heidegger, establish reason in the role of 'the most stiff-necked adversary of thought.'[43]

The ideas of reason in Kant's thought do not show us given or present objects; rather, they *represent* the 'unity of the articulated manifold of a realm as a totality' (SB, 36). It is this regulative orientation of the ideas towards comprehensive unity that marks out 'the highest ideas' in Kant's philosophy as 'those in which the essential main realms of beings are represented: the ideas of God, world, man' (SB, 36). These ideas are, until the analogical presentation of the idea of freedom in the *Critique of Judgment*, only present as ideas. The conception of system in Kant is that of the unifying of manifold knowledge under an idea, but the problem of grounding this system especially in the analogical mode of presentation in the *Critique of Judgment* is immense given that it would require a founding unification of what are only heuristic, regulative ideas.

Nonetheless, the significance of Kant's conception of reason as the faculty of ideas for the modern systematisation of reason is that this conception provides the mechanism under which 'ordinary knowledge' is transformed into a 'systematic unity' and what would otherwise be 'a mere aggregation of cognitions' is made 'into science' (SB, 37). How this conception of system designates what is scientific in a science is important for Kant's contribution to the modern conception of a correspondence between thinking and being: systematic reason designates the quality of scientificity not according to an external principle under which areas are arranged into arbitrary categories but as 'the anticipatory selection of the inner stringent essential unity of respective areas.' This 'anticipatory selection' is what 'at the same time' prefigures 'the articulation of the connection in which the manifold appearances of the area stand' (SB, 38). Kant, then, conceives of system as the anticipatory organisation of experience for the subject that is also the conditioning of being into the order of an object ('the manifold appearances').

In Heidegger's reconstruction Kant's attempt at articulating his conception of system ran into 'an indissoluble difficulty' (SB, 40). This difficulty, that what the highest ideas represent 'is not itself presented and presentable as a being' (SB, 40), opens the path to the 'completion' of Kant in German Idealism. The German Idealists add to the will to system in Kant 'the *essential* insight . . . that such a system could only be found and formed in accordance with knowledge if knowledge were *absolute* knowledge. In addition, system itself became the *absolute requirement* and thus the key term for philosophy as such' (SB, 35). The change in the idea of system 'presupposes' the self-understanding of philosophy 'as absolute, infinite cognition.' In turn this self-understanding of philosophy places a 'heightened emphasis on what is creative in human reason' (SB, 35).

This aspect of the will to system in German Idealism links up, in Heidegger's account, with Nietzsche's professed renunciation of system. In both cases the central feature of modern metaphysics as willing is affirmed.[44] The will is the pivot of modern metaphysics. It designates the act of representing by which man defines himself to be at the centre of 'beings as a whole.' Crucially this self-definition means that 'man' at the same time *wills* himself to be at the centre and willing is what secures him in this position. In the ancient world it was the order of the cosmos, or in the medieval period it was God who placed 'man' in the centre. In the modern period the formation of system means not only that 'man' must place himself in the centre, but also for this event to take place he has to arrange things around himself *freely*. This places beings under his disposition at the same time that this will to 'a freely forming and knowing *control* over beings as a whole projects for itself the structure of Being as this will' (SB, 34). In other words, 'willing' designates here the sense in which this *description* of man's control over beings is also a *projection* that wills this control. In the essay 'The Age of the World Picture,' first presented two years after his Schelling lectures, Heidegger emphasises that what is decisive about the position of 'man' in the modern age is not that his position 'in the midst of what is' contrasts with the medieval and ancient 'man,' but that he 'expressly takes up this position as one constituted by himself, that he intentionally maintains it as that taken up by himself, and that he makes it secure as the solid footing for a possible development of humanity' (AWP, 132). It is this account of modern metaphysics as 'man's' view that he *is* at the centre of beings but, as Heidegger adds, is only 'secured' as this centre by also willing himself there that culminates in Nietzsche's 'completion' of metaphysics in his conception of being *as* a valorising will.[45] Heidegger understands Nietzsche's countermovement to the passive nihilism that would rather will nothing than not will at all in a valorising will as a closing of the circle in which being is the effect of the will's calculations.[46] In the case of German Idealism, as we will see in a moment, the will to system also has an effect of closure that consists in absorbing finitude to a moment in the absolute and thus sealing the gap that leaves the problem of presentation in Kant as a force and hence impetus to think.

The 'stormy will to system' in German Idealism that is 'supported and guided' 'above all' by 'a dispute' with Kant's *Critique of Judgment* (SB, 42) aims to force a presentation for 'highest ideas.' Against Kant's faith that these ideas of reason 'necessarily belong to the nature of human reason' (and the fidelity to the project of system as finding an adequate presentation for these ideas), Heidegger queries not just why it is that these and only these ideas are considered by Kant to be necessary but also how the connection between these ideas can be grounded 'if these Ideas are not drawn from the beings themselves which they mean and from the corresponding immediate comprehension of these beings' (SB, 40). The significance of this question for the articulation of the key concerns of Heidegger's thinking cannot be overstated. Heidegger in fact reverses Kant's perspective to argue that the ideas of reason do not, as Kant thought, precede the elements and context of material life but are in fact drawn from this context in the first place. It is because Kant raises the question of presentation downstream from the ideas which require presentation that his aim of systematisation remains inherently unfulfillable.

The significance of Kant's abortive system is retrospectively illuminated by the central place of system in German Idealism. In respect of the problem of presentation, the 'achievement' of the latter makes apparent the reasons Kant had to 'fail.' In contrast to the prominence of the problem of presentation that in Kant negotiates the divide between the absolute and the dependence of a finite subject on sensible forms, the definition of system in German Idealism automatically resolves the problem of presentation. The complaint of the German Idealists that the Kantian ideas of reason are not ostensive but form only a 'prelude to reason' is resolved by their achievement of system as making possible the grasping of being for a subject. System is now less a 'framework of knowledge of beings,' as it was in Kant, than it is concerned with 'the jointure of Being itself, and toward shaping it accordingly' (SB, 39). As we will see, this concern with the 'jointure of Being' differentiates system from an arbitrary, external imposition on raw data and defines instead the inherent pliability of being once it is conceived *as* system. The ideas, which form the basic representations of reason in Kant, cannot for the German Idealists just be guiding concepts. Rather they insist that, in Heidegger's words, '*something* is thought in these Ideas; and *what* is thought, God, world, man, is taken to be so essentially determinative that *knowledge* is possible only on the basis of what is thought here' (SB, 43).

The distinctive mark of the change to Kant's split between ideas and their presentation is that the totality of what is known is 'released from all relations' and as thus absolved becomes the '*Ab-solute*' (SB, 43). The key to this release from all relations is that the German Idealists define the absolute knowledge of system in terms of self-relation. From their perspective the problem of presentation raised by Kant follows from the block he placed on the intellectual intuition of the Absolute. For Kant, a finite being is restricted to sensuous knowledge and on this count restricted also to an approximate relation to the absolute. Such knowledge is mediated by a sensuous relation and thus also by a 'thing' (SB, 43). In contrast, the German Idealists insist on knowledge of the ideas, and script this knowledge as

nonobjective knowledge of beings as a whole [that] now knows itself as the true and absolute knowledge. What it wants to know is nothing other than the structure of Being which now no longer stands as an object somewhere over against knowledge, but which itself becomes in knowledge, and this *becoming to itself* is *absolute Being.* (SB, 45)

This revision of Kant alters the constituent elements that make presentation a problem for him on account of its dissolution of the division of terms in his conception of knowledge into the greater unity of system. In German Idealism knowledge

explain[s] itself in terms of its correspondence to mathematical knowledge. In mathematical knowledge, thinking (the concept thought) is adequate to Being (object). Here one cannot ask whether what is correct in 'thinking' is also correct in 'Being.' Accordingly [and in defiance of Kant], there is also an absolute unity of thinking and Being in intellectual intuition. (SB, 46)

What is significant here is that the relation between the knower and the known and with it the question of 'whether what is correct in "thinking" is also correct in "Being"' is removed. The self-standing, self-relation that is absolute knowledge contains within itself the knower and the known in an original unity. There is not an Absolute *outside* the knower as an object, nor *within* the knower 'as a thought in the "subject"' (SB, 47). Thus the question of a meaningful relation to an outside that creates the problem of presentation of a totality that is beyond any particular relation (but which Kant nonetheless adapts to particular, analogous 'things,' as I argued in previous chapters) is already resolved:

The philosopher as the knower is neither related to things, objects, nor to 'himself,' the 'subject,' but, in knowing, he knows what *plays around* and *plays through* existing things and *existing* man and what *prevails through* all this as a whole *in existing*. (The subject-object and the object-subject.) (SB, 47)

The German Idealists can thus be understood from Heidegger's perspective as having an ambiguous relation to Kant's thought. On the one hand, they follow the thread of Kant's aim to systematise reason, but in doing so they absorb the relation to an outside that, as Heidegger's Kant book emphasises, finitude imposes in Kant. In the German Idealists finitude is reduced to a moment within the Absolute. However, like Kant, the Idealists leave the question of the *need* for this determination of system in terms of the presentation of ideas hanging. The system is *presented* as the solution of the problem of presentation, but only on the condition of the elimination of finitude.

In resolving this problem of presentation in its systematisation of reason *as* an 'immediately grasping' faculty (SB, 44), the German Idealists also suppress the problem of presentation *as it occurs* in Kant. Nonetheless we need to be careful of the nuances that condition Heidegger's position on Kant: for Heidegger it is also clear that Kant himself suppresses this problem and, moreover, provides the ground from which this suppression is 'completed' in post-Kantian thought (SB, 47–48). Indeed after Kant's suppression of the primacy of presentation over ideas in the B version of the *Critique of Pure Reason,* the requirements of the critical system (the faith in the nature of human reason, the conception of philosophy as a reflection on reason, and the drive to ground the unity of reason's ideas and to comprehend beings as a whole in this systematic unity) only attain their accurate elaboration 'when the knowledge of Being—*en route* through Kant's philosophy—understands itself as absolute knowledge' (SB, 47). Heidegger writes:

For only from that moment on when this idea of system as the absolute system of reason knows itself in absolute knowledge is system absolutely founded in terms of itself, that is, really mathematically certain of itself, founded on absolute self-consciousness and comprehending all realms of beings. And where system knows itself in this way as unconditioned necessity, the requirement of system is not only no longer something external, but what is inmost and primary and ultimate. (SB, 47–48)

This elaboration of the presuppositions of the Kantian idea of system in German Idealism has a profound effect on the understanding of philosophy. From the perspective of German Idealism the whole history of Western philosophy now comes to be understood in terms of 'system.' Each 'earlier' form of system is now configured through the prism of 'absolute system,' and 'system' becomes 'understood as what is innermost in history itself. And the thinkers of German Idealism are aware of themselves as necessary epochs in the history of absolute Spirit' (SB, 48). The way that German Idealism institutes a history of philosophy that transforms history into 'a path of absolute knowing on the way to itself' (SB, 48) completes the project whereby presentation (material and historical life) is bent to the absolute and embodies this absolute in a self-relation. Kant plays a crucial role in the completion of this project because his call for systematicity presupposes that beings must, as a whole, be objects for the intuition of a subject (SB, 45).

Against the metaphysical reduction of being to an object for a subject, Heidegger argues that being shows itself precisely by and in manifesting its inscrutability to calculative knowledge. This presentation moreover is the modality for being's occurrence in the history of modern metaphysics

as a 'concealment' or 'refusal.' In each of the different epochs of being, being occurs in philosophical language in a specific way. This understanding
of being as an occurrence in philosophy requires for Heidegger a reflection
on the history of philosophy that is also a destruction of its skewed ontology. Now the recasting of the question of being in purely historical terms
is complete.

In the 1935 *Introduction to Metaphysics* he says that it is only in philosophy 'that essential relations to the realm of what is take shape' and this
means that 'this relation *can,* indeed *must,* for us today be a fundamentally
historical one' (IM, 44). Heidegger suggests that the foundations of the
Greek world, though now distorted, still sustain our world. We need to re-
build this world 'authentically anew, i.e. historically,' and this rebuilding
depends on knowing the tradition in a 'stricter' and 'more binding' way
'than all the epochs before us, even the most revolutionary' (IM, 126). The
'radical historical knowledge' that is required for this task of rebuilding
saves us from the false hope of anthropology (AWP, 140) and refines the
question of man as a 'historically metaphysical' rather than an anthropological one (IM, 140).[47] This project of rebuilding remains a pressing
theme in his late writing, although its import, I think, is dramatically altered by Heidegger's thinking of technology.

## 'Experience' and 'Metaphysics as the History
of Being' in Heidegger's Thinking

In my opening remarks to this chapter I gave a provisional schema
for the itinerary of Heidegger's thinking and noted the problem, given
Heidegger's views and those of his leading interpreters, of describing
breaks or 'turns' in the path of his thinking.[48] So far in this chapter I have
tried to identify some of the points of discontinuity that affect the course
of Heidegger's thinking. To my mind, the shift in the framing of the
question of being is of such a nature as to require attention to these discontinuities. To this end the problem of presentation, which is operative
in his thought from the beginning but which first surfaces as an explicitly
historical topic in his reading of Kant, gives us a point of reference from
which to identify and describe two distinct locales of emphasis in Heidegger's approach to the thinking of being. While each of these locales draws

on Heidegger's understanding of presentation as the key problem for thinking, and in this respect attests to the continuity of certain points of reference in his approach to and formulation of the question of being, they are discontinuous in their orientation and consequences.

On one side, there is the approach to the question of being through metaphysics as the history of being. In Heidegger's reading of metaphysics as an historical unfolding of the 'giving' of being, metaphysical doctrines are not understood as arbitrary points that have accrued to this history but are related by Heidegger to how being 'is' or holds itself forth. It is this conception of metaphysics as the history of being that frames Heidegger's understanding of history as the ultimate horizon of meaning.[49] Thus in his reflections on technology Heidegger situates technology in terms of the history of metaphysics and develops, from that understanding, an expectation of the path of how technology will unfold in the future. In the lecture series of 1951–1952, 'What Is Called Thinking,' he discusses the decisive event that had already destined this path in the Greeks' metaphysical questioning (WIT, 319). The split between a given being and its ideal form in Plato 'already presupposes that the duality of being and Being does exist' (WIT, 222). This dualism which 'is the thing most used, and thus most usual, in all our stating and ideas, in all we do' (WIT, 227–28) is the ground on which 'all movements of our modern age take place' and the ground, too, of 'the growing wasteland' we inhabit (WIT, 90).[50] The oblivion of being is the 'destining' that occurs with the decisive duality of beings and being in ancient Greek philosophy and from which perspective it is possible to account for 'the growing wasteland' in which, under the reign of the technological *Gestell,* the relation to being is forgotten and 'man' everywhere encounters only himself.

On the other side, there is the thematic of 'saying' the 'experience of being.' Although I noted in my opening remarks that this approach to the question of being is emphasised in Heidegger's later work, the topic of an experienceable relation to being is a crucial theme in his earliest publications as well as in his writing on the history of philosophy.[51] In *Being and Time,* moods like care or anxiety are qualified as 'fundamental' on account of their giving access to the question of the meaning of being; and, later, in the perspective of the history of being, the experience of beings as such always takes place in the context of an implicit relation to their being. In this respect we can cite the fact that throughout his thinking 'philosophising' retains the existential sense of a staking of the questioner in the question.[52] However, the claim of experience, particularly in its treatment in Heidegger's late work as the orientation for the task of 'saying' the experience of being, seems to me to form quite a distinct reflective constellation to the perspective of metaphysics as the history of being. In my concluding remarks to this chapter I would like to note some of the pertinent points of contrast between these constellations by focusing on the understanding of presentation that Heidegger uses, in each case, to frame them. By this approach, I hope to identify the split motivations that generate the contradictory tendencies in Heidegger's thought, which go some way to explain the ambiguous threads that we will examine in the next chapter in his conceptions of art and technology as specific relations of presentation.

In terms of the analysis of metaphysics as the history of being, presentation emerges as a key problem because it leaves open the question of the meaning of being. Similarly the question of presentation is important from the perspective of 'saying' the 'experience of being,' because it keeps open the possibility of a reflective relation to the experience of being.[53] Despite their surface compatibility, these two approaches seem to me to be framed by distinct, if not irreconcilable, considerations. From the perspective of metaphysics the problem of presentation can be fruitfully formulated as the question of what historically, or in the epochal formations of philosophy, it means for something 'to be.' This formulation is a long way, however, from the perspective that asks how language might 'say' the experience of being. In the latter case, 'presentation' is an adaptation, in a generalised form, of the features that Kant had ascribed specifically to aesthetic experience.

We can characterise these two different emphases in provisional terms as responding to two different types of questions. The first addresses the problem of understanding the present by the means of the historical inquiry able to ground such an understanding. This problem also acts as a way of opening up the present age to questioning reflection. Hence Heidegger's inquiry into the history of philosophy can be represented as opening this history to reflection in asking, 'How did we get to the point where we are?' In the case of the second, a contrasting set of motives inquires after the conditions of our existence at the present moment and can be schematised as asking: 'given our circumstances, how should we live?' The 'answers' to these questions are not necessarily commensurable because there is a tension between their guiding frameworks and motivations. The perspective necessary for one seems to be all but foreclosed by the other, and this is nowhere clearer than in the fact that the type of experience or attunement of the self required by the imperative of 'saying' the experience of being is rendered unavailable by the 'destining' of being, by metaphysics.

In both cases Kant is an important figure. From the perspective of metaphysics as the history of being, Kant might be understood as preserving in his questioning relation to presentation what German Idealism and Romanticism later abandoned. The questioning relation to presentation also sustains the other theme of Heidegger's reflections insofar as it keeps open the possibility of experiencing being in the philosophising questioning. Nonetheless, if we look at texts other than those in which the question of presentation and the status of Kant in its formulation are at issue, it is clear that the historical and experiential perspectives on presentation suppose heterogeneous reflective dispositions and cannot, therefore, be reconciled simply by an appeal to Kant.

Comparing Heidegger's 'destinalism' with Hegel's philosophy of history is illuminating in this regard. The view that being is a disclosive questioning within the history of metaphysics gives Heidegger a different set of resources to conduct a meaningful history to the one Hegel develops in his *Phenomenology of Spirit*. According to Heidegger, Hegel's achievement is to make history meaningful, rather than an arbitrary lurching from one contingent event to another. Despite Hegel's importance for orientating a historical perspective on philosophy, he is criticised by Heidegger for the way he organises this perspective in terms of system. This perspective is what licenses Hegel to bend experiential and historical events to the grounding self-relation of the absolute. Heidegger's view that the forgetfulness of being is not a moral fault of human beings depends on the idea that history is essentially, rather than incidentally, important in the destining of being as oblivion of being (WIT, 314).

On the other hand, the statements Heidegger makes concerning the task of 'saying' the experience of being are indicative of a perspective on the question of being that follows a different point of departure. In *What Is Called Thinking?*, he excoriates the 'habit' of dualism that prevents us from hearing 'what the Greek words tell us' (WIT, 227–28) and contrasts being 'gripped by thinking' with the vague and abstract distinction between being and beings (WIT, 225–26). The 'saying' of 'recollective thinking'

that he practices in these lectures calls on the listener to understand thinking first and foremost *as* experience, or to be more precise, as the experience of being. This difference in orientation between recalling the traces
of being in the history of Western philosophy and saying the experience
of being naturally leaves its marks on the stakes of Heidegger's thinking.
It is because what is at stake in this final lecture series is the saying of an
*experience* of being that Heidegger's expressions become more spatial and
demanding of self-involvement. The vocabulary of the 'leap' and the 'step
back' are indicative of the view that to understand metaphysics is to experience it from 'out of' its ground. In Heidegger's late works, this means
that the call to experience being in such a way as to see how this historical
destiny of the oblivion of being unfolded is fused with the call, that issues
from a different perspective, to *say* this experience.

It is because these competing considerations of 'history' and 'experience' are at play in Heidegger's thinking that topics such as 'art' and 'technology' are, I believe, ultimately handled in an ambiguous fashion in his
work. As we will see in the next chapter, the work of art may be exemplary
in the perspective of the experience of being, but not for the perspective of
metaphysics as history of being. Art is arguably a privileged moment of access to an experience of being for the thinker, but thinking about being in
the horizon of history may call this use of art into question, especially if
we ask what technology 'is' in such a perspective.

# 4

## 'Technology' and 'Art' as Relations
## of Presentation in Heidegger's Thought

Heidegger's writing on technology has a unique position in his approach to the topic of presentation. As I mentioned in the last chapter, for Heidegger, 'technology' is, like 'art' and the formulations of being in the history of philosophy, a specific relation in which things are understood 'to be.' The significance of technology within the framework of the topic of presentation is, however, paradoxical: *as* technology, relations of presentation become more immediately visible; but because, as a specific set of relations of presentation, technology is planetary for this reason finding a way of articulating a reflective relation to them becomes more difficult. This difficulty is given clear expression in Heidegger's famous 1955 essay 'The Question Concerning Technology.' In his closing remarks to this essay Heidegger suggests that art may provide a counter-term to technological revealing, but given his view that the 'danger' of technology is that it threatens to close down all other modes of *poiesis*, these comments on 'art' are equivocal.[1]

In Heidegger's account of technology the ambiguities in his approach to the topic of presentation, and specifically the status of this topic as the mode for a critical engagement with philosophical dualism, are in the foreground. His writing on technology emphasises the dramatic alteration made to the stakes of the topic of presentation in the epoch of the technological *Gestell* but also, despite the contrary indications in this essay and other late writing, reveals the difficulties of an adequate path of reflection on this epoch. In particular, his writing on technology, in my view, rules out any straightforward interpretation of art as constituting an available and viable critical view on the technological world. We can cite, as indicative of the difficult position left for 'art' in the epoch of the *Gestell*, two features of Heidegger's writing on the topic of technology. First, the language he uses to describe the *Gestell* as the 'first flashing of appropriation' and as a 'prelude' to the event of appropriation [*Ereignis*] indicates that technology is not simply a negative term in Heidegger's thinking. Second, and further to this, the rationale for recuperating 'technology' from the status of a negative term comes from Heidegger's historical approach to the question of being according to which the reflection on the 'essence' of technology is also, in terms we will need to qualify, a reflection on what being now 'is.'

Admittedly, this perspective on the status of 'art' and 'technology' is somewhat controversial given the value of 'critique' invested in 'art' by recent Heidegger scholarship. This scholarship generally tends to contrast the texture of experience in the age of technology with the experience afforded by artworks. However, as we saw in the previous chapter, a contrast that pivots solely on the claim of 'experience' in Heidegger's writing risks overlooking the importance of Heidegger's historical approach to the question of being. It is not enough to use art to criticise the 'distorted' form of experience in the age of technology. It is necessary to ask how these very technological relations enable a saying of being. Despite the difficulties in interpreting 'art' as a locale for critique in Heidegger's thinking of technology, this type of interpretation is indicative not of an 'error' but rather, I think, of the ambiguities that structure Heidegger's discussions of art. Indeed, given the distinction to be made in his thought between the locale of 'experience' and the historical framework he uses to treat the topic of technology, art does exercise a claim for a specific kind of experience. However, the distinction between the historical perspective and the claim of experience also means that art's potential as a venue for critique within the terms of Heidegger's thinking needs to be radically qualified.

According to recent interpretations of Heidegger the distinction between his own so-called post-aesthetic approach to art and the conception of the artwork in modern philosophical aesthetics hinges on Heidegger's attempt to prise art away from the status of an 'aesthetic object' in a 'cultural field.'[2] The noncalculative conception of the 'work' of the artwork that is the result of this attempt not only organises his 1937 'Origin of the

Work of Art' essay but also is sustained in his 1955 essay 'The Question Concerning Technology,' where art plays the role of a counterforce to the instrumental thinking of the technological epoch. The role of art as a counter to instrumental thinking outlined in the 'Origin' essay acts in these interpretations of Heidegger as an operative contrast to the otherwise totalising instrumentalism of the technological *Gestell*.

Art's capacity to counter instrumentalism follows its differentiation from the status of a merely 'aesthetic object.' In a number of recent publications, Krzysztof Ziarek has cited the distinctive features of post-aesthetic art in support of art's ability to confront 'the impact of technological modernity on experience.'[3] This confrontation signals the importance of renegotiating in a post-aesthetic context 'art's relation to social and political dimensions,' because this context opens up the specific 'possibility of an emancipatory, post-Enlightenment thinking' able to sustain a critical relation to 'experience in the age of technology.'[4] This ambitious social and political scope may not be endorsed by other commentators, but the terms in which Ziarek describes art's confrontation with the technologisation of experience in Heidegger often are. Ziarek emphasises the negative effects of the technologisation of experience and argues that Heidegger's account of *poiesis* in the technological epoch delineates 'the obscured yet potentially emancipatory significance of the juncture between technological practices of schematising experience and the poetic.'[5] What is stressed in this reading of Heidegger is the particular relation of art 'to (everyday) experience, where art, taken to be disclosive and enactive rather than representational and reproductive, produces (reveals) the world as the play of differences and heterogeneities, which disappear within the intuitive immediacy of experience.'[6] Art is able to resist 'the dominant schema of experience' because its emphasis on the contingent and the singular contests the general and schematic mode of experience in the technological age.[7] The possibility of this resistance is a feature of the 'co-belonging' of *poiesis* and technology in the technological epoch such that '*poiesis* in modernity is unthinkable without or apart from technology. *Poiesis,* as unfolding of experience, works on the inside, as it were, of *techne,* as the "tain" of the technological mirror of modern reality.'[8] The co-belonging of *poiesis* and *techne* testifies to the continuing significance of *poiesis* in the technological epoch, but it does so by emphasising that the artwork (*poiesis*) is a positive, resistant term to the encroaching and negative technologisation (*techne*) of experience. The distinctive feature of this conception of the technological epoch is that particular features of the artwork motivate an evaluative framework within which the technical can be assessed and criticised.

This contrast between the instrumental and the artwork that empowers art with a critical mission in the age of technology also surfaces in recent accounts of Heidegger by Beistegui and Wright. Wright names art as the 'saving power' able to counter the technological *Gestell* in its embodiment of 'places which preserve and hence save a place for dwelling.'[9] Not only is art a stable counter-term to technology, but its capacity to disclose the world as 'a dwelling place' against the 'homelessness' threatened by the age of technology is made 'manifest in a new way' with 'the discovery of the essence of technology.'[10] Beistegui, who criticises the utility of Heidegger's favoured examples of art and architecture to resist the epoch of the *Gestell,* nonetheless still uses the features of art described in the artwork essay to explain how architecture might counter or 'resist' the technologisation of space. Beistegui uses the definition of the essence of art in Heidegger's 'Origin of the Work of Art' lectures ('the truth of beings setting itself to work into the work' [*das Sich-ins-Werk-Setzen der Wahrheit*]) to explain how the question of the possibility of place is posed for Heidegger in the 'taking *place* of truth in the work or building.'[11] According to Beistegui, the following question is posed from the time of Heidegger's work of the 1930s: 'can space, in the age of techno-science, be conceived otherwise than mathematically and objectively? Is there still room for another space? And does the artwork, the architectural work, free such a space?'[12] On this account, it is not the contrast between the techno-spatial world of the *Gestell* and the 'counter-techno-spatial activities' of art and architecture that is troublesome, but the provincial mindset that leads Heidegger to contrast an 'authentic dwelling to the technological residing.'[13] Instead of the 'peasant house in the Black Forest,' Beistegui argues that 'some instances' of contemporary architecture 'open up a space beyond' 'the technological, machinic fate of an inhabiting reduced to the macroeconomic demands of late capitalism.'[14] Thus, Beistegui uses the vocabulary of the 'Origin' lectures to describe how particular cases of contemporary architecture 'set to work into the work of truth' not the negative features of the technological age but a 'space for architectural resistance' to them.[15] Beistegui and Wright both reiterate Ziarek's positive evaluation of specific features of post-aesthetic art in relation to the negative effects of the technological epoch.[16] Admittedly, such interpretations echo the tone of certain passages in which Heidegger refers to technology, and they can also call on considerable textual support in the role they attribute to art in the positive, suggestive remarks that Heidegger makes from the time of his 'Origin' lectures to his late commentaries on architecture and poetry.[17]

Despite the support that can be found in Heidegger's work for these interpretations, they tend to emphasise one-sidedly the negative features of the technological age, even against substantial ambiguities that are present in Heidegger's account, thereby obstructing the view of these. But more importantly, since the picture they give of the impact of technology on human existence and its fundamental worldly relations is systematically built up in reference and as a counter-image to the experience of the artwork, they abort Heidegger's own epochal approach to the meaning of being. In particular, they render incomprehensible a number of important claims Heidegger raises in regard to the technological opening up of a more adequate relation to being. I will argue here that the theses on post-aesthetic art in the 'Origin' lectures are unable to serve as a clear evaluative framework for the technological *Gestell*; instead, the distinctive features of Heidegger's relational understanding of being need to be heeded in analysing the respective status of art and technology in the economy of his thinking.

Two compelling factors recommend this approach: first, Heidegger's own ambiguous description of the reign of the technological *Gestell* as the 'first flashing' of appropriation,[18] and second, the fact that the 'essence' of technology is elaborated in the course of and in terms of his historical-hermeneutic reflections on 'being' as elaborated in the philosophical tradition. The core of Heidegger's historical reflection on the question of being is a relational approach to beings that inquires into the sense of their 'being' within more or less distinct, epochal frameworks of presentation, that is to say, the fundamental manner in which beings are given to us in each epoch, what Heidegger also calls their 'truth.' It is these frameworks of presentation that locate the continuity between the approach Heidegger takes to the artwork and to the technological and, more importantly, explain why it is that by the time of the essay on technology art is no longer able to play the role of a stable and constant reference point for the thinking of technology. It is a significant feature of Heidegger's account of technology that the epoch of the *Gestell* is a 'prelude' to the 'heat lightning of a new beginning' called for in his Schelling book (SB, 3). The *Gestell* has the status of a Janus-head, a 'first flashing of appropriation,' because its mode of ordering everywhere displays its potential to dissolve entities in its mode of relating to them and bringing them into relation.[19] In other words, understood as a mode of presentation, technology leads the metaphysics of the subject (and the object) to a close.

This chapter has four main parts. The first two parts will address through the framework of the problem of presentation the substantial alteration that the conception of art undergoes in Heidegger's writing from the time of the 'Origin' essay in 1937[20] to his essay on technology in 1955. This perspective, I will suggest, is crucial for understanding the changing way that Heidegger positions the work of art and the calculative relations of technology between 1937 and 1955 as modalities in which this reflective relation to relations of presentation occurs. Next, I will consider the implications of this alteration for the distinction between art and technicity that is often used in Heidegger scholarship as a 'ground' for the critique of the technologisation of experience. Finally, I will outline some of the factors involved in Heidegger's writing on art and technology as a provocation for the thinking of Lacoue-Labarthe and Nancy, each of whom also, I believe, identify presentation as *the* central question of modern thought.

## 'The Origin of the Work of Art': Modern Art as the Presentation of the Ordinary

In his 'Origin of the Work of Art' essay, Heidegger laments the forgetting of that which 'once struck man as strange and caused him to think and to wonder.'[21] Although Heidegger locates the beginning of this process of forgetting of the Greek questioning disposition in the Latinisation of the so-called authentic Greek language,[22] he targets the sedimentation of this forgetting in the modern philosophical categories which, under the cover of 'their semblance of self-evidence,' 'preconceive' and 'assault' 'all immediate experience' of the thing.[23] The ready answers that the expansive philosophical couplets such as form/matter give 'to the question "What is the thing?" are,' Heidegger complains, 'so familiar that we no longer sense anything questionable behind them' (OWA, 22). Indeed, the 'boundless presumption' of the familiar categories used for thinking the thing belie the remarkable fact that 'the unpretentious thing evades thought most stubbornly' (OWA, 32). Heidegger's essay thus introduces the topic of the work of the artwork by first of all foregrounding what he calls 'the most difficult of tasks,' namely, how 'to let a being be as it is.'[24] Heidegger takes as his example to approach this task a pair of peasant shoes, and uses for the 'visual realization' of this example 'a well-known painting by Van Gogh, who painted such shoes several times' (OWA, 33). In carefully attending to the pair of shoes in the painting, Heidegger discovers the 'essential being' of the equipment. He calls this being 'reliability.' In discovering the 'essential being' of the equipment as 'reliability,' Heidegger flags too a specific conception of the nature of art as bringing the truth of beings to stand out. Art, in this precise sense, meets what he had earlier called 'the difficult task' of letting a 'being be as it is' in its letting the truth of beings happen. Hence despite his prefatory remarks, the van Gogh artwork is no mere example:[25] it did not, Heidegger emphasises, 'serve merely for a better visualizing of what a piece of equipment is'; rather, the work *first* discloses 'what . . . the pair of peasant shoes, *is* in truth.'[26] The artwork, in this account, brings out what the peasant woman 'knows . . . *without* noticing or reflecting' (OWA, 34, my emphasis).

This disclosure of the truth of the peasant shoes in the artwork needs to be understood from the perspective of Heidegger's combative conception of truth. The very work-being of an artwork, that is, its character as a work, is its opening up of a unique space in which beings presented in the work are revealed in their truth. This space Heidegger calls 'world.' The world opened and 'kept abidingly in force' by the work is a space in which the recipient of the work is put in relation to beings *in respect of* their truth (OWA, 44). This truth is not present as a statement, but as an experience of an event, more precisely as the experience of strife. The beings are susceptible to being questioned in respect of their truth precisely because they stand on their own. They stand on their own thanks to a preserving 'agent' that stands as their 'ground,' what Heidegger calls the 'earth.' It is this relation between world and earth, understood as a conflict between the appearing and opening of beings (world) and withdrawing and sheltering of beings (earth), that sets Heidegger on the path of thinking what he terms the 'double concealing' of truth (OWA, 54).

Heidegger's adaptation of the Greek term *aletheia,* defined by him as an interplay between concealing and unconcealing, characterises 'truth' in this essay in terms of the important theme of the refusal of being to calculative inquiry. In the case of the artwork, this refusal means that even as the artwork opens a world and 'is present in, and only in, such opening up'(OWA, 41), it also presents the unfathomable reserve, or earth, that is at the core of what is disclosed. It is this dual struggle of the work, its status as a work through which and as which the world is opened, and within which the struggle between earth and world is waged, that makes of art an essential way that 'the uncanny [*das Ungeheure*] [is] thrust to the surface and the long-familiar thrust down' (OWA, 66). However, Heidegger maintains, truth occurs under a double concealing condition according to which we can 'never' be 'fully certain' whether the concealment is 'a refusal or merely a dissembling.'[27] What follows is the radical absence of a normative measure for truth, or for art as a way in which truth is related to. This threshold is reached in the modern work of art when 'we can say no more of beings than that they are' (OWA, 53).

In this respect the reflective relation to the ordinary that the struggle in the work presents is also to be understood as installing a questioning relation to our familiar conception of truth as 'correctness in representation' (OWA, 52). This conception, Heidegger writes, 'stands and falls with truth as unconcealedness of beings' (OWA, 52). The definition of truth as *aletheia* is not, he insists, a mere 'refuge in a more literal translation of a Greek word' but a reminder of what 'unexperienced and unthought, underlies our familiar and therefore outworn nature of truth in the sense of correctness' (OWA, 52). Against 'the appearance of mastery and of progress in the form of the technical-scientific objectivation of nature' Heidegger argues that that which is unconcealed, that which 'shows itself,' does so 'only when it remains undisclosed and unexplained.'[28] The unconcealing of beings does not just underpin the possibility of scientific truth as correctness[29] but is understood by Heidegger to interrogate this scientific conception in so far as it refuses in the mode of concealing—in the case of the shining of the beautiful—'every calculating importunity' (OWA, 47). The artwork is thus rescued from its forgetting in modern philosophical aesthetics, because the work of presentation it performs puts in play in the mode of an event the crucial transition from the familiar framework that asks 'what the being is' to the questioning attitude in the face of the bare fact 'that the being is' [*daß . . . ist*] (OWA, 65).

It is just this fact, 'that it is a work,' that marks out the seemingly 'least feature of the thing,' the 'that it is' [*es gibt*] (OWA, 53). It is in opening this feature that the artwork questions the relations of presentation that have become familiar to recall that '[a]t bottom, the ordinary is not ordinary; it is extra-ordinary, uncanny' (OWA, 54). As I have already noted, the context for the discussion of art's attention to the truth of beings is the familiarity of those thing-concepts under which the thing itself is forgotten. In this questioning of familiarity it is above all against the 'familiar' conception of truth as 'correctness in representation' that the opening created by the artwork reminds us 'of what, unexperienced and unthought, underlies our familiar and therefore outworn nature of truth' (OWA, 52). Understood this way, the work of the artwork is a doubly reflective relation to that which is: next to the presentation of the bare but remarkable fact that it, the work, is (rather than is not) is that it establishes the clearing that goes beyond any particular being—such as the peasant shoes—that is. The painting works as a reflective relation to relations of presentation because unlike the degraded conception of truth as correctness, it attends to that which this conception presupposes as merely given, namely, the 'there is' [es gibt] of the thing. The importance of art as a truth happening lies here: it is in the artwork that the clearing occurs and a shift from what-a-being-is to that-it-is occurs.

This is important not just for understanding the points of continuity with the modern philosophical tradition of aesthetics that this essay, at first glance, appears to simply repudiate, but also for understanding the combative interplay of concealing/unconcealing as it concerns the ordinary or familiar in Heidegger.[30]

Van Gogh's painting is a work of modern art, and as such its subject matter, according to the Hegelian verdict followed by Heidegger in his lectures on Nietzsche, is the everyday or the ordinary. Unlike the other examples in this essay—the Greek temples at Paestum, the Aegina sculptures in the Munich collection, Sophocles' Antigone, and the Bamberg cathedral[31]—this painting presents a secular, specifically modern truth:[32] in its attention to how and that the peasant shoes are, it shows the truth of these shoes as the 'reliability' of equipment, and does so by bringing into the open what the peasant woman knows 'without noticing or reflecting' (OWA, 34). One may conclude that the peculiar privilege of modern art is to open the possibility of a reflective relation to relations of presentation. The importance of this historicisation of that which art presents as a happening or event of truth cannot be overstated: it introduces the important idea that 'differences relating to the history of Being may yet also be present in the way equipment *is*' (OWA, 32). It is this idea that radically transforms the world of the peasant depicted in the van Gogh painting. But it also inflects Heidegger's thinking of the artwork in the direction of understanding it as a reflective relation to relations of presentation. This understanding is given further impetus and becomes more articulate in Heidegger's reflections on existence and experience in the technological world.

## 'The Question Concerning Technology': Technological Relations as Relations of Presentation

In 'The Question Concerning Technology' the 'essence of technology' is defined as a mode of 'revealing' that installs, but also conceals that it is, a particular relation of presentation. 'Challenging-revealing' is Heidegger's way of describing presentation in the epoch of technology as an ordering of what is that does not simply use nature in the mode of equipmental use but that fundamentally reorders what is meant by equipment. A windmill was a form of equipment that relied on the wind's blowing to produce energy. Whereas the windmill 'does not unlock energy from the air currents in order to store it,' modern, industrial technology actually 'challenges' 'a tract of land . . . into the putting out of coal and ore. The earth now reveals itself as a coal mining district, the soil as a mineral deposit.'[33] Whereas the peasant's work had not 'challenged' the soil of the field, the cultivation of the field in the modern food industry '*sets* upon' (Heidegger's emphasis) 'the air' to deliver nitrogen, and the old 'cultivation of the soil' is drawn into the arranging of nature which 'challenges forth' (QCT, 15). Even to the extent that the Rhine remains 'a river in the landscape,' it is such a river in 'no other way than as an object on call for inspection by a tour group ordered there by the vacation industry' (QCT, 16). The ordering of the *Gestell*, as Heidegger describes it here, becomes total; nothing seems able to escape it, even the 'beauty' of the 'scenery' in the case of the Rhine is a 'setting-upon, in the sense of a challenging-forth' (QCT, 16). This 'challenging-forth' installs a particular relation to the real that 'reveals' it as a specific relation of presentation: namely, the ordering of what is.

We would seriously misunderstand Heidegger and the historical tenor of his reflection on technology if we imagined a sort of pure or primordial 'nature' as the target of this ordering. As Heidegger understands it, the essence of technology is not just an ordering of nature or an application of the exact natural sciences. It is modern physics that is the forerunner to technology in its use of pure theory to order experiments (QCT, 21–22), and its objects, as Gaston Bachelard first described them, are themselves the products of procedures of experimentation rather than 'natural givens.' Heidegger's terminology, in which technology is defined as a 'challenging-revealing,' has to be understood along the lines of the structure of innovation in modern physics and industrial technology whose view of reality, as it were, it generalises. The forms of challenging-revealing described in 'The Question Concerning Technology' are relations of presentation under which technical, calculative thinking provides the context in which things appear as they are as such. The force of this mode of presentation encroaches on the beautiful, which is no longer able to draw attention to the relations of presentation under which equipment becomes reduced to a given ordinariness, as beauty itself is thoroughly instrumentalised and integrated within the ordering specific to the technological *Gestell*. If we give his characterisation of *Gestell* the full weight it demands, we are left with a seemingly intractable problem. For, according to the framework of an epochal understanding of being that structures Heidegger's thinking of truth of being, the problem is how to reflect on and articulate the technological relation *as* a relation of presentation.

Let me expand on how one arrives at this aporia. Heidegger is at pains to define the essence of technology as a revealing that exceeds and also defeats the merely instrumental and anthropological reduction of technology to a 'mere means' (QCT, 12). It is as a revealing that technology is a *poiesis* or 'bringing-forth' and also a 'granting' that 'gathers' (QCT, 12–13). Heidegger defines *poiesis* in such a way that it spans both 'the growing things of nature as well as whatever is completed through the crafts and the arts' precisely because he means it to refer not just to the 'bursting of a blossom into bloom' (*physis*) or the bringing-forth of the work of the artisan or artist, but to what comes 'at any given time to their appearance' (QCT, 11). The revealing of technology is a 'bringing-forth' in this sense as it, like the 'growing things of nature' or the work of the artisan or artist, brings 'something concealed . . . into unconcealment.'[34] In other words, it is on account of its being a way of revealing that technology belongs to the realm of truth and thus calls for a conception other than that of a 'means': technology calls for a reflective relation to its mode of revealing. In this respect the mode of revealing installed by modern technology is analogous to art in its status as one way in which thinking *as* a reflection on historicised presentation can occur. However, it is the peculiarity of the relations installed at the historical moment of modern technology that gives the task of thinking in 'The Question Concerning Technology' an urgency it lacks in his criticisms of the forgetting of the thing in modern metaphysics (or of the artwork in modern aesthetics). This urgency has to do with the all-encompassing way in which technological relations (whilst they are a mode of revealing and thus a way that truth happens) conceal, or (because Heidegger is ambiguous on this point) threaten to conceal, their status as relations of presentation and block the 'bringing forth' of *poiesis* for a mere ordering relation to 'what is.'[35] It is in the context of the urgency raised by technological relations that the approach taken to the artwork in the 'Origin' essay is no longer tenable. What becomes clear in Heidegger's attempt to think technology, fundamentally, is the following paradox (and the concomitant pathos): precisely the point where the problem of presentation (the reflective relation to relations of presentation) becomes potentially articulable in its full scope is also the point at which finding a path to it becomes all but impossible because of the thoroughgoing and all-encompassing nature of technological relations and of their self-concealment.[36]

Here it is worth considering carefully the place of the history of philosophy for Heidegger's reflection on the technological *Gestell*: it is Heidegger's view that there has not yet been a thoughtful experience of the thing. In modern philosophy, aesthetics distorts the experience of the artwork by having already determined the artwork according to the subject/object schema of modern metaphysics. Although the ancient Greeks had a 'luminous' knowledge that did not rely on the abstractions of the modern aesthetic disposition, neither was it the case that their experience of the thing was thoughtfully grounded. Hence the theme of forgetting in Heidegger does not refer to a past event or state of affairs that has been forgotten, but to an activity of reflection that could *for the first time* thoughtfully ground the experience of the thing. It is the forgetfulness of a call, not of its fulfilment, of a questioning attitude, not an answer and self-satisfied certainty that Heidegger addresses in his so-called step back. The step back is a reflection on the history of thinking that 'points to the realm which until now has been skipped over, and from which the essence of truth becomes first of all worthy of thought.'[37] This is not a 'step back' to an earlier place or occurrence of truth but a 'step back' to a path 'out of metaphysics into the essential nature of metaphysics.'[38] For Heidegger this means both that the 'step back' concerns 'the manner in which thinking moves' and that it 'calls for a preparation . . . in the face of beings as such and as a whole, as they *are* now and are visibly beginning to show themselves ever more unequivocally.' He continues,

> What now *is*, is marked by the dominance of the active nature of modern technology. This dominance is already presenting itself in all areas of life, by various identifiable traits such as functionalization, systematic improvement, automation, bureaucratisation, communications. Just as we call the idea of living things biology, just so the presentation and full articulation of all beings, dominated as they now are everywhere by the nature of the technical, may be called technology. The expression may serve as a term for the metaphysics of the atomic age. Viewed from the present and drawn from our insight into the present, the step back out of metaphysics into the essential nature of metaphysics is the step out of technology and technological description and interpretation of the age, into the *essence* of modern technology which is still to be thought.[39]

The 'step back' meets the aporia of technological domination by reflecting on how that which appears to us in the epoch of technology is given in certain constellations of meaning. This approach dissolves the schema in which authentic modes of worldliness such as the artwork can oppose a degraded instrumental and calculative relation to beings. Indeed the peculiarity of the technological age is that it makes clear the constitutiveness of presentation (that is, the historicity of the 'truth' of being and hence the groundlessness of 'things') but also leaves no room for the 'authentic' mode of reflection on being. Heidegger leaves open whether 'this step of thinking will develop into a proper . . . path and way and road-building.'[40] What is crucial here, however, is that his attempt to meet through the 'step back' the aporetic point reached by technology does not retreat to art as a counter-image to technology. Rather, because this step is guided by what 'now *is*,' it is able to query whether the framework of technology in which man and being 'reach each other in their nature [and] achieve their active nature by losing those qualities with which metaphysics has endowed them'[41] does not itself 'overcome the mere dominance of the frame to turn it into a more original appropriating.'[42]

The conception of this reflective relation to what is (which I have interpreted here as the inflection of relations of presentation as a question) in Heidegger's work on technology dramatically qualifies the place of the artwork in the 'Origin' essay. Two main deficiencies in the earlier discussion of the artwork stand out immediately: first, the way of life depicted in the van Gogh painting can no longer be taken as a given by Heidegger. It is under assault from two directions. The technological *Gestell* has fully reordered this way of life[43] and, aside from altering the texture of this experience, the atomic age goes one step further in actually placing all things under the threat of annihilation. Second, just as the way of life depicted by van Gogh can no longer be taken as a given, so too what Heidegger refers to as art's 'primal' significance loses its status as a *given* counterforce to the technological *Gestell*. The cautious questioning of the riddle of art in Heidegger's earlier essay can be cited in this respect against the place he gives to art in his later essay on technology. Does the assault on the peasant life mean that modern art, the art of the everyday and the ordinary and with it 'the world of the work . . . has perished'? Does it suffer the same fate as the Greek temple for which '[w]orld withdrawal and world decay can never be undone' (OWA, 41)? It is because of the way Heidegger conceives of modern art as *not world founding* (unlike earlier art which 'first gives men their outlook on things') that the perishing of modern art and its capacity to be world founding is not a question for him. After all, the van Gogh puts us into a particular relation with the ordinary. The limited role of modern art seems to preserve it in this role. The difficulty for Heidegger is that he is tempted in places to use art as a positive counter-term to the technological, but given his historicisation of the way things are, the 'ordinary' that modern art questions is not the new 'ordinary' of technological relations. It is indeed the perpetualism of the relations that technology has set in place which, for Heidegger, is the 'Janus-head'[44] according to which the essence of technology is a 'first flashing' of appropriation that supersedes the earlier role of art as a special way in which truth occurs.

Heidegger deliberately cultivates an ambiguity around the lost status of modern art as a uniquely unsettling force. Despite the incontrovertible evidence that 'art' is no longer secure in its position as a mode of questioning of relations of presentation, it is a telling feature of his essay on technology that Heidegger equivocates on the implications for art of his analysis of modern technological relations. This equivocation can be read as a function of the use to which Heidegger puts art in this essay. Heidegger uses art as a compelling rhetorical effect: it is art, in the form of Hölderlin's poem on the Rhine, that brings the ubiquity of the technological ordering that reaches as far as the beauty of the landscape into view.[45] It is art that, by virtue of its connection with technology as a form of *techne,* is still able to offer a (heavily qualified) questioning reflection on the essence of technology. Without 'art,' as it is used in this essay as the point of contrast to the merely technical, how would the all-encompassing sway of the technological *Gestell* be identifiable as a mode of presentation at all, let alone able to be characterised and questioned as a danger? However, Heidegger also strips art of its epochal, which is to say, its modern-day historical, characteristics in this use. The waning significance of art described in Heidegger's *Nietzsche* lectures in terms of the detachment of art from the sacred is underlined by the choice of van Gogh's painting as the example of modern art in his 'Origin' essay. It is significant that after his posing of the question of the technological, according to which the way of life of the peasant would itself *require* presentation, the essay on technology is unable to call on an art that belongs to the epoch of the technological *Gestell.*[46] It is under this restriction that Heidegger, in this later essay, calls on art either in modal or entirely unhistoricised terms.

Heidegger's statements concerning art in this essay do not square with the historicised conception of the artwork advanced in the 'Origin' essay. In contrast, the element that is consistent throughout this period is the questioning of relations of presentation. Questioning technology is, like the reflective relation to things opened by modern art, a reflective thinking about or relation to things present.[47] In each case the ground for the appearance of things turns out, given the epochal conception of Being, to be an *Ab-grund.* Against the attempt to retain art or certain of the features ascribed to it in the 'Origin' essay in a critical relation to technology, it seems to me that the priority of relations of presentation over *what* is presented in the case of *both* art and technology is the most consistent thesis able to be drawn from these essays.

## Art and Technology as Relations of Presentation

This thesis concerning the place of relations of presentation offers more than an account consistent with the epochal approach to the question of being taken in Heidegger's thinking after *Being and Time;* it also allows us to identify the evaluative language put to work in the very contrast between 'art' and the 'technical.' The features of the technological *Gestell* that carry a negative valence can, indeed, easily be described in terms of a deprivation of those relational features attached by Heidegger to the artwork: the prevalence of calculative thinking threatens to reduce all things to the status of 'standing-reserve' and results in the loss of the distinctive feature of a relation to truth as a 'letting-be' in his earlier art-work essay; similarly, there is a loss of an experience of a 'dwelling place' as the epoch of the *Gestell* closes down distances to the 'space' of techno-science, and it was art that was able to open our relation to place in the art-work essay. These examples, regularly used in the interpretation of the *Gestell* from the perspective of the artwork essay in Heidegger scholarship, explain the temptation to deploy the artwork, or the features associated with its 'work,' as a counter to instrumental values. As I have argued here, such deployments overlook the very features of the epochal conception of being that make the technological *Gestell* so significant: the defining feature of the *Gestell* is not to be had in a contrast with the features of the re-lation to being that are now lost, although this contrast is used to great rhetorical effect by Heidegger in the essay on technology. Rather, the sig-nificance of the *Gestell* is the prospect for a new relation between human being and being that it suggests. It is this prospect that underpins the am-biguity in Heidegger's description of the technological *Gestell* as an abyss that is also the promise of another beginning. Further this other beginning is engendered out of the very extent and perpetualism of the calculative re-lations set in place by technology.[48]

The features of the artwork that oppose it to the technical, that is, the breach with the familiar that lets beings be and the nonscientific expe-rience of space as a dwelling place, have to be seen to be reliant on a constellation of relations of presentation that, in his account of the technological *Gestell,* Heidegger takes to be past.[49] Further, if we accept Heidegger's diagnosis of the epochal relations set in place by technology, then it must be asked of those interpretations that make the modest claims for contemporary, nonscientific expressions of place whether these expres-sions can intervene at all in technological relations or whether they do not reinstall the dichotomy between a negative technology and a positive counter-term that Heidegger's own statements on the future event of ap-propriation discount. If, as Heidegger remarked, he was writing between the 'no longer art' and the 'not yet technology,'[50] what does this mean for interpretations of Heidegger that, in however modified or nuanced a form, use the vocabulary of art as a counterpart to the instrumentalism of technology or see in it an antidote to a technical nihilist culture?

These doubts about the ability to sustain the role of art, even when art is defined in a minimal sense as the features capable of an evocation of an alternative experience of space, in a position of dissent without undermining both the significance of Heidegger's account of technology as a 'Janus-head' and the historical-hermeneutic orientation of his epochal approach to the relation between being and human being as a relation of presentation, are, I believe, indicative of the implications for art of Heidegger's historicising approach to the topic of presentation. Equally, however, the ambiguities in Heidegger's account of technology, which are expressed by his consistent attachment to the critical potential of 'art,' may be understood as a function of his reluctance to fully accept the implications of historicising relations of presentation. Both perspectives, it seems to me, are operative in Heidegger's late writing. To conclude my discussion of Heidegger, I would like to briefly outline the key indicators of his reluctance to treat technological relations as historicised relations of presentation and foreground thereby the motivations that sustain 'art,' despite the implications of the epochal inflection of the question of being, in the ambiguous position of both a past experience of being and a counterforce to technology. It is important to canvass this ambiguity in the treatment of art in Heidegger's writing, because it is the prominence of presentation as the key question of thinking that, in the post-Heideggerian thought of Lacoue-Labarthe and Nancy, also brings the capacity of art as a vehicle of critique under scrutiny. In Heidegger's thinking the tension between the competing perspectives on the experience of being and the history of being has ambiguous consequences for the arts, but for that very reason is peculiarly well situated to frame *as a question* one of the central elements in the post-Kantian reflection on aesthetic presentation: the claim of art to a privileged position of critique.

## 'Presentation' in Heidegger's Path of Thinking

In *Being and Time* Heidegger examined the constitutive role of *Dasein,* or worldly and practical human existence, for the ways in which things appear. This phenomenological approach to the question of the mode of being of things made clear to Heidegger a problem that his subsequent thinking explored: the historicisation of Dasein's constitutive relations to things revealed their variability and raised the question of understanding their 'ground.' This 'turn' takes Heidegger to the history of philosophy and the way that this history thinks being. The path of this reflection, as is well known, leads to the development of an epochal conception of being in which being is thought of as an *Ab-grund.* The salient feature of this conception is Heidegger's historicisation of the constitutive relations under which things appear or are given to us. These constitutive relations for the appearance of things are the very relations that Heidegger's thinking invites us to reflect upon. It is this reflective relation to the relations under which things appear that forms the framework for Heidegger's approach to 'art' and 'technology' as relations of presentation.[51] It is just because Heidegger conceives of the task of thinking as the reflective relation to our relation to things that this reflective relation is directed towards the historical presentation(s) of things being what they are for us, that is, *that* beings are what they are. Considered in these terms, it is impossible to overstate the centrality of the question of presentation within Heidegger's thought: at the very least the reflective relation to relations of presentation is the question of thinking as such.

The difficulties in this orientation towards thinking appearance in terms of historicised relations come out clearly in the main themes of Heidegger's final lecture course (delivered between 1951 and 1952), *What Is Called Thinking?*[52] The prominence in this lecture course of the theme of 'saying' recollective thinking (WIT, 319–20) brings to a head many of the issues canvassed in these last two chapters on the articulation of thinking as a reflective relation to relations of 'presentation' in Heidegger's thought. The question of being is cast in these lectures in terms of an 'artless' and 'fateful relation' to 'the calling' of being that is, above all, an *experience* of this calling (WIT, 166–67). Heidegger's criticism of the thinking that furnishes 'representations and concepts'[53] as too vague to grip the thinker and throw into question the habit of dualism has an historical inflection in this course because he asks us to 'hear' what the Greek words 'tell' (WIT, 226), but the scope of this inflection is diminished on account of the fact that it operates at the level of the experience of the individual thinker and does not lead (as the technological *Gestell* arguably does) into the 'other beginning' first proposed in his Schelling lecture course as an historical path.

The structure of this call seems to me to parallel the verdict on modern art in his 'Origin of the Work of Art' lectures: such art has lost the capacity to be world founding, but nonetheless 'art' like the project for 'saying' the experience of being does offer an alternative venue to the habit-bound experience of the ordinary. It is the capacity of art to place us in a reflective relation to the prevailing relations of presentation that, I have argued, embodies its status as an exception that carries critical potential. However, if, as I have tried to show here, the project of thinking appearance as a historicised relation places the ability of art to sustain such a relation beyond the experience of the individual in question, it needs to be asked why this question is not more thoroughly pursued in Heidegger's late writing.

This question about art can be approached from a slightly different set of resources by examining the writing of Lacoue-Labarthe and Nancy. Each of these thinkers, like Heidegger, argues that the question of presentation is the key question of thinking. However, these thinkers, unlike Heidegger, are faithful to the context of aesthetics in which Kant first poses this question. The criticisms they make of Heidegger's approach to this question, accordingly, do address the status of 'art' in his thinking. However, it is because of the central status the arts occupy in their thought as the venue for posing or 'staging' the topic of presentation that art still claims, as it does in Heidegger, a position of exception.

# 5

## Lacoue-Labarthe: Aesthetic Presentation and the Figuring of the Political

In his Introduction to the English translation of Lacoue-Labarthe's *Typography,* Derrida states that Lacoue-Labarthe's work 'resembles, for me, the very *trial* of the ineluctable: insistent, patient, thinking—the experience of a very *singular* thought of the ineluctable.' 'The word "singularity," ' he goes on to explain,

Might lead us to think of novelty. And in fact the reader will have to recognize something quite evident: a very new configuration, following unprecedented schemas, joins here the question of Being and that of the subject in its philosophical, political, ethical, poetic, literary, theatrical and musical dimensions, in the reasons and madness of its autobiography. A different thought of mimesis and of the *typos* gives access *today* to these figures and this configuration.[1]

Immediately, however, Derrida unpacks the difficulties that plague this tentative characterisation: the so-called new configuration that Lacoue-Labarthe's work 'evidently' presents is one that disturbs the presuppositions of epochal thinking (as in Heidegger) or gestures of periodisation, and thus the valence and meaning of 'novelty' that Derrida had claimed was available to us in Lacoue-Labarthe's work '*today.*' Further, his writing has these effects as a result of its insistent questioning of 'the very possibility of the configurable.'[2] The 'very different thinking of mimesis' that Lacoue-Labarthe articulates is telling in this context. This thinking expounds on the logic that hollows out in advance, as it were, the conventions of theoretical filiations and breaks that would allow an author to be described as a 'figure.' It is the patient elaboration of the consequences of this 'different thinking of mimesis' that Derrida has in mind when he describes the *experience* to be had of the 'ineluctable' in Lacoue-Labarthe's writing.

In light of the difficulty of characterising this writing, it is interesting that Derrida places less emphasis in his Introduction on extracting 'theses' from Lacoue-Labarthe than he does on the experience to be had by reading him. The reader, he advises, 'must learn to read Lacoue-Labarthe, to listen to him, and to do so at his rhythm.' Lacoue-Labarthe's 'rhythm,' which 'multiplies caesuras, asides, parenthetical remarks, cautions, signs of prudence and circumspection, hesitations, warnings, parentheses, quotation marks, italics—dashes above all—or all of these at once,' has 'the necessity of a scansion that comes to fold and unfold a thought.'[3] These comments need to be read, I think, against the tendency in the reception of Lacoue-Labarthe's writing to emphasise his relation to Heidegger, as if this relation could help the reader to anticipate the motivations that drive his writing and thus provide for them a scheme of intelligibility that would save them from the trying experience of reading him.[4] Derrida, in contrast, points out that Lacoue-Labarthe constantly encourages us 'to break with the family atmosphere, to avoid genealogical temptations, projections, assimilations, or identifications' and that, above all, '[h]e uncovers their fatal character, the *political* trap they hold.'[5]

In this respect, it is important to make a preliminary note of the multiple fronts of critique that Lacoue-Labarthe opens up on Heidegger's thinking, which range from his critical analyses of its political commitments to its archaic tone, its 'manipulative' 'tampering' with Hölderlin's poetry and the 'unbearable' 'soothing thematics' of 'dwelling' and 'religiosity' in his late writing.[6] As far as his own thinking is concerned, then, it is not surprising that, to quote again from Derrida, although his 'entirely different thinking of mimesis' may well be 'borne by the impetus of Nietzschean-Heideggerian deconstruction,' Lacoue-Labarthe 'nevertheless impresses upon it, a supplementary torsion, reorganizes the entire landscape and brings out, or brings into play, new questions: on another dimension of the subject, of politics, of literary or theatrical fiction, of poetic experience, of auto- or hetero-biography.'[7]

If it is impossible to adequately explain Lacoue-Labarthe's writing in relation to the questions or figures that provide its impetus, the important features of Lacoue-Labarthe's style and the 'subtlety' of his strategies also make it impossible to adequately 'recount' the intricate movements of his writing.[8] Perhaps even more significantly, there is also the difficulty of the task Lacoue-Labarthe imposes on himself. Derrida indeed strikes a note of caution on this score and goes so far, I think, as to concede that Lacoue-Labarthe necessarily yields to the temptations his writing insistently guards against. Does not Lacoue-Labarthe 'himself,' Derrida politely wonders, 'risk a reduction' in his discussion of Heideggerian deconstruction? When Lacoue-Labarthe names the question of the subject as the 'unique central question,' does he 'not continue to reflect, or to collect in its gathering force, in the unicity of its question, something of the Heideggerian un-thought?' Derrida pulls these comments back from the status of 'a critique' because, he states, 'I do not believe that this gesture of gathering is avoid-able.'[9]

### The Filigree of Mimesis

We need to keep in mind some of these difficulties in approaching the topic of presentation in Lacoue-Labarthe's writing. It is because, as Derrida notes, the 'gesture of gathering' is not avoidable that our own topic will stifle some important themes and ideas in Lacoue-Labarthe's work, but it is also the case that the difficulties of his writing will need to be carefully considered in defining the status of the topic of presentation there. It is clear, for instance, that the ambitious scope he gives to the project of his 'entirely different thinking of mimesis' places enormous constraints on his writing and that these constraints have no evident connection with the topic of presentation. The task of rethinking mimesis entails scrupulous analyses of the operation of the machinery of mimetic identification and the resilient interrogation of what he sees, most evidently in his critique of Heidegger's 'unacknowledged mimetology,' as its 'political dangers.' Some of these constraints are most obvious in his own practice of reading or translating philosophical works, in which, with an almost obsessional intensity, he follows a single word in writing by Heidegger, Girard, or Rousseau. On the other hand, his writing is ideally suited to the analysis of poetry and some of his best essays deploy this cautious and de-tailed approach to unpack the poems of Celan and Hölderlin. At the risk of oversimplifying the differences between his treatment of philosophy and poetry we could say that the 'dangers' he describes in philosophy in terms of 'the machinery of identification' that operates there are disturbed by the relief that the experience to be had in poetic writing provides from mechanisms of identification. In this regard, I think it is significant both that the metier of his cautious practice of writing is the essay and that Lacoue-Labarthe has explained his interest in philosophy as driven by a 'passion' and even a 'vocation' for literature.[10]

Lacoue-Labarthe's 'passion' for literature has, from his earliest writing, always been supplemented by an interest in the history of the philosophical 'idea' of literature. It is in this early writing on literature that we can begin to elucidate some of the important differences between the treatment of the topics of presentation and mimesis in his work. Indeed, in one of his early books with Nancy he unpacks the constellation in which 'ideas' claim a forming position in relation to 'materiality' in Jena Romanticism's conception of 'the literary absolute.' In *The Literary Absolute,* the authors examine the Jena Romantics not in the terms of the pursuit of 'a literary project,' or as opening up 'a crisis *in* literature,' but as the response to the 'general crisis and critique (social, moral, religious, political)' in Germany in the late eighteenth and early nineteenth centuries 'for which literature or literary theory will be the privileged locus of expression.'[11] The privilege the Romantics give to literature 'opens the entire history, up to the present, of the relations literature is *supposed* to have with society and politics' (LA, 5, my emphasis). The key feature of the Romantics' 'overdetermination' (LA, 6) of literature in this way is their concept of the 'literary absolute,' which relates less to 'the production of the literary thing than . . . [it does to] *production*' (LA, 12, my emphasis). The literary absolute is the 'absolute *literary operation*' (LA, 12, their emphasis) in which 'literature [is] producing itself as it produces its own theory' (LA, 12).[12] The conception of literature as an exercise of critical formation that constructs the work at its origin (LA, 110) would be misunderstood if it were cast as 'a matter of a relation between "literature" and "philosophy"' (LA, 122). Instead Lacoue-Labarthe and Nancy argue that in its very conception of criticism as formative, 'romanticism *completes* idealism and opens up the ongoing history of its completion' (LA, 122).

The Romantics' conception of the 'auto-production' of literature is philosophical because it presupposes the forming relation to materiality of ideas that is the core of the speculative response to the Kantian dualism of appearances and ideas.[13] In their 'Preface' to *The Literary Absolute,* the authors comment that the Romantics' belief in the 'effectivity' of auto-productive literature, in the idea that literature could 'intervene' in politics, remains 'our naivety' (LA, 9). Their advocacy in this work for an attitude of critical 'vigilance' or 'lucidity' (LA, 17) in the face of such naivety inflects the idea of literature's 'effectivity' through the historical determination of this idea of literature by the Kantian approach to the topic of presentation. The Romantics' conception of literature embodies the belief in the symbolic effectivity of the absolute (i.e., its full presentation in sensible form) and carries into the literary domain the signal features of the attempt in speculative philosophy to overcome the inexact or analogical determination of 'ideas' in Kant's technical conception of presentation.

On the other hand, this interest in the political determinations of the concept of literature is given a different schema of articulation in Lacoue-Labarthe's rethinking of mimesis. In his writing on this topic Lacoue-Labarthe indicates that philosophical concepts owe their comprehensibility to the fact that they engage and are shaped by a prior literary understanding. There is more force to this view than a commentary on the literary devices used in the articulation of philosophical concepts, or in a bold assertion of the priority of literary devices over 'concepts.' Lacoue-Labarthe, I think, aims to show that the functioning or force of philosophical concepts is aesthetic. As in his historical approach to the topic of presentation, this position is geared to a set of political questions, but these questions have a different point of departure and aim in view than the critique of the formative position of the idea of criticism in relation to literary forms that he undertakes with Nancy in relation to Jena Romanticism.

Lacoue-Labarthe detects a deep-seated ambivalence in philosophers such as Heidegger and Nietzsche regarding the insight that meaning is entirely governed by the materiality of its existence and communication. The sign of the attempt to deny this insight and to contain the aesthetic force of philosophical concepts is the evidence he displays of an antimimetic prejudice in their writing. Nietzsche's comment 'Are you genuine? Or merely an actor?' embodies the Platonic view of the actor as a dissimulator of meaning as well as the more general Platonic view of dramatic poetry or theatre as a false staging of feelings, expertise, and opinions.[14] Similarly, Lacoue-Labarthe locates a contradiction in Heidegger's discussion of tragedy in which he describes its value in terms that reject any relation between tragedy and the dis-appropriating effects of the staging of theatrical form.[15] Against these instances of the attempt to minimise mimetic effects, Lacoue-Labarthe argues against Heidegger that the problem of mimesis 'is older and deeper down than the discourse on being'[16] and that 'the ineluctability of the fact of mimesis'[17] concerns the 'impropriety' that is the originary structure of identity. Two elements, in his view, operate the logic of mimesis: (1) there is the unsurpassable fact of impropriety; and (2) this 'fact' draws attention to the 'infinite malleability' of identity (TYP, 129, n. 128). Identities neither have set boundaries nor can account for how they 'are.' Rather, identities are 'figures,' which is to say that they are always exaggerated or surplus to any grounds or causes that may be given for them and that the absence of any set boundaries renders them temporary or provisional.

The fundamental significance of 'mimesis' can be schematised in the following way: mimetic relations reposition the notion of an intrinsic identity, origin, or essence in terms of a prior relation to a role that is copied, borrowed, or, as in an originary mimesis, devised as a futural act of projection.[18] The operation of mimesis, described by Lacoue-Labarthe as a 'hyperbologic,' recasts categories such as 'identity,' 'origin,' or 'essence' as secondary terms worked into form by a figure. His view that the figure itself is the originary locus of meaning implies that there is no 'authentic origin' that the figure incarnates as a 'secondary' act. With this fundamental disturbance to the notion of a mimetic derivation from an original or authentic communication, meaning is itself understood by the terms of this analysis to be a fiction. I understand 'fiction' to operate in Lacoue-Labarthe's writing in both a generic (so that 'truth' is also a fiction) and a specific sense (so that fiction works against 'truth,' as in Nietzsche's aphorism 'art is there lest we perish from truth').[19] The clear implication of this analysis is that meaning has its force because it is, in its genesis and functioning, aesthetic, which is also to say that meaning is (de)constituted in the disappropriating field of its operation.[20]

Lacoue-Labarthe's rethinking of mimesis may be understood as generating a local model of explanation for the contradictions in thinkers like Nietzsche and Heidegger, but also as providing a general outline of the conceptual presuppositions that underpin the aporetic structure of identity, whether this identity is personal, as in theories of the subject, or political, as in conceptions of national or group identity. For example, on Lacoue-Labarthe's account Lacan fails to follow the consequences of the mimetic mechanism he himself locates at the basis of identity because he still founds identity on a *Gestalt,* or figure. Lacan's significance is that he approaches subjectivity as a fiction forged from a mimetic mechanism. The mimetic moment that, in Lacan, conceals the infant's 'real' state of physiological fragmentation under the cohesive force of the image of the Other, promises a radical rethinking of the subject's identity given that it describes identity as constituted in a series of acts of misrecognition. Yet, Lacan stabilises the mimetic constitution of the subject in his reference to the Other as a structuring, cohesive force that figures the self as a split from a primary 'image' or *Gestalt.* Despite his radicalism, Lacan still conceives identity in the form of a *Gestalt* or figure and not in terms of a constitutive disappropriation.[21]

In Rousseau the conception of the moderns is bound to the ancients by a mechanism of mythic imitation, and in Heidegger 'originary mimesis' is the path he takes to circumvent this mechanism of imitation by locating the 'model' for authentic German identity as a future production. For Lacoue-Labarthe, Heidegger's philosophy criticises the idea of mimetic depreciation in his view of the thinking of the Greeks as an origin from which we have fallen; but he also sanctions a mimetic mechanism as a solution to this fall in encouraging the project of a future production able, not to reappropriate, but to supersede this origin. It is significant that Heideggerian mimesis is not a mimesis at the level of 'products' (as in Plato) but of 'acts' of installation.[22] This 'originary mimesis' or 'mimesis without models' is the basis for Lacoue-Labarthe's description of Heidegger's political project as a 'mimetic' installation of 'authentic' German identity. In Lacoue-Labarthe's account this political project is tied to the philosophical project of overcoming the depreciation, with the Greeks, of an originary experience of being.

Lacoue-Labarthe binds together the consequences of the mimetic foundations of political identity and the identity of 'the subject.' The account given in classical psychoanalysis of the mechanism of the identification of an 'exterior' as the 'origin' in a 'fiction' of subjectivity is a major theme in Lacoue-Labarthe's work and informs his view that today 'murder is the first thing to count on, and elimination the surest means of identification.'[23] In his introduction to *Poetry as Experience* he states that the

' "cancer of the subject" ' is the principle that operates the atrocity of the 'extermination' (PEX, 8). In an essay coauthored with Nancy, 'The Nazi Myth,' their thesis that myth is an 'instrument of identification' leads to an examination of how this mechanism for the forging of political identity relates to the extremities of political violence.[24]

In all these cases, Lacoue-Labarthe interprets the place of models, forms, myths, fictions, the figure [*Gestalt*], and the type as attempts to purify the 'improper' mechanism that constitutes identity, and he catalogues them accordingly as part of 'a great machinery of identification which is entirely founded *upon* imitation itself.'[25] It is notable that in his essays dealing with the topic of mimesis in philosophy he thinks that the undertow of impropriety elicits a 'virile' response, as in Nietzsche's frequent imprecations against 'jews' and 'women' (TYP, 129, n. 128). In Plato, too, feminization and madness are the risks attributed to, but also by this description projected outwards as, the external 'forms' of malleable or lacking identities. In all these cases Lacoue-Labarthe points out that the real fear mimesis awakens is not so much the dissimulation that is the premise of theatrical representation as the splintering or dispersal of identity that is the consequence of the mimetic 'deconstitution' of the 'subject':

> What is threatening in mimesis . . . is exactly that kind of pluralization and 'fragmentation' of the subject provoked from the outset by its linguistic or 'symbolic' (de)constitution: an effect of discourses, the 'self'-styled 'subject' always threatens to 'consist' of nothing more than a series of heterogeneous and dissociated roles, and to fraction itself endlessly in this multiple borrowing. Thus, the mimetic life is made up of *scenes from the life of one who is suited for nothing*—or of a Jack-of-all-trades. Let us say that the 'subject' de-sists in this, and doubly so when it is a question of man (of the male), since there the roles, which are themselves fictive, are moreover passively recorded, received from the mouths of women. In short, what is threatening in mimesis is feminization, instability—*hysteria* (TYP, 129).

In this passage, Lacoue-Labarthe develops his thesis concerning the disturbing, ineluctable force of mimesis in relation to themes in Plato (the fictive roles 'received from the mouths of women') and Lacan ('linguistic or "symbolic" (de)constitution'). He argues that the constitutive incompleteness of the subject fosters a 'resentment against the original maternal domination and original feminine education,' which concerns the 'natural incapability of self-engender[ment].' The Hegelian philosophy is antimimetic in response to this incapability, its 'dream' is 'absolute (in)sight, the subject theorizing its own conception and engendering itself in seeing itself do so—the speculative' (TYP, 127). Against Heidegger, who still tries to delimit onto-typo-logy, to 'gather' it in the unicity of the question of 'being,' Lacoue-Labarthe suggests that 'under the rhythms and melodic variations of the history of metaphysics, indeed under the quasi-permanence of "aletheic" withdrawal and forgetting, there is a kind of continuous or persistent bass in the insuperable formalism (or "figuralism") of the endless repetition of the typographical motif. As also—through the hollow depths of the "question" of writing and on the threshold of the vertigo of dissemination–in the *obsession* with the "subject"' (TYP, 128). The general thesis that emerges from this different thinking of mimesis seems to be the following:

> An entire Western *discourse* on the subject—a discourse that after all could well be Western discourse itself—right away seems to find its limit here; a limit that would lie less, as Heidegger has nevertheless had reason to say, in the supposition of a *suppositum* [*suppôt*], of a matrical identity or substantial *hypokeimenon*, than—on the very borders, perhaps, of the possibilities of *discourse*—in *the necessary reversibility of the motifs of engenderment and of the figure, of conception, and of the plastic*, or, if you will, in this kind of reciprocal and insurmountable metaphorical (figural) exchange between the concepts of *origin* and *fiction*. (TYP, 127–28)[26]

Lacoue-Labarthe describes here the way that origins are only describable and given their semantic force in discourse as fictions, and that equally, the very concept of fictiveness carries with it an inevitable reference to engenderment, to the 'always anterior circulation of discourses' from which fictions are made (TYP, 128). Hence the irrecoverable 'origins' of the subject may be read in the modes of 'virile' resentment of women, but also may be found in the compensating interest in philosophy in the topic of education (Plato) or of a supplementary formative *Bildung* (German Idealism and Romanticism) able to reestablish an origin that could supersede and refigure the sexual relation of birth. The discourse of education is, in other words, to be understood as a fiction of origins that supplants the anxiety of maternal origins as well as an alternative mode of dealing with the fictive force of the description of these origins.

From this preliminary discussion it is possible to identify some important points of overlap between Lacoue-Labarthe's approach to the topics of mimesis and presentation. Like the relation between ideas and sensible forms in his discussion of the historico-political context of the Jena Romantics' conception of literature, mimesis, I think, is shown, if it is not explicitly understood, by him to be an irresolvable problem for modern thought and especially for conceptions of the political [*le politique*]. Is not 'identification,' he asks at the end of his essay 'Transcendence Ends in Politics,' 'the essential problem of the political?'[27] Given the terms of his analysis of mimetic identification, this would mean that the 'essential problem of the political' is understood by him to be irresolvable. Similarly, in his discussion of the relation between ideas and material forms of presentation he defines the modern dilemma of the political in terms of the forming relation of ideas to materiality. In both cases he puts into view the intimate relation between the theme of genesis, whether this is phrased in the vocabulary of mimesis or presentation, and the strategic interest in shaping or forming this irrecoverable origin. From the role Rousseau gives to the figure of the legislator at the end of *The Social Contract,* to the 'effectivity' of literature that is construed as a *poiesis* of sense in Romanticism, to the 'virile' code that organises Heidegger's idea of authentic German identity, 'the problem of the political' is met by myths, conceptions of literary auto-engenderment and figures of national identity that also encounter, as much as they engage and put in play a machinery of identification, an insurmountable logic of imitation. Or, to put this thesis solely in the terms of the topic of presentation, 'ideas' are not constitutive or orientative in respect to meaning because they face an insuperable incapacity in relation to the project of imposing form on the register of appearances, not least because they themselves first come into being as forms *in* this register. It is worth noting here the amendment Lacoue-Labarthe makes to the terms in which Kant raises presentation as a technical problem. In Kant the problem of presentation places the accent on the need to give sensible form to ideas. It is the sensibilisation [*Versinnlichung*] of ideas that gives them force for a finite being and saves them from the impotent status of errant speculation. In Lacoue-Labarthe the coherence of this dualism between ideas and sensible forms of presentation has broken down. As a result, it is the aesthetic force of sensible forms that becomes the central focus in his reflection on the topic of presentation, and it does so because 'ideas' have lost their orientative force and claim to intelligibility as frameworks for the experience of meaning. In this respect, Lacoue-Labarthe still reaches for the radical, or the most basic impulses and elements of the conditions of experience of meaning. By virtue of this gesture, he is still doing 'philosophy,' but a philosophy that is practiced against philosophy.

There is a notable convergence in Lacoue-Labarthe's approach to the modern dilemma of the political between his understanding of the topic of presentation (in the forming relations he analyses between ideas and material forms of presentation) and the modes of his analyses of mimetic identification (as the impossibility of self-engenderment that is worked out through figures and myths). A further convergence between these frameworks of analysis can be found, I believe, in his treatment of the topic of literature. Further, he invariably examines literature in connection with his interest in political topics and questions. In *Poetry as Experience,* for instance, he situates the Heideggerian question of the ability of poetry to 'open' an alternative future to our technicist culture in relation to the mimetic and political question of the historical relation between the ancients and the moderns (PEX, 7). At the same time, his analysis of Celan's poetry takes up a different perspective on the failed conception of literary effectivity in Romanticism to ask whether poetry could be effective in disabling the machinery of modern politics as an 'art' or '*techne*' able to 'form' material conditions as, let us say, seminal. In the place of attempts to 'aestheticise' politics (Heidegger) or poetry (Romanticism) as the terrain of 'virile,' forming ideas, Lacoue-Labarthe wishes to foreground specific instances of poetic writing, which 'stutter' and 'de-form' classical ideals such as the beautiful, and in doing so open the possibility of a de-figuration of the mimetic projects of philosophy. It is significant that Lacoue-Labarthe describes such poetry in the vocabulary of 'experience' and thus concedes the restricted terrain, but not the force, with which poetic writing has its effect (PEX, 18).

It should be clear from this preliminary discussion that Lacoue-Labarthe's thinking on the topics of presentation and mimesis have considerable points of overlap, not least in their status as contexts in which his treatments of political and literary themes are developed. In the rest of my discussion of Lacoue-Labarthe I will analyse some of these points of overlap with a view to unpacking in more detail the role that the topic of presentation plays in his understanding of the aesthetic force and functioning of 'ideas.' This approach will necessarily skirt over many of the important frameworks and themes, such as the relation between the mimetic (de)constitution of the subject and madness, which are attached to the project of a different thinking of mimesis in Lacoue-Labarthe's writing. My approach here is necessarily selective because, leaving to one side the impossibility of accounting for all the intricacies of his writing, I would like to draw out and comment on just two themes that are apposite to the relation between his discussion of mimesis and his treatment of the topic of presentation: first, the reflection on the classical duality of the sensible and the intelligible that it is possible to extract from his analyses of the operation of political 'figures' in modern philosophy, and second, the reflective and critical position he develops on the modern conception of the arts as the presentation of ideas in sensible forms. In both of these cases it is possible to build up a picture of the characteristic features of Lacoue-Labarthe's understanding of presentation. The emphasis he gives to the irresolvability of this topic in his discussions of politics and literature and the intimate relation between the way he treats the topic of presentation and the themes that guide his reflections on the hyperbologic of mimetic 'origins' reveal in his reflection on presentation the experience of poetic yearning.

## Aesthetic Presentation and Political Figures

Figures may operate as a shaping schema for the meaning or self-representation of philosophy as in Plato's figure of Socrates or Nietzsche's figure of Zarathustra, but they may also have the status of a shaping schema for political ideas as in Junger's figure of 'the worker,' Marx's figure of 'the proletariat,' or Freud's figure of 'Oedipus.'[28] More fundamentally, there is a kinship between these modes of operation in so far as Lacoue-Labarthe thinks that the 'figure,' rather than the 'idea,' is the meaning of the 'political' [*le politique*]. His view that there is an original reversibility or semantic promiscuity between the concepts of origin and of the figure does not lead to an attack on the presence of mythical figures in conceptions of the political; rather, Lacoue-Labarthe believes that such figures are the indispensable constituent element of politics [*la politique*], and he is interested in analysing the aesthetic or 'fictional' dimension of the mechanisms of identification they set in play.

One of the major themes in Lacoue-Labarthe's writing is his critique of the formative position of ideas with respect to materiality. To my mind, his description of this formative relation as the basis of modern politics as 'art' or 'techne' is significant not just because it elucidates the way that the very functioning or force of political ideas is aesthetic, but also because it makes this point from the perspective of a reflection on the topic of presentation.[29] His criticisms of the various speculative responses to Kant, whether it is the conception of literature in Jena Romanticism or the conception of history in Hegel, specifically isolate the 'virile' motif of the shaping or forming status of ideas as different modes in which the 'original' status of ideas as aesthetic presentations or figures is suppressed.

Rousseau is exemplary of this combination of the aesthetic dimension of figures and their political, shaping role. In Rousseau, history is viewed in theatrical terms as the stage on which human freedom is shaped and brought into being. His appeal to the devices of a civic religion or lawmaker to shape and install such freedom inscribes a contradiction between his mimetic conception of history as acts of imitation and identification that work at the level of appearances and his well-known intolerance to the false, mimetic stagings of theatrical art and the emotions, premised on false identifications, that they solicit.[30] But it is in Heidegger that the combination of these themes brings into view the connection between Lacouc-Labarthe's treatment of the topics of political mimetology and aesthetic presentation. Heidegger's so-called originary mimesis is important not least because, unlike the example of Rousseau or the characterisation Lacoue-Labarthe gives of speculative thinking, its ostensible aim is to think the meaning-depth of appearance. The impetus for the critique Lacoue-Labarthe develops of Heidegger's political mimetology is the contradiction he finds between Heidegger's thinking on the topic of presentation and his reliance on a mimetological model of politics. Furthermore, this reliance is used by Lacoue-Labarthe to point out the continued dependence on a dualistic conception of presentation in Heidegger's thinking.

It is, I think, striking that in his readings of Heidegger the framework of mimesis often works in concert with an analysis of Heidegger's own discussion of presentation. Such a combination is not unusual in his analyses of the contradictory status of reflections on art in the philosophical tradition. In the exemplary case of Lacoue-Labarthe's account of the mimetic structure of theatre, for instance, Plato criticises the inauthentic form of the theatrical spectacle: emotions are only 'performed,' and actors pretend to incarnate experience and expertise they do not have. The mechanism of theatrical verity is mimetic, and this system, in which the author 'does not say directly what he has to say' but uses the staging of theatrical mechanisms, is described as well by Lacoue-Labarthe as a 'system of *indirect presentation.*'[31] The phrase 'indirect presentation' recalls the terms of the provocation that speculative philosophy sought to overcome in its response to Kant's technical conception of presentation. Moreover it is this mixing of the problematics of 'mimesis' and 'presentation'—so that the rejection of the impropriety of mimesis is comparable to a rejection of the inexactitude of 'indirect presentation'—that underscores the significance of Lacoue-Labarthe's account of Heidegger's contradictory relation to Platonic theses on the arts.

Like Heidegger, Lacoue-Labarthe identifies in the historical moment of philosophical aesthetics an important marker of the breakdown in the hitherto coherent relation between intelligible ideas and sensuous forms. He notes also that many modern thinkers misunderstand or inadequately assimilate this specific effect of the aesthetic moment. He describes Hegel, for instance, as attempting to suppress this effect in continuing to assert the primacy of the concept over the sensuous element of its presentation.[32]

The tone of his own thinking on this topic becomes clearer, however, if we consider that the breakdown he describes in the relation between intelligible ideas and sensuous forms is not able to be adequately mastered even by those who identify and treat this breakdown. Hence his ambitious argument that Heidegger's deconstruction of aesthetics yields only partly to the radical insight of aesthetics into the breakdown of the coherence of intelligible ideas and sensible forms. In his 'Origin of the Work of Art' lectures, Heidegger displaces truth from the field of intelligible ideas to the field of sensuous presentation. The attention to sensuous forms of presentation that one finds in Heidegger is, according to Lacoue-Labarthe, undercut by his displacement of truth there. Heidegger's commitment to truth is read by Lacoue-Labarthe as an attempt to stabilise the abyssal structure of sensuous presentation.[33] But he also reads this attempt in the terms of the problematic of mimesis, as an assertion of the primacy of the unthought 'question of being' or the 'quasi-permanence of "aletheic" withdrawal and forgetting' as a prior meaning, which Lacoue-Labarthe duly submits to the more primary 'hyperbologic' of mimetic disappropriation.[34] Put in the language of figuration, Heidegger does not analyse truth itself as figuration, but puts truth behind the staging of appearances in figures, as an anterior moment, a pure or un-figured giving.

Lacoue-Labarthe's critique focuses accordingly on what could be de-scribed as contradictory elements in Heidegger's deconstruction of the aes-thetic categories that stem from the founding opposition between the sensible and the intelligible in Western thought. In particular he locates a contradiction between Heidegger's condemnation of the 'Hegelian defini-tion of the work of art as the sensible presentation of an ideal or "spiritual" content' and his equally vehement intolerance towards mimesis.[35] In Heideg-ger's fear of the disappropriating mimetic effect of theatre, Lacoue-Labarthe reads the desire for an authentic *Gestalt* that is separate to its aesthetic staging or presentation in and as a 'figure.' In his discussion of Heidegger's eviscer-ating comments on Wagner's music-dramas, for instance, he explains that what Heidegger 'incriminates' in Wagner is

obviously the dubious erotics, simultaneously sentimental and voluptuous, effu-sive and 'mystical,' that are the clearest content of the 'affective state.' But in the same movement, it is also its 'theatricalization' that reinforces the music in dilut-ing the stage itself, thus forbidding all presentation, all real *Darstellung,* ruining in advance any possibility of the appearance of an authentic *Gestalt.*[36]

It is important to be clear on the relation between these problematics of 'presentation' and 'mimesis.' After all, if it is the case that what Heideg-ger subjects to careful analysis in his deconstruction of the concept of pre-sentation in Western aesthetics, he unthinkingly reintroduces in the figure of a 'real *Darstellung*' or 'authentic *Gestalt*' in his failure to think through the disappropriating effects of theatricality, we may well ask whether these prob-lematics are equivalent. Are the same issues at stake for Lacoue-Labarthe in the conceptual problematics they represent?

In his essay 'Transcendence Ends in Politics,' Lacoue-Labarthe tries to reconstruct the elements of Heidegger's thinking that permitted his in-volvement with National Socialism in the early 1930s.[37] Rather than assume a given continuity between philosophy and politics by arguing that Heideg-ger put the thought and language of *Being and Time* into the service of Na-tional Socialism, Lacoue-Labarthe wants to pose as a question whether it is 'his philosophy or his thought which engages Heidegger in politics (in *this* politics), and allows him to state and justify his position.'[38] His examina-tion of Heidegger's 'Rectoral Address'[39] in relation to his philosophical writing concludes that his thinking is determined by an unacknowledged mimetology. This mimetology not only bends fundamental ontology to give Germany a special historical mission but also does so through the mimetic mechanism that frames freedom (which Heidegger understands as transcendence without a ground since it is a 'throwness') within the 'destiny' of a people that constitutes the 'truth' of that transcendence.[40]

There is, no doubt, some evidence for this reading of Heidegger. In the *Fundamental Concepts of Metaphysics*, Heidegger describes metaphysics as 'a fundamental occurrence within human Dasein.' He goes on to define metaphysics as 'a questioning in which we inquire into beings as a whole, and inquire in such a way that in so doing we ourselves, the questioners, are thereby also included in the question, placed into question.'[41] This definition inscribes a constitutive link between metaphysics and human *Dasein*: the kind of being which is capable of putting itself into question, first of all, has to be in the mode of finite transcendence; neither an infinite being nor the one which fully coincides with itself can call itself into question. The finite transcendence of *Dasein*, however, questions itself in a special way, which Heidegger calls 'philosophising.' *Dasein* authentically questions itself only when it also questions 'beings as a whole.'[42] The two questionings—of beings as a whole and of human *Dasein*—proceed from the thought of nothingness, from a mode of being which holds itself out in the Nothing, from 'philosophising existence.' Anxiety towards death, in this perspective, is the condition of having metaphysics, of being able to question beings as a whole.[43]

The structure of metaphysics shares with the finite transcendence of *Dasein* a mimetic structure. *Dasein* occurs in the mode of (finite) transcendence. Through this mode of transcendence man has a 'world,' which means that man relates to things through a world and that things exist for him through his having a world. This is the structural feature of his mode of existence.[44] From the perspective of the encounter with things, the world is, in Lacoue-Labarthe's formulation, 'the condition of the general possibility of all relation to what is,' what *Vom Wesen des Grundes* calls the 'transcendental concept of the world.'[45] From the perspective of *Dasein*, the world is the 'project of its possibilities' or the 'projection' of these. The identification not only of things but also of the self always takes place against the world. Yet this world can be only insofar as *Dasein*, whether it knows it or not, projects from out of nothing. In *Dasein*'s being anxious about death, this lineage of the world manifests itself.[46] This is why the authentic mode of

*Dasein* (i.e., being death-anxious) shares the structure of metaphysical thinking as a withdrawal from its absorption in the proximal and a putting into question of the *being of* beings. It is the address made to things from the viewpoint of nothing that questions things as to their ground. Heidegger writes: 'The certain possibility of death discloses Dasein as a possibility, but does so in such a way that, in anticipating this possibility, Dasein *makes* this possibility *possible* for itself as its ownmost potentiality-for-Being.'[47]

Hence the link to metaphysics as philosophising activity: experiencing itself in the mode of possibility (i.e., as possibility: from beyond the fact that it is or through 'anticipating its death'), *Dasein* is delivered to the possibility of questioning the possibility of things.[48] There is no philosophy without philosophising, no comprehensive (metaphysical) questioning without also involving the questioner: 'in the philosophical concept [*Begriff*], man, and indeed man as a whole [by 'man as a whole' Heidegger means man rounded off by death], *Dasein* is in the *grip of an attack* [*Angriff*]—driven out of everydayness and driven back into the ground of things' (FCM, 21). Thus the kind of being which the anxiety about death (or being gripped with terror) opens to *Dasein* is nothing but the experience of its own fundamental mode of being or its essence which, precisely put, is its being in the mode of transcendence. It is in these terms that Heidegger talks of the 'fundamental attunement of philosophizing' (FCM, 9). This anxiety about death reveals the transcendental ground of things; it puts the questioner in question and *thereby* throws the world into question. The qualification 'authentic' (that *Dasein* recapture its structural possibility of being the place of the disclosure of the being of beings) signifies the mimetic ex-istence of *Dasein*.

For Lacoue-Labarthe the significance of the word 'mimetic' here is twofold: it signifies the mimetic logic of Heidegger's political commitment, and it does so by describing the structure of a mimetic *act* (rather than the mimesis of an image) through which the world takes form.[49] Philosophy relates to the world through the forming function of a relation, through a sort of 'schematism.' As in Kant's schemata where the world is formed out of a transcendental relation, Lacoue-Labarthe alerts us to the value this forming relation carries in Heidegger (politically and philosophically) when this mimetic act binds the *future* to the schematism of the 'world.'

Heidegger *historically* locates the ex-istence of *Dasein* in the metaphysical comportment of the Greek philosophy. 'This beginning is the setting out of Greek philosophy. Here, for the first time, Western man raises himself up from a popular base and, by virtue of his language, stands up to *the totality of what is,* which he questions and conceives as the being that it is.'[50] 'Ek-sistence . . . is exposure to the disclosedness of beings as such. . . . The ek-sistence of historical man begins at that moment when the first thinker takes a questioning stand with regard to the unconcealment of beings. . . . The primordial disclosure of being as a whole, the question concerning beings as such, and the beginning of Western history are the same.' Just as the authentic mode of *Dasein* is a recalling of its primordial or originary ground, of exposing itself to the summons of, and resolutely relating to itself from out of, that originary ground, likewise the historical destiny of *Dasein* (in its essentially existing in the mode of Being-with-others: the people) is to place itself under the authority of the beginning and of holding itself to the task of making the beginning happen. In both cases 'making it happen' is given as a task, but (and here the precedence of the historical becomes clear) this task is handed down to every individual *Dasein* as a 'tradition.'[51] It is not a tradition of achievements but of a call or a commandment. Thus it forces a destiny: a saying yes to the call, but also a greatness. 'As what is greatest, the beginning has passed in advance beyond all that is to come and thus also beyond us. The beginning has invaded our future. There it awaits us, a distant commandment bidding us catch up with its greatness.'[52]

Mimesis, as an imitation of a model, is originary when the imitation of the model is also the inauguration of this model. In the structure of transcendence as in that of (its refounding of ) metaphysics (this repetition is also a repetition of the Kantian refounding), Heidegger's thought is structured by such an originary mimesis. *Dasein*'s ex-istence is mimetic because through it the world is possible (originates) and this possibility is itself historically figured as 'the beginning,' which must be brought to pass. The Greek opening of the question of being and the return to this question in Kant constitutes the model that regulates what is to be done in philosophy as a *repetition* of this model.[53] The possibility of the questioning of the being of beings is thus mimetic not least because it follows the model that first discloses the questioning of being. As a projection of *Dasein*'s possibilities (finite) transcendence gives the world its shape from nothing. This thought of nothingness is the perspective from which metaphysics throws beings as a whole (including the questioner) into question. The originary structure of this mimesis derives not just from the fact that its model (in the Greeks and Kant) remains unfinished (which makes of this model a project to institute, thereby claiming the future) but the structure of transcendence and metaphysics themselves mime this originarity in their departure from a supposed Nothing.

Heidegger, in Lacoue-Labarthe's account, is caught within the 'double bind' of a *repetition* of a model (the philosophising act of the Greeks) which is nevertheless only about to receive its *initial* articulation. In this sense Heidegger's original mimetology is a problem of imitation in a thought that refuses imitation. Alongside the philosophical purism of Heidegger (the fact that Heideggerianism claims for itself a foundational epoch-breaking position within philosophy) is the account of finite transcendence that understands the world as an original mimesis. The significance of the mimetology that runs through Heideggerianism lies in the ontic determination that structures its 'neutral' ontology. If the possibility of the world is that of relation in general, the neutrality of the ontic being's relation to Being is given. But in 'great art' as in 'philosophy' the German people are credited with a special vocation that predetermines ontology.[54] This predetermination receives its 'political' expression in Heidegger's national socialism and the possibility of its 'philosophical' endorsement in the subordination of freedom to truth in Heidegger's 'national aestheticism.'

This originary mimesis subscribes as well to the dualistic logic of presentation: it looks past, as it were, the exigencies of figuration to mark its faith in an authentic figure still to come. The figure it wishes to install as a future project, to extrapolate a little from Lacoue-Labarthe's analyses, is behind the stage of material forms of presentation. It is because Heidegger's constellation of an authentic meaning-figure presupposes a place exterior to figuration that it treats its constellation of meaning-figures as if they were orientating meaning-ideas rather than operational fictions.

In this analysis of the mechanisms of political identification in Heidegger, the perspectives of mimesis and presentation work in concert. To be sure, Lacoue-Labarthe foregrounds the mimetic structure of Heidegger's antimimetic project of an installation of 'authentic' identity, but he also shows that this project, which claims an authentic form for the presentation of identity, may be understood in terms of a desire to produce an exact presentation, that is, an adequate and full presentation. It is because Lacoue-Labarthe does not think that 'ideas' can exist independently of the materiality of their existence and communication, but that they are rather 'fictions,' that he focuses upon the aesthetic form or figure that is constitutive of Heidegger's very 'idea' of 'authentic' German identity. No less important in this context is his analysis of the fiction of production that is inscribed in Heidegger's transcendentalism.

In his argument that the revision Heidegger wishes to make to the formative role of figures in modern philosophy falls short because it seeks to surpass the exigency of material forms of presentation with a conception of 'authentic' presentation, which is an unacknowledged 'figure,' as well as in his diagnosis of the mode of operation of this speculative approach to presentation in Heidegger's preference for 'virile' shaping or styling forces over 'passive' material forms of presentation, Lacoue-Labarthe points to the presence of a model of political identification in Heidegger that may be described, I think, not just as 'originary mimesis,' but as 'originary mimetic presentation.'[55]

### Literary Experience and Yearning

Lacoue-Labarthe's writing is almost obsessional in the way it recounts the irresolvability of the relation between ideas and figures, as well as in his assertion of the mimetic logic that disappropriates the appeal to origins in philosophical writing. Further, the way he treats these themes raises questions concerning the implications of his analyses: after all, if there is an irresolvable relation of promiscuity between ideas and figures, does this mean that there is no alternative to the mechanisms of political identification he identifies and criticises in philosophical writing? What does Lacoue-Labarthe propose as an alternative to the desire and recurrent attempts to shape sense at its 'origins' and resist the effects of mimetological disappropriation in philosophical writing?

These questions are engaged from an oblique angle in his writing on poetry, although it needs to be noted that the way that he pits literary 'defiguration' against the forming powers of the subject in this writing raises other questions regarding the historical parameters of the issues addressed in his thinking. In the practice of his writing, Lacoue-Labarthe seems to subscribe to Heidegger's view that 'aesthetics' is difficult to confine to the period of modern philosophy. Despite the emergence of the philosophical field of aesthetics in the eighteenth century, aesthetics for Heidegger emerges *with* philosophy in the Greeks' reflection on the essence of art and the beautiful in which art as the object of *aisthesis* is gradually reduced (i.e., with modern aesthetics) to the aesthetic feeling of a subject.[56] Similarly, Lacoue-Labarthe uses the themes and topics that are first given an explicit formulation in modern aesthetics as a framework of legibility for his readings of the canon of premodern philosophical texts. His use of aesthetics in this way, however, has ambiguous consequences, and these can be seen most clearly in the comments he makes concerning language. In his view, our existence in language defines us as actors who 'perform' roles and 'stage' meanings. This performative quality of existence is also the feature that puts us 'outside' of 'proper' identity. In this way Lacoue-Labarthe gives an explicitly aesthetic or 'theatrical' cast to the Heideggerian view of the constitutive relation to an outside that defines human existence as an ex-istence in time. However, Lacoue-Labarthe's view that language hollows out, defigures, or desubjectivises experience means that the distinction between poetic speech and everyday language in his writing is a reversible one and that the aesthetic steering he gives to the topic of existence by treating it in the terms of the vocabulary of theatre also entails a critique of the aestheticising tendency, pejoratively understood, to consecrate poetry as a sublime use of language.

On the other hand, his writing on poetry defends the thesis that poetic language stages the de-figuring and de-constitution of experience that philosophical writing suppresses. This thesis, moreover, aims to address the specific question of the effectivity of poetic language to stage experience and meaning after the caesura of the Holocaust, and its treatment of poetic language is therefore framed by historical considerations. In *Poetry as Experience,* for instance, he asks whether poetry is still a venue in which one may have a singular experience of meaning. Could such an experience stand as an alternative to the prevailing frame of meaning as *techne* in the West? Can poetry place us in relation to 'the post-Auschwitz era' when nothing seems to 'escape this era's shadow: a cancer of the subject, whether in the *ego* or in the masses?' (PEX, 8). He is critical of those who deny the 'caesura' the Holocaust represents on the 'pretext of avoiding the pull of pathos' but also of those who attempt to 'transform it into pathos, so as to be able "still" to produce art (sentiment, etc.)' (PEX, 8–9). His repetition, post-Auschwitz, of Hölderlin's now 'heavily layered' question '*Wozu Dichter?*' wants to avoid giving the arts a consecrated position, and this care is primarily exercised against the aestheticism that the category of 'the arts' represent. The 'impossible, exhausting combat' that modern poetry wages against 'the arts' in its motifs 'of panting, babbling, or stammering' needs to be understood as a combat against the genius and thus as a rejection of the philosophical conception of the arts as the presentation of ideas in sensible forms (PEX, 69). The gesture that rejects art on the grounds that it renders reality palatable (as in Bataille's 'hatred of art,' which Lacoue-Labarthe describes, after Barthes, as 'precious') is itself placed to one side in order to examine the possibilities of staging in art an opening for experience away from the classical expectations of the arts as vehicles for edifying ideas. This is undoubtedly a difficult topic for Lacoue-Labarthe given the consistent critique he makes of the Romantic faith in the 'effectivity' of literature as well as his reservations regarding the mimetic determination of historical 'openings.'

The breakdown [*défaillance*] of the constitutive, forming powers of the subject that he argues is staged in Celan's poetic language draws out the salient points of contrast between Celan's de-figuring prose and the Jena Romantics' 'literary absolute,' which seeks an identity between ideas and material forms.[57] There are other features in Lacoue-Labarthe's discussion of Celan that highlight the distinct way that he approaches the stakes of the topic of presentation in poetic writing. Against the productive and constitutive powers of the subject to bring ideas into form, he focuses specifically on the process that is (de)constitutive of meaning and form. The critique of the classical conception of the arts as presenting ideas in sensible forms is extended in his writing on poetry by the insistent attention to the technique or mode of poetic presentation (the 'how') over the self-subsisting entity (the 'what') that is 'presented.'[58]

This contrast between the technique or the 'process of appearing' over a product or an 'already present' (PEX, 67) builds up a further perspective in Lacoue-Labarthe's writing on the topic of presentation that can be characterised in terms of a poetic experience of yearning. We may cite as evidence for this call to poetic experience his critical references to Lyotard's formula for the sublime as well as his commentary on the evocation of the theme of the 'fallen' in Celan. In reference to the way that Celan surpasses the prayer with the poem, he writes:

> The poem arrives in the prayer's stead and in its place; the poem as it is henceforth uttered by the 'deposed' or 'fallen,' the desublimed (*der Enthöhte,* who no longer inhabits the heights), revealing precisely through this that 'there is no longer a God,' rather than that 'there is no God.' (PEX, 86)

The description of the desublimed as those who experience the withdrawal of a divine presence casts poetic language as the place in which the experience of the ebbing away of 'meaning' (rather than the presentation of the meaning 'that "there is no God"') is staged. Meaning, we might say, does not exist; rather, the *experience* of meaning does. What is significant here is the temporal structure of the poetic revelation. It is not that yearning produces a desire to project an 'object' to replace the withdrawal of divine presence. Rather, yearning is a disclosive experience of meaning that shows the difference between a coming to be (divine presence) and a falling away (the process of its withdrawal).

A similar set of themes may be detected in his criticism of Lyotard's view that the sublime in Barnett Newman's painting 'presents that the unpresentable exists.' Lacoue-Labarthe objects that this formula separates out the unpresentable and thereby 'substantialises' or 'hypostasises' it as if it were something 'beyond' presentation. 'By definition, only the presentable is presented. Therefore the unpresentable, if such a thing exists, cannot present itself' (PEX, 90):

We would thus need to think . . . that there is presentation, not *of* what is beyond presentation, but *that* there is something beyond presentation. In which case the presentation would indicate, in what is present or in so far as it *does* present, its beyond.

But this beyond is nothing; it is not *a part of* the unpresentable (PEX, 90). When presentation, he continues, 'attempts to indicate its beyond, or rather the (baseless) base, pure nothingness or pure openness, from which it detaches itself as presentation . . . the difference of the presented from presentation presents itself.'

Instead of a meaning 'beyond' presentation—even if this meaning is conveyed as lost, as in the absence of God ('there is no God'), or as an 'unpresentable' that is substantialised or hypostasised as intact beyond presentation—the 'difference of the presented from presentation,' he argues, is indicated by 'the *disappointment* of presentation, or, more broadly, the disappointment that *the presentable exists*' (PEX, 91). Yearning can be understood in opposition to 'satisfying and edifying' meaning, the meaning that is beholden to the needs of 'reason.' Celan's 'stuttering' language, for instance, opens a critical relation to the claims of the present that has an effect at the level of 'experience': it 'stages' a 'disappointment' that the presentable exists. More generally, it is technique or style in the arts that allows the experience of 'the difference of the presented from presentation.' This difference can be met neither by the cultivation of the 'not beautiful' (Adorno), which as in modern art attempts to exit from the logic of presentation in the in-adequation of form to content, nor by the purity of 'the white square of the "minimal" that, in its attempt to retreat from presentation, is the end point of negative theology' (Lyotard) (PEX, 91). Rather, the experience of yearning which is disclosed in the temporal structure of the experience of the difference between the coming to be and the falling away of meaning is had nowhere else than in the 'stuttering' evocation of the experience that 'there is no longer a God' or in the 'joy' or 'serenity' that 'shows the pain of presentation' (PEX, 91). It is in these forms that the staging of meaning is now *shown to exist* and, we might add, is *felt to be* on the register of appearances alone. Style is the reminder that meaning is not beyond presentation, that all occurs in history, God and all, as experience. Is then the experience of yearning born of the monstrosity of Auschwitz and our resourcelessness, our poverty in the face of it?

The way that Lacoue-Labarthe describes the staging of meaning in sensible forms and especially the tone of pathos that characterises his choice of themes and his style of elucidating them point to the tension that structures his discussions of poetic writing. On the one hand, he seems to be drawn to poetic writing because it is there that an experience of yearning is to be had. His discussion of Celan's surpassing of prayer with the poem is exemplary in this regard. On the other hand, his consideration of modern poetry is motivated by the need for a critical perspective on the constituent elements of this experience of yearning and the tenor of his analysis is directed toward showing how incommunicable deep meanings are, now that such meanings are only to be had in the experience of the meaning-depth of solitary exposures.

In this chapter I argued that a number of persistent themes warrant examining Lacoue-Labarthe's writing in relation to the topic of presentation. His writing aims to provide an account of the aesthetic element in which meaning exists and is communicated. The emphasis he places on this theme of the materiality of meaning may be read as an aesthetic steering of philosophy by means of which he raises the question of the genesis of meaning in sensible experience. In contrast to Nancy who, as we will see, questions the contemporary theme of the exhaustion or crisis of meaning, which is without a point of 'ideal referentiality,' Lacoue-Labarthe focuses instead on the way that meaning is without an idea at its 'origin' because semantic cogency is, for him, only ever forged from out of sensible forms. His view that, rather than starting with ideas or orientating meanings, philosophy starts with figures that aesthetically 'present' its meaning gives rise to the distinctive features of Lacoue-Labarthe's own approach to the topic of presentation. He scrutinises literature as the 'originary' site of meaning, because rather than a technical problem concerning the co-articulation of the intelligible and the sensible domains as in Kant, presentation has become for him an ontologically posed problem of an experience of meaning. It is in its literary or theatrical forms that meaning most evidently displays the tools, resources, and place of its elaboration in the aesthetic register. Whether it is in his criticisms of the way philosophy suppresses the aesthetic form in which meaning is experienced and communicated or in his view that poetic writing discloses the experience of the infirmity of meaning in a world where 'there is *no longer* a God,' his reflection on the topic of presentation is driven towards the poetic evocation of the experience of yearning.

# 6

## Nancy: Touching the Limits
## of Presentation

The writings of Jean-Luc Nancy share some of the central concerns of Lacoue-Labarthe's critique of Heidegger. Like Lacoue-Labarthe, Nancy recalls that the problem of presentation is first raised in the context of philosophical aesthetics and he, too, is faithful to these origins in foregrounding the contemporary arts as the privileged place for the formulation of presentation as a question. Nonetheless, Nancy's philosophy has wider ambitions, which we can phrase, in provisional terms, as articulating an ontology that is not beholden to an originary meaning. The central topic in Nancy's thought is the question of presentation as sense or meaning. Nancy inflects this topic through the frame of Heidegger's approach to the question of the meaning of being and uses this frame to develop his own ontology. Just as Lacoue-Labarthe criticises Heidegger's dependence on an orientating figure, Nancy is critical of the thought of a unitary origin that frames the topic of presentation in Heidegger, and thus his own conception of meaning is partly expressed through a critique of what he takes to be Heidegger's continuing reference to the dualist structure of metaphysical thinking. On Nancy's view, this structure is not adequate as a framework to fully comprehend what is experienced in our epoch as the withdrawal of meaning. As we will see, the source of dissatisfaction for him in Heidegger's thinking of the problem of presentation is that the dualist structure of metaphysics is still operative here.

Nancy's complaint against Heidegger has two main sources of evidence: first, Heidegger's existential analytic in *Being and Time* retains the traditional order of ontology in which being is thought of as a primary term that is logically prior to being-together or *Mitsein* and thereby overlooks the primary feature of ontology as being-in-common.[1] Second, this dualistic structure is represented in Heidegger's view that being occurs more authentically at its point of origin with the Greeks.[2] It is this conception of an authentic or original occurrence of being that underpins the constant ambivalence in Heidegger's late work about an authentic counterterm able to critique the technological *Gestell*.

It is not just these deficiencies in Heidegger's writings that motivate Nancy's complaint regarding dualism: according to him, phenomenology in general has the structure of a search for something more authentic (as in the impulse to go back to a point of origin) or essential (to discover an underlying condition).[3] It is precisely Nancy's critique of this dualism that is the core framework for raising presentation as a question in his thought.

If we were to characterise Nancy's position on this question in more positive terms, we would have to see it in the context of his understanding of contemporary art. The place given to art in Nancy's work can be read as paralleling Heidegger's treatment of art in the 'Origin' lectures. There, as we saw, art was understood as a significant way in which truth occurs. In Nancy, however, it is not truth but meaning or sense on the verge of its emergence that art presents.[4] This is a crucial difference whose implications for Nancy's ontology we will discuss in detail later in this chapter. The Heideggerian conception of the artwork becomes in Nancy's ontology the paradigmatic category of praxis of 'sense-making' that emerges solely from the senses. Nancy's attempt to get away from a structure that assumes a point of orientation for meaning makes the central problem in his deconstruction of ontology that of showing how sense emerges from the exteriority of the senses. This is important because if Nancy is to avoid the resurrection of an ontology that relies on a dualistic structure, he has to be able to show that sense emerges from the active involvement of the senses in the world. In this context we can appreciate better the significance of art for his ontology given that in art meaning is not given but is rather sensuously staged or presented but always underway, so to say, and never complete as a 'truth' would be. This feature of the arts qualifies them as a ' "presentation of presentation," '[5] but also makes the way they stage presentation a general model for the ontology of sense.

The other connection that seems to me to be important between Heidegger's 'Origin' lectures and Nancy's ontology of sense is the theme, which Heidegger underlines, of the comportment of wonder that has been forgotten in the modern age. This theme becomes a crucial reference point in Nancy's ontology because art is the privileged place for exposing this forgotten comportment to things. But, at the same time, he criticises Heidegger for restricting the experience of wonder to the sphere of art: in Heidegger the comportment of wonder revived in our attitude toward art is radically distinct from the fallen relation to the everyday. Nancy gives to this comportment the status of a basis for the relation to the everyday. Thus Heidegger's discussion of wonder in the arts as the staging for this forgotten comportment to things is cultivated by Nancy as the framework for our relation to things in general.[6]

The negative axis that, I suggest, structures Nancy's approach to the topic of presentation as a critique of 'referential ideality' is evident in his earliest published works. In Nancy's first published book, *The Title of the Letter: A Reading of Lacan,* coauthored with Lacoue-Labarthe, they criticise the structure of theological thinking still operative in Lacan's critique of the classical metaphysical subject in his use of the notions of Law, Subject, and Other.[7] Nancy's later works extend this criticism of Lacan, to include Levinas's formula of 'otherwise than being' and Heidegger's 'Being' as examples of thinking that, despite their authors' intentions, sustain this dualist structure of 'referential ideality' (BSP, 26; SW, 199, n. 164).

The topic of the praxis of sense making, which is the frame for Nancy's recent writing on the arts and the positive axis on which he develops the central problem of his ontology, also receives an important, nascent formulation in his earlier works. In another early collaborative work with Lacoue-Labarthe, *The Literary Absolute: The Theory of Literature in German Romanticism,* the suppression of the problem of presentation in Romanticism is described in terms of the Romantic conception of the literary work as fashioning, in its productions, the sources of sensibility.[8] It is precisely the Jena Romantics' conception of literature as an 'absolute,' as a fashioning or *poiesis* of sense, that Nancy's later works will describe as an attempt 'to appropriate the generativity of sense' and to close down the question of *praxis* of sense making (SW, 162).[9] In his later discussions of the arts,[10] the opening that artworks provide for posing the question of praxis of sense making becomes a positive countertradition to the Romantic conception, described in this early text, of the 'literary absolute.' Finally, the conditions of possibility for such praxis are outlined in *The Experience of Freedom,* which anticipates the quasi-historical framework, in which this possibility is systematically treated in more recent works like *The Sense of the World* and *Being Singular Plural.* One may view this treatment as a philosophical reply to what he takes to be the fundamental experience of our times, namely, the waning of all compelling existential regime of meaning.[11]

In this chapter I would like to give a systematic consideration of the implications of Nancy's reflection on the key question of aesthetic presentation for his ontology of sense. My thesis is this: Nancy's ontology is developed from a reflection on what happens in art and to art in our time. In the earlier discussion of the place of the artwork in Heidegger's thought we pointed to the problem for him of retaining art's relation to truth in the epoch of the *Gestell.* Nancy, in contrast, generalises the features of the artwork into the topics of a 'first philosophy' and thereby reinstates art in precisely the position of exception that, in Heidegger's late work, is a matter of considerable ambivalence and debate. Can Nancy's use of the arts in this way be justified by the particular terms in which he gives the arts an interrogative relation to presentation? How does his understanding of our age, in which the emphasis is placed on the operations of capital rather than technology, influence the role he gives to the contemporary arts as staging the question of presentation?

The following discussion of the problem of presentation in Nancy's philosophy, guided by the preceding questions, is divided into five main sections. The first two sections deal with the historical impetus given to Nancy's ontology by, respectively, the approach to the topic of presentation in modern philosophy and the modelling of presentation as 'co-appearing' within the operations of capital. These operations, as the prevailing schema of our times, are interpreted by Nancy as impenetrable to any dualistic frame of analysis. The operations of capital thus raise in a profound way the question of not only where to look for a locus of sense but also what exactly this sense could be in an epoch that has no essential point of orientation. The third section provides a brief account of how Nancy's ontology turns to the affectability of the senses to answer this question, and the final two sections attempt an assessment of (1) Nancy's view that sense-making occurs paradigmatically in the arts and (2) his defence of a 'first philosophy' able to connect the paradigmatic sense-making activity of the arts to everyday existence.

## Nancy's Account of Presentation in Modern Philosophy

Heidegger's account of the epoch of technology, as we saw in earlier chapters, culminates in an aporia: the point at which the problem of presentation becomes potentially articulable in its full scope is also the point at which finding a path to it becomes nearly impossible because of the all-encompassing nature of technological relations and of their self-concealment. Heidegger seems to resolve this aporia by his construction of a 'step-back' into the history of metaphysics, out of which the thinking of a new relation between being and human being is supposed to emerge. In Nancy's thinking, too, Western metaphysics is understood as having reached an end, and as in Heidegger's thinking this 'end' is understood as an 'opening' that requires a rethinking of Western philosophy. Nancy takes the question of ontology raised at the 'end' of Western metaphysics to be the 'question of social Being' (BSP, 57). In terms of the structure he gives to this ontology and the terminology he uses to articulate it, Nancy draws on two different trajectories: on one side, there is Nancy's account of the history of philosophy in terms of 'the exhaustion of significations' presented there; on the other, there is his political-economic diagnosis of the impact of capitalism on social being. These two trajectories, whose respective significance for Nancy's ontology will be analysed in greater depth in the next section, converge in Nancy's contrast between History (as a system that gives a sense or direction to existence) and what he terms the 'historiality of history' (SW, 77). The exhaustion of significations in Western metaphysics and the operations of capital both expose the 'event-character' or 'historiality' of history, the emergence into view of the contingency of the 'sense of the world' (SW, 24, 77). Nancy uses the phrase 'sense of the world' in the same way that one would have referred in earlier times to God or History to construct 'the meaning of life' or 'the sense of existence.' In fact, his quasi-historical typology of systems of sense leaves no doubt in this regard. According to him, there are three formal structures of sense constitutively oriented to (1) observance of a pregiven all-encompassing order (i.e., the ancient philosophy); (2) salvation, that is, recovery from alienation (the Christian Fall or the expropriation of labor); and (3) existence with no guiding and justificatory foundation, but in accordance with an ethics of praxis of sense-making, which is an ethics of the sensibility or 'affectability' (the ability or 'aptitude' of the senses to be affected). 'The sensible,' he writes in *The Sense of the World,* 'or the aesthetic is the outside-of-itself through which and *as* which there is the relation to itself of a sense in general, or through which there is the *toward* of sense' (SW, 129).

In his reading of the texts of Western philosophy, Nancy argues that the aporia presented there is, like the Heideggerian *Gestell,* an epochal event. This event is given an exemplary formulation in Nietzsche's diagnosis of 'nihilism.' In 'The Forgetting of Philosophy,' Nancy puts in stark terms the impossibility that this event places in the way of any project for a return to an earlier system of 'meaning.' This work, written as a critique of humanist philosophers such as Ferry and Renaut who advocate just such a return puts the realities of our times, as Nancy sees them, in the barest possible terms:[12]

Nietzsche's age is the age when all the projects of Humanity come to recognize themselves under the heading of 'nihilism,' that is, as doomed from the outset and by essence to the exhaustion of their signification.

The fact that this event has happened, and that it is still under way . . . this inevitably delivers us over to *another history* which opens up before us beyond signification, a history whose meaning could never consist in a return of 'meaning' (no more than Plato could make the meaning of Egypt return, or Christianity could make the meaning of Socratism return, or industrial society could make the meaning of the Christian community return) . . . this [event] happened to our time as its destination. (G, 44)

Nancy contrasts the sedimentation in signification of a 'located meaning' and '[t]he dimension of the open . . . according to which nothing (nothing essential) is established or settled,' since the emphasis here is on the '*coming* of a possible signification' (G, 10, my emphasis). In 'The Forgetting of Philosophy' he uses this narrative of the history of metaphysics to present a credible platform for questioning the idea of essence. On the level of ontology this takes the form of trying to show how 'everything essential *comes to be*' (G, 10). He takes this revised approach to ontology as a 'coming to presence' as the key topic for the 'thinking [of] the present, the presence and presentation of reality' (G, 15). Our epoch has as its defining characteristic the 'exposure' to meaning because, as Nancy likes to put it, the limit reached in this epoch by the exhaustion of systems of signification cannot be met with revived significations. But, thanks to this exhaustion, this limit is also where our exposure to the event of meaning or 'existence' takes place. This important, partly diagnostic, notion of 'exposure' is intimately connected, in my view, with Nancy's analysis of sense in terms of presentation.

As the 'destination' of 'our time,' this event of exposure to meaning is the moment at which the history of Western philosophy, for the first time with Nietzsche, comes to be understood in general as the history of metaphysics and, according to the slant Nancy wishes to give it, specifically as the passing of 'signified meaning':

This exhaustion does not imply that all significations will have been null and void. They had their *meaning;* they cleared the way for this destination that leads beyond them without itself, perhaps, leading toward some other signification. Christianity and empiricism have led us to ourselves, they have destined us, just as democracy, axiomatics, the critique of reason, human rights, art for art's sake, and the total man, and so on have. But in the end, the system and history of signification have come to signify their own annulment, turning upon themselves only to reveal the infinite withdrawal [*éloignement*] of signified meaning, that is, of a meaning that is immobile, inaccessible, or else infinitely evasive, thus slowly becoming, as if before our very eyes, insignificant. (G, 48)

For Nancy, the exhaustion of signification needs to be understood as a 'limit' in Heidegger's sense of 'that from which something *begins its presencing* [*Wesen*].'[13] This exhaustion is the event of the gradual emergence into view, and in its full scope, of presentation not, as it was for modern philosophy, as a project but as a question. It is the sustaining of presentation as a question in an historical context in which there are no orientating points of reference that can be considered the major task that Nancy defines for his work. He argues that the comportment to take towards the limit reached by projects of signification is that of *Gelassenheit:* 'letting be' (as opposed to the reassertion of new projects of signification) is, for Nancy, the only way to experience the full 'weight' of the exhaustion of signification or withdrawal of meaning that occurs in our time.[14] This comportment of *Gelassenheit* is contrasted by Nancy to the will to the presentation of meaning that is, for him, the defining feature of modern metaphysics.

In metaphysics there is a 'will to presentation' that 'constantly makes meaning return,' and this will suppresses the question of the 'presentation of meaning' (G, 24). As in Heidegger's double reading of Kant, Kant is used by Nancy to represent both the metaphysical will to presentation and the awareness of a question overhanging the projects of presentation that commence with his philosophy. Kant is unusual because his thought 'never forgot the question' of presentation, and 'this project [for total presentation] nonetheless began in Kant's work itself ' (G, 23–24). Signification, which takes place in Kant's thought, in Nancy's account of it, certainly 'takes on different modes, ranging from the ostensive mode of mathematics to the analogical, symbolic, and even 'negative' modes of morality, aesthetics, and history—but it is still essentially signification, it is still the demand and the logic of its closure (Kant speaks of the "satisfaction" of reason) that are at stake' (G, 23–24). The Kantian ideas of reason are thus the orientating ideas that in the symbolic and negative forms of morality, aesthetics and history precede, govern, and arrange presentation.

'[T] he great lineage' of modern philosophy 'from Kant to Husserl' does nothing but 'modulate the will to presentation in various ways'; but it is precisely in its various modulations of this will that modern philosophy has also 'come to touch on the limit of signification and put it into question . . . as such.'[15] Instead of the 'immobile,' 'infinitely evasive,' or 'inaccessible meaning' that stimulates the various projects of presentation in modern philosophy, Nancy wants to turn our attention to the forgotten *accessibility* of meaning *as* a coming to presence, rather than a given and prior signification.

The culmination of the 'referential ideality' of metaphysics is reached, for Nancy, in phenomenology (SW, 7). Phenomenology wants to stay with the things themselves, and this 'posture' makes possible 'a new access to the world' 'as the absolute horizon of sense' that is neither subordinated to a ' "beyond-the-world" or to mere representation' (SW, 17). However, it is because phenomenology 'still irresistibly convokes us to the pure presence of appearing' and maintains 'a proper . . . point of origin for sense, a point with which, consequently, all sense is confounded' that its project retains a will to presentation that structures the projects of signification in modern philosophy (SW, 17). Phenomenology cannot pose the question of the *sense* of appearing, or of the *coming* of sense, because its method, as Nancy reads it, attempts to contain sense to what is given in the interiority of thought or of consciousness. This attempt, described by him as 'the incessant will to turn back on itself in order to appropriate its own process, in the reduction to the "immanence" of an origin (subject, consciousness) that contains all "transcendence,"' loses precisely the excess of sense to an origin that is the topic that structures Nancy's ontology (SW, 18).

One may draw attention in this regard to the emphasis prepositions receive in Nancy's writing. Indeed, careful attention to the terminology he uses can further illuminate his understanding of the structure of existence. In the next section we will see how he deploys this terminology for his analysis of the operations of capital.

The most striking feature of Nancy's writings is the central place given to prepositions. Prepositions are used by Nancy to deconstruct certain representative approaches to ontology within the philosophical canon. As he characterises them, these latter approaches attempt to appropriate the generativity of sense by containing the excess of sense to an origin. The different modes of such appropriation can be readily schematised in terms of the essence/appearance distinction. Ontology, according to the parameters of this distinction, is understood as going back to an origin; the origin or essence is understood as an enabling and determining condition for appearance. On the one hand, essence determines and enables appearances, but on the other, this determining and enabling condition is not given to the senses and needs ontological investigation to be disclosed. Against the understanding of ontology implied in the essence/appearance distinction, which basically constructs appearance as a derivation from a point of origin, Nancy's ontology understands existence according to the ontological structure of 'co-appearing.' Traditional ontology neglects the shared nature of being because it tries to think the meaning of being apart from co-existence as an origin. But, Nancy suggests, this is an erroneous path because being is first of all shared, or 'being-in-common.'[16] He reverses the conventional order of ontological exposition. By this reversal Nancy redefines being as acts in relation.[17]

In this context, the 'co' of co-appearing underlines Nancy's point that meaning is not appropriable, because, as in the Derridean conception of *différance,* it belongs to the spacing of being that 'remains between us' (BSP, 84). Meaning, which has its location in the 'between' and the 'with' that is the shared dimension of being cannot be an essence, an origin or pure presence; rather, meaning begins when 'Being does not identify itself *as such* (*as Being of the being*), but *shows itself* [se pose], *gives itself, occurs, dis-poses itself* . . . as its own singular plural *with*' (BSP, 38, his italics). The 'as,' like the 'co,' the 'between' and the 'with,' marks the originary duplication of Being according to which it is meaningful only as an element of communication or happening in common. The duplication necessary for the functioning of language is cited by Nancy to mark out the 'element' and the 'space of . . . declaration' of this being-in-common (BSP, 88):

> Language constitutes and articulates itself from out of the 'as.' No matter what is said, to say is to present the 'as' of whatever is said. From the point of view of signification, it is to present one thing as another thing (for example, its essence, principle, origin, or its end, its value, its signification), but from the point of view of meaning and truth; it is to present the 'as' *as such*. That is, it is to present the exteriority of the thing, its being-before, its being-with-all-things. (BSP, 88)

This attempt to redefine the 'origin' of sense, not as 'being-within or being-elsewhere' or as an 'essence, principle, origin,' but as the exterior surface of the network of 'co-appearing,' is also ventured in Nancy's recasting of the interiority/exteriority distinction according to his view that being is 'at' the surface of the senses. He thus uses the preposition 'at' to define his new conception of the source of sense as the affectability of the senses that occurs 'at' the point of contact between bodies. I will discuss this conception of the source of sense in detail in the third section. Finally, the view that sense is not an appropriable term is marked in Nancy's modulation of sense as 'coming' or 'toward'; both terms are used to critique the immanent/transcendent distinction of the canon which locates meaning either in an interiority without relation or in a term external to all relations.

## The Operations of Capital and the Ontological Relation of Co-appearing

It is interesting to consider what it is that makes Nancy think the ontology of co-appearing can be formulated in a comprehensible way in *our* time. My understanding of Nancy's thought is that when he comes to reflect on this question two distinct trajectories provide him with an answer. The evidence from the history of Western philosophy is called on to support his view that our era raises in stark terms the exhaustion of systems of meaning. Western philosophy is the place where this exhaustion is first laid bare.[18] However, the second trajectory that provides Nancy with a schema of legibility for his ontology surpasses Western philosophy in one crucial respect. In Nancy's systematic account of his ontology in his 1996 essay 'Being Singular Plural,' he states that the distinctive features of our age need to be examined in relation to the 'question of capital' (BSP, 22). This question of capital itself needs to be understood, he argues, in more radical terms than those offered in Marx and contemporary post-Marxist critical theory, and in the terms already offered in the analysis he gives of Western philosophy, as the withdrawal of meaning. However, in contrast to Nancy's discussions of the philosophical canon, his examination of the 'question of capital' brings to a head, in a way his analysis of the canon could not, the key problem of his ontology: namely, what is the experience of meaning in a context of social relations in which meaning withdraws. His examination of 'the question of capital' is the significant trajectory for his ontology, in other words, because through it the problem of meaning can be posed in terms of the real conditions of its social or communicative possibility.

At first glance, the operations of capital in Nancy seem to be analogous to those of the technological *Gestell* in Heidegger: in both cases the absolute nadir reached under the conditions of capital/technology brings with it an opening that greatly complicates the issue and questions the adequacy of schematically representing either capital or technology in simply negative terms. The operations of capital have the structure of an antinomy for Nancy: they both 'strip bare' *and* nullify 'co-appearing' (BSP, 64). However, the way Nancy articulates this double effect distinguishes the significance of capital for his ontology from Heidegger's analysis of the *Gestell*. Heidegger's account of technology, as we saw in earlier chapters, is ambiguous: the oppressive relations set in place by technological revealing suggest the opening of a new relation of appropriation between human being and being, but Heidegger also wants to criticise technology, the apex of Western metaphysics, as a decline from the 'authentic' space of philosophising in the Greeks. According to Nancy's analysis of capital as stripping bare relations of 'co-appearing,' the 'referential ideality,' which, for Heidegger, permits the identification of an 'authentic' origin that precedes and is corrupted by these relations is no longer possible. Capital, like the 'historiality' of Western thought, undermines systems of signification at the same time as it reveals meaning to be a feature of a network of exterior exchange relations. In *Being Singular Plural* Nancy criticises three perspectives on capital that distort or suppress this insight into meaning: (1) conceptions of spectacle in political philosophy, (2) Marxist and post-Marxist discourses of social criticism, and (3) the angle of capital itself.

In the Western discourses of political philosophy and even in the Marxist and post-Marxist discourses of social criticism, there is not yet a thinking 'adequate' to the problem of sense raised by the disclosure of capital (BSP, 64). In these latter discourses Nancy detects the symptoms of ambivalence that he locates in Heidegger's thought on technology: the 'insight' of capital, 'buried' in Marx's work, is to show that there is no 'proper,' 'self-identical,' or 'given' meaning, but only relations of 'co-appearing' (BSP, 64). However, Marxist and post-Marxist discourses of social criticism retain the dualistic reference according to which capital happens to 'a primitive, authentic subject,' or 'some prior community . . . within a continuous historical process' (BSP, 74).

In this dualistic frame, these discourses of social criticism carry over the reflection on 'collective existence,' or the problem of social being, in the mimetic terms in which it is conceived in the tradition of Western political philosophy (BSP, 71). This conception, according to Nancy's schematic outline, separates the 'authentic' form of sociality from 'false' collective existence, or the origin and essence from its mere appearance. The two examples that give the clearest indication of the terms of Nancy's critique are, from the classical tradition, Rousseau's *Social Contract* and, from post-Marxist discourse, Debord's *Society of the Spectacle*.

Rousseau, 'despite himself,' shows the necessity of the spectacle in the account he gives of 'the best spectacle, and the only one that is necessary': 'the spectacle of the people itself, assembled in order to dance around the tree they have planted as their own proper symbol' (BSP, 68–69). In Rousseau, Nancy finds the constituent elements of the theory of society in modernity in which it 'takes place as a *subject*'; more specifically, society takes place as '*representation as subject*' (BSP, 69, his emphasis). His criticism concerns the operational problem at the core of Rousseau's political reflection: Rousseau shows that rather than a self-identical, self-aware term that secondarily discharges institutional functions, society first comes to be as self-spectacle; or, as Nancy puts it, society takes place as '*representation as subject*.' There are two key points here: first, having fused authentic sociality with the spectacle, Rousseau can only generate a distinction between a good and bad spectacle rather than an authentic and illusory sociality;[19] second, the coming to presence of society in its spectacular representation means that the 'togetherness' of the people that is represented needs to be defined in the terms of acts not of an essence, of 'being-in-common' rather than a given 'togetherness.' Hence Rousseau's social contract is reinterpreted by Nancy not 'as the conclusion of an agreement; [but as] . . . the stage, the theatre for the agreement' (BSP, 69). This reinterpretation of Rousseau frames Nancy's reordered ontology according to which we 'are' the staging of ourselves as 'being-exposed' to, rather than bearing pregiven, meaning.

The position Nancy takes against the dominant post-Marxist accounts of contemporary culture follows from his view that they are continuous with the mimetic presuppositions of classical political philosophy. For him, there is no given, collective identity or individual subject that is not already a co-appearing. This position is deployed against those conceptions of a prior, 'authentic' preexisting group or 'pure' community, but also against those explanations of the 'we' that depict it as only an illusory coexistence, as in the manufactured idea of the 'we' described in Debord's 'society of the spectacle.' For Nancy being-with is not an already given 'we' that is secondarily distorted. The problem of social-being is not anterior to, nor is it independent of, the technological proliferation of the spectacle, it *is* this spectacle. The motivation and the credibility of critiques of the 'spectacular' turn on their claim to possess 'the key to what is an illusion and what is not' (BSP, 202, n. 60). However, such a claim relies on designating what is 'proper' as beyond mere appearance, when this 'nonappearance' can only be 'the obscure opposite of the spectacle' (BSP, 51). It is because in Nancy's view there is nothing beyond co-appearing that the denunciation of 'mere appearance' also and only 'moves within mere appearance' (BSP, 51). Thus, his treatment of the theme of criticism in political thought raises the question as to whether social criticism can work with no positively valued, emotionally invested counter-image, however vague this would have to be.

The post-Marxist versions of critical thinking obscure their own intuition 'of society exposed to itself, establishing its being-social under no other horizon than itself,' preferring to scrutinise this intuition in terms of 'the reign of appearance' (BSP, 52). Critique thus 'remains obedient to the most trenchant and "metaphysical" tradition of philosophy, "metaphysical" in the Nietzschean sense: the refusal to consider an order of "appearances," preferring, instead, authentic reality (deep, living, originary—and always on the order of the Other)' (BSP, 52). In his critique of the commitment to classical metaphysics in critical theory, Nancy is guided by the concern that this critique remains bound to 'another, symmetrical alienation' that suppresses the problem of social being (BSP, 53). Against it, Nancy argues that the problem of social being lies in the spectacle and in the technological and has to be considered and understood with their parameters; it is, after all, ' "our" comprehension of "our-selves" that comes up with these techniques and invents itself in them' (BSP, 70). For this reason the dualistic conception of technology as a *poiesis* that acts on and shapes social being is replaced in Nancy's thinking by a conception of technology as a *praxis* that 'transforms its agent . . . more than it fashions a product' (SW, 101).

Finally, the operations of capital tend to suppress the insight they themselves make available into the primacy of co-relation. In capital the operations of exchange determine 'value' (or meaning) not as an essence but according to the surface network of exchange relations in which value is defined and has to be defined in terms of disappropriation. However, this very feature of capital that lays bare the constitutive ontological relations of 'co-appearing' is retracted in its assertion of this 'being-together' as 'being-of-market-value' (BSP, 74). In this respect, the criticisms Nancy makes of post-Marxist social criticism, when it holds onto a conception of 'use' value not corrupted by the disappropriating effects of 'exchange' or when it entertains the idea of a prior authentic community that is only secondarily acted on or alienated by the operations of capital, are also levelled at capital. In both cases an orientating meaning (the corruption of a prior community or anthropology, or the determination of co-relation as market value) suppresses the insight of capital into the constitutive ontological relations of 'co-appearing.'

There is an important distinction to be made between the disappropriation of identity in the operations of capital (which Nancy uses to confirm the features of an ontology of sense as co-appearing), and the way that these operations raise the question of the *source* of sense. Capital, as I understand it, does not raise this latter question merely as a function of its disappropriation of identity, but because of the scope and form of this disappropriation. Rather than using the 'infrastructural' terminology of the 'economic,'

Nancy defines the operations of capital as '*ecotechnics,* the global struc-
turation of the world as the reticulated space of an essentially capitalist,
globalist, and monopolistic organization that is monopolizing the world'
(SW, 101). He sees two possible outcomes of this 'reticulated space':[20] in the
first, described by him as a 'windowless monad,' there is a 'process of indefinite self-expansion' whose 'entire sense' is claimed by 'indefinitely growing
totalization'; in the second, there is the 'disruption of all closures of signification' that 'opens them up to the coming of . . . sense' (SW, 102). The first
option would make the global system of capital a new grounding system of
signification, which can perhaps be rendered as living the 'sense' of senseless
totalisation, whereas the second would sustain the 'disruption of all closures
of signification' by following the 'global' insight of capital that sense is made
or more accurately practiced, not given, in relations of exteriority.

As we have seen, the operations of capital have significance because
their exteriorisation of meaning in relations of exchange articulates the ontological framework in which, for Nancy, the question of sense emerges in
its full scope. The operations of capital show that this question is not answered in the reassertion or reappropriation of meaning in the politics of
nationalism, fundamentalism, and fascism, likened by Nancy to the naïve
conception of nature as a modality that excludes exteriority and contingency.[21] They also show that the 'non-alienated community' that animates
post-Marxist critical theory depends on a conception of sense that fails to
absorb the implications of the exteriorisation of meaning in a system of
exchange. Wherever post-Marxist discourse holds out a new authentic
form of community, it overlooks the insight of capital that there is no
'other' mode of social unity that could claim to be in tune with human nature. Instead of gesturing towards a community beyond 'commerce' and
'exchange,' or implementing or applying these essentialising ideas of community (representing them, so to say), all that is left, Nancy writes—having
also discounted the new systems of signification proposed by capital—is
'understanding ourselves as moderns' (BSP, 73).

The operations of capital define the terms of this task in the extent and
form of the 'reticulated space' of 'exterior relations' that they assert. It is the
impact of capital on modern society that raises the question of the real origin
or real source of sense. In placing the 'source' of meaning in our exposure
to the exterior relations of sense, Nancy draws on the ontological insight the
operations of capital provide, but also rejects the possible nihilistic outcomes

of its processes (the 'sense' of 'senseless' 'indefinite . . . totalization'). Or better, in the light of his use of the operations of capital to critique the idea that interiority could be a source of meaning, Nancy is able to ask what the source is and what the processes are through which meaning may emerge. Such questions are not answered by the theory that modernity is an abyss of senselessness. Rather, nihilism is another regime of signification and thus, like the interior essence operative in nationalism or the dualistic function of the 'authentic' community in critical theory, a failed reflection on the question of sense.[22] This question cannot be resolved, or really understood, in purely conceptual terms, albeit those of a critical social ontology of co-appearance, because it asks, not merely after an ontological idiom, but about the experience of the emergence of meaning. It is the surface of the senses that are the site for the experience of meaning for us moderns; they alone, Nancy argues, do not pin the generativity of sense to an origin, but experience sense as it is made in relations of exteriority (SW, 101–2).

## Affectability: The Senses as the Source of Sense

The key problem of Nancy's ontology is the 'epochal' question of where the actual experience of sense or meaning comes from now that the grounding systems of signification, as capitalist relations set in, have collapsed. The category of affectability is used by Nancy to argue for the general claim that meaning has its locus in exteriority. Instead of the subject being the site or source of meaning, meaning is exteriorised; its 'origin' is being-in-common, between bodies. Nancy, indeed, explicitly sets up 'affectability' as the network of relations where meaning takes place against 'the subject.' In Heidegger's late thinking of appropriation he tries to give primacy to the co-belonging of being and human being over the terms to be related. Nancy radicalises this gesture in the centrality he gives to 'affectability.' Just as a subject presupposes itself in classical philosophy as the ground for experience and meaning, affect 'presupposes itself ' (SW, 129). But affect gets away from the grounding or essentialising presuppositions of classical philosophical terms such as the 'subject' or the terminology of 'being' in Heidegger because what it presupposes is 'the passive or passible actuality of a being-subject-*to*' (SW, 129). What affect presupposes, in other words, is *relationship* 'in the form of being-affected-by, and consequently in the form of being-affectable-by' (SW, 128).

Nancy argues that to describe how sense emerges in our time requires an ontology that starts from the contemporaneity of the body *with* other bodies (the co-belonging of bodies) but also that this co-belonging is the locus of sense because the contact or touch between bodies generates sense from materiality alone. As a consequence of these two theses, the body is not understood as brute matter but as *already* a source of sense. In Nancy, 'exteriority' of the body against not just the eloquent interiority of the subject but also the silent brutishness of the Cartesian extended things, in short against any form of self-closure, is comparable to the openness of Heidegger's *Da-sein* and is marked in his texts both by the hyphenation used in Heidegger's late work and, as previously noted, by the use of prepositions such as 'at,' 'along-with,' and 'with.' Aside from this use of prepositions to mark the exteriority of sense, there are two elements in Nancy's characterisation of affectability that sustain the thesis that sense takes place in exterior relations: (1) Sensation is eroticised; and (2) the structure of sensation is thematised by the sense of touch. Let me briefly describe these elements before turning to examine how they are developed in Nancy's view of art's relation to affect.

1. The conceptualisation of the body in terms of affectability means that it is understood in terms of relation and thus already characterised as sense and meaning. Indeed, Nancy describes affectability as a kind of point zero of sense (SW, 129): The sense of existence is 'right at' [*même à*] the surface of the sensible body where its material exposure to other bodies is structured with the syntax of pleasure and pain. Nancy uses pleasure and pain to describe the exposure to meaning in the contact of bodies: bodies are not indifferent to one another; because the origins of sense in exteriority are forgotten, the erotics of the body better 'expose,' or perforate, the supposed interiority of meaning. Indeed, pleasure and pain do not belong to the 'body,' nor do they have their origin in the 'outside world,' but right at the surface where contact occurs. The syntax they give is not able to restore a structure of signification capable of grounding meaning; rather, it is used by Nancy to provide a glimpse of the *coming* of meaning, 'at the very point where pain and joy mixed together compose the nonsignifying origin of significance itself ' (SW, 146; cf BSP, 93). The eroticisation of sense thematises the idea that affectability rather than 'the subject' is the

locus and condition of the practice of sense-making. Suffering and joy *per se* (separately) have no sense, but together, conjoined and dissociated, their 'insignificance is significance itself. Although there is nothing left to say about them, everything we see, and every interruption of our discourse, is exposed to their demand' (SW, 151).

2. Nancy uses touch to give a general schematisation of sense as emerging from 'exteriority.' Rather than the surface itself, touch places meaning 'at' the surface. It deconstructs the conceptual oppositions used in traditional philosophy such as passivity/activity and exterior/interior, by rendering the boundaries between these concepts undecidable.[23] Thus Nancy uses the indissociability of touching/touched to describe the 'originary *act* of passibility' (SW, 129, my emphasis) at the origin of sense, and the indistinguishability between exterior/interior to depict the 'intimate exteriority' of sensation (SW, 129). But my concern here is less with the mechanics of such a deconstruction of terms than with the fact that 'touch,' as the structure for the affectability of the senses, is the basis for Nancy's attempt to describe in general terms how sensible flesh can be a source of meaning. In *The Sense of the World,* Nancy states that 'sense *is* touching' (SW, 63). 'Touching' in this text is used by Nancy to make the general claim that sense emerges from a 'circuit' (SW, 60) and that this circuit includes 'all bodies' (SW, 63). Against Heidegger's description of the stone as 'world poor,'[24] Nancy includes the stone in the circuit of sense not because it 'has' any 'interior' sense, but because 'sense touches the stone: it even collides with it' (SW, 63). Thus the general terms in which the world is understood 'as the network of all surfaces' (SW, 61) rather than any nodal point within it schematise the source of meaning in terms of the touching/touched relation.

## Art as Praxis of Sense Making

Our discussion of Nancy's thought to this point has established the context in which the full significance of the place of art within his ontology can be gauged.[25] Art offers an answer to the problem of presentation posed in Western philosophy and by capital: in the arts the emergence of sense from sources of sensible materiality is staged or presented. In this respect art exemplifies the core precepts of Nancy's ontology: specifically, that sense takes place in relations of exteriority and that affect is the hinge that joins materiality and sense as an act rather than a passive state of being. The arts are crucial for the articulation of Nancy's ontology because they develop these propositions along two axes (1) The arts provide an ontological rehabilitation of pleasure; pleasure is no longer a private function of the body or the subject that has no serious claim on politics, life, or sense (SW, 133–34). Rather, pleasure in art is an opening of sense and thus shows that the source of sense is affectability. (2) The praxis of sense is understood by Nancy in terms of creation, itself understood in terms of origins of sense (SW, 131). Nancy understands by 'origins of sense' the emergence of sense from relations of affectability. The arts give an access to these origins because they allow for the possibility of describing how a new, surprising, or affectable sense can emerge (BSP, 14–15).[26] Nancy indeed emphasises that the arts are an actual praxis of sense making because any praxis, as opposed to the productions of a subject, is already a modality of sensible experience.[27] In each of these respects, in my view, Nancy uses distinctive features of the arts to develop an ontological discourse able to describe the forgotten 'wonder' and 'surprise' of sense as a *coming*-to-presence. Art, furthermore, corroborates the stakes of this ontology because it does not just detail the emergence of sense from sensuous sources, but does so as the emergence of a new or surprising sense.

The importance of art for Nancy's ontology can also be schematised according to his historical ontology of systems of sense. He reverses Hegel's view that philosophy captures the essence of modernity (SW, 127). In Nancy, the artwork captures the 'essence' of the new form of existence as an *existence* that is without any *essence*.[28] This view of the historical significance of the arts is formalized in Nancy's writing by the joining of classical philosophical oppositions in the description of the artwork: the artwork is ' "a fractal essence" ' (SW, 124), 'trans-immanence' (TM, 87), '[t]he in-finite explosion of the finite' (SW, 132), or an 'in-finite finishing' (TM, 87).[29]

Although Nancy follows Heidegger in finding in art the forgotten comportment of wonder, it is important to emphasise that for Nancy it is the presentation of sense rather than truth that is at stake in this comportment.[30]

He posits as the key features of the artwork (1) that it is a sensuous surface that opens sense as such and (2) that it is structurally incomplete (e.g., the artwork is always open to further elaboration). These two features combined qualify art, in Nancy's words, to give a 'presentation of presentation.' Put in other words, art could be described as presenting out of sensible relations the genesis or process of meaning.[31] Nancy's view that sense emerges from a network of relations and does so as an act or praxis of affectability is phrased by him in terms of the '(k)notting' of sense (SW, 112). This network of affectability in which sense emerges is 'before or beyond' the truth of being (SW, 138). Art can claim to be more originary than truth because it presents the *process* of presentation. There is no 'truth' of things in Nancy's historical ontology because things are (k)notted. In its presentation of the process of presentation, art presents the network taking precedence over the nodes, or the coming of sense over the event of taking place.

The corroboration the arts give to Nancy's ontology can, finally, be explained in terms of their modelling of the symbolic operation of the senses-sense (affectability–coming of sense). Nancy understands symbolicity in terms of the basic orientation of his ontology: the 'symbolic' is the name he gives to the fact that things take place alongside each other. The symbolic is not a 'consistent link and a continuous circulation' but the 'condition of possibility of a link or exchange' in exposure to the network or chain from which sense emerges (SW, 136, cf: BSP, 54–55, 58, 59). Nancy finds in art a model for the symbolic operation of the senses-sense because art is the relation that 'does not close itself off into a circle of signification. . . . It exposes sense as the secret of that which contains nothing hidden, of that which comprises nothing other than the multiple, discreet, discontinuous, heterogeneous, and singular truth of being itself ' (SW, 137).

At the same time that art corroborates Nancy's ontology, he is explicit that 'Art' cannot be invoked in the singular as an authentic term able to service a critique of inauthentic existence in the fashion suggested by Heidegger and the discourses of post-Marxist critical theory. Such a use of 'Art' would reinstall a position of 'referential ideality' at the core of his ontology. For this reason, and despite the importance of the arts for Nancy's ontology, the very term 'art' is also a topic of critical discussion in his writings. In works devoted specifically to the arts, such as *The Muses,* this ambivalent relation to the arts is marked. Nancy refers to 'the arts' in the plural in *The Muses* and does so in the spirit of following the indication given in *The Sense of the World,* published in France in the year preceding the former work, that 'art' should not be relied on 'for the "coming" . . . of another sense' (SW, 127). The discussions of 'art' in *The Sense of the World* and *Being Singular Plural* emphasise the *aisthetic* dimension of the arts as loci of affectability and occasionally follow up on this point by including in the category of 'the arts' so-called minor arts such as taste and smell (SW, 83). In *The Muses* the pluralisation of the arts towards minor arts becomes part of a critique of the view of 'art' as a stable, continuous 'region or domain . . . to which one could address oneself, to which one could address demands, orders, or prayers' (TM, 86). Nancy's criticisms of 'art' need to be seen from the perspective of his attempt to sustain sense as a question. Nancy, unlike Lacoue-Labarthe, thinks that the question of sense points to the exigency of figuration. Moreover, it is because the 'referential ideality' of an authentic term or origin misunderstands the very problem of the withdrawal of sense that the exigency of figuration also, or especially, means that no particular kinds of figures can be consecrated above others:

> How are we to let it be *seen* that meaning exposes itself as impenetrable, and exposes us to this density? With what figure? By de-finition—that is, by the absencing of the ending [*finition*] there will not be only one. By right, any figure is already such an exposure. This is why 'art' can no longer suffice for us, if 'art' signifies a privileging of chosen, sublated, sublime, exquisite figures. For meaning has, on the contrary, no chosen or privileged ones, no heroes or saints, and it is rather a formidable density of *common destiny* that is brought to light, to our light, the entire weight of a community of equals that does not come from a measure, but from the incommensurable opacity of meaning, which is the meaning of all and of each (and of no one). We need an art—if it is an 'art'—of thickness, of gravity. We need figures that weigh upon the bottom rather than extracting themselves from it. We need a thought that would be like a mass out of true, the fall and the creation of a world. (G, 84)[32]

Despite these reservations concerning 'art,' it is because of the way the arts model the stakes of Nancy's ontology as the coming of a new sense out of material surfaces and modulations that, I believe, it is Heidegger's 'Origin of the Work of Art' lectures rather than *Being and Time* that are the defining reference for his writings. Indeed, the way that Nancy generalises the features of the artwork into a 'first philosophy' seems to me to warrant describing his ontology as an operationalised conception of the artwork.

## Everyday Existence, the Artwork, and the Praxis of Sense Making

There are several clear indications, it is true, that Nancy understands his ontology as a radicalisation and extension of theses in Heidegger's *Being and Time*. Indeed, according to Nancy, it is not just his own thinking that follows this path: 'The existential analytic of *Being and Time* is the project from which all subsequent thinking follows, whether this is Heidegger's own later thinking or our various ways of thinking against or beyond Heidegger himself ' (BSP, 93). The 'seismic tremor' registered in this analytic introduces the analytic of *Mitsein* but leaves it as 'nothing more than a sketch' and in a 'subordinate position' to *Dasein* (BSP, 93). Nancy frequently refers to the necessity of thinking the originary implication of *Mitsein* in *Dasein* in order 'to forcibly reopen a passage somewhere beyond that obstruction which decided the terms of being-with's fulfilment, and its withdrawal, by replacing it [in Heidegger's notorious politics] with the "people" and their "destiny" ' (BSP, 93).[33]

Given these indications of the importance of *Mitsein* for a rethinking of Heidegger's existential analytic and its political consequences, it is not surprising that Nancy's own elaboration of *Mitsein* often frames the critical reception of his work. Nancy's emphasis on the need to reorientate the existential analytic of *Being and Time* around the axiom of co-existentiality has led François Raffoul, for instance, to argue that Nancy's ontology of the 'with' is a radicalising of Heidegger's fundamental ontology. Nancy, on Raffoul's account, praises Heidegger for 'the recognition that Being-with belongs constitutively to the essence of Dasein,' but criticises his failure to 'fully draw the consequences of this statement.'[34] Heidegger is taken to task in the vocabulary of the 'retreat' he had himself used to criticise Kant: in pursuing the task of a consideration of *Dasein* 'in itself ' in the second Division of *Being and Time*, Heidegger, for Nancy, retreats 'before his own discovery.'[35] Following Nancy's view that '*all* thinking' follows the 'seismic tremor' registered in Heidegger, Howard Caygill has noted that, indeed, the task of thinking the 'with' that arises from the dissatisfaction with Heidegger's 'retreat' in the existential analytic in *Being and Time* is not peculiar to Nancy but can be seen as a guiding motif in the call to reflect on the ontological priority of 'community' in a number of diverse contemporary thinkers, including Blanchot, Agamben, Dastur, and Lingis.[36] In Nancy's case the problem of the order of ontological exposition in Heidegger is undeniably crucial for an understanding of the impetus driving his emphasis on co-existentiality.

However, I believe it can be shown that the form Nancy's ontology takes relies less on a social radicalisation of the terms of Heidegger's existential analytic than it does on his conception of the artwork. Nancy's conception of sense as 'coming to presence' and the emphasis thus placed on the modality of praxis of sense-making are best understood not through the revision of the existential analytic of *Being and Time* but as a generalising thinking through of the core theses of Heidegger's 'Origin' lectures. This radicalisation accounts for the path Nancy's ontology needs to take through the thesis of the affectability of the arts, in a way the revision of the existential analytic of *Being and Time* is unable to do. My discussion of this link will be guided by the following hypothesis: Nancy's philosophy gives ontological force to Heidegger's notion of the work of the artwork. The features ascribed to the work of the artwork in Heidegger (its presentation of the emergence of meaning and its capacity to thereby revive the forgotten comportment of wonder) are mobilised in Nancy's ontology as a framework from which to approach beings in general. Despite offering a 'first philosophy' (BSP, 26), a philosophy of beings in general rather than a 'regional' social ontology, this 'first philosophy' of being as being-with is modelled on and articulated through the praxis of sense making that occurs paradigmatically in the arts. Moreover, examining this link between Nancy's ontology and the 'Origin' lectures allows us to evaluate the implications for art of Nancy's radicalisation of Heidegger, given the pivotal position of art in Heidegger's own critique of the technological *Gestell*. This link, in short, will allow us to examine the full breadth of Nancy's critical engagement with Heidegger's 'referential ideality.'

Nancy's ontology uses the praxis of affectability in contemporary art to characterise the forgotten features of everyday existence. Art is taken to be an exception in an important sense on account of the way it presents the genesis of sense. At the same time, however, the presentation of the genesis of sense in art is used as a paradigm to characterise the canonical themes and categories of Western philosophy, such as Nature, human sociality, and alienation. Art is able to answer the driving question of how existence in its nudity (stripped of all significations) can sustain meaning. On Nancy's view, the arts are the exceptional category able to withstand the passing of metaphysics because the affectability of sense that takes place there is 'essentially fractal.'

Contemporary art lays bare, he writes, 'the fragmentation that is happening to us and to "art"' (SW, 124). Nancy distinguishes this fragmentation from the 'classical fragmentation' of Romanticism. In Romanticism 'the fragment' is a form with finality. It 'retracts its frayed and fragile borders back onto its own consciousness of being a fragment . . . [and] converts its finitude . . . into finish. In this finish, dispersion and fracturing absolutize their erratic contingency: they *absolve themselves* of their fractal character' (SW, 124–25). In Romanticism the fragment has 'all the autonomy, finish, and aura of the "little work of art." Ultimately, it is only the "little" size of the fragment that differentiates here between the art of the fragment and the art of the "great" work' (SW, 125). In contrast, the 'fractality' of contemporary art deals not with a finished and complete 'fragment' but with the presentation of the excess of sense to a point of origin: it is the presentation of a '*coming* that no presence could ever *finish*' (SW, 126). However, the presentation in the arts of the fractality of sense also implodes the category of 'art' because the birth to presence staged there 'can neither be assumed nor subsumed in either the work, form, art (little or great), or any finish' (SW, 127). The arts are thus in the ambiguous position of spectacularly staging the question of sense but also, because this question is *the* ontological question, neither having an exclusive claim over it nor being shielded from its implications.

There are two features in Nancy's discussion of the arts that seem to me to radicalise core theses in Heidegger's 'Origin' lectures, (1) the use of the arts to provide a model of the *genesis* of meaning, and (2) the crucial role that 'strangeness' plays in the exceptional position claimed for the arts. What I would like to emphasise here is that each of these features becomes the constitutive term, not for a conception of the artwork, but for the articulation of a general ontology. Heidegger's 'Origin' lectures prefigure the focus on sense in Nancy's ontology because Heidegger identifies in the 'strangeness' of the work of the artwork the coming of a new sense that is beyond any present thing. Nancy, who understands the coming-to-sense in the artwork in terms of the presentation of the genesis of meaning (rather than truth, as Heidegger does), suggests, following Heidegger, that in art the forgotten origins of sense are presented as extraordinary.

Heidegger, as we saw in Chapter 5, sees art as an exemplary way in which, beyond any merely given thing, attention is drawn to how and that a thing is. I suggested there that this attention is best understood in terms of the reflective relation that the artwork establishes to relations of presentation. The work of presentation the artwork performs puts in play in the mode of an event the crucial transition from the familiar framework that asks 'what the being is' to the questioning attitude in the face of the bare fact 'that the being is' [*daß . . . ist*].

It is just this fact about the artwork, 'that it is a work,' that marks out the seemingly 'least feature of the thing,' the 'that it is' [*es gibt*]. It is in opening this feature that the artwork questions the relations of presentation that have become familiar to recall that: 'At bottom, the ordinary is not ordinary; it is extra-ordinary, uncanny.'[37] In Heidegger, the context for his discussion of art's attention to the forgotten truth of beings is the familiarity of those thing-concepts under which the thing itself is forgotten. In this questioning of familiarity it is above all against the 'familiar' conception of truth as 'correctness in representation' that the opening created by the artwork 'works.' This opening reminds us 'of what, unexperienced and unthought, underlies our familiar and therefore outworn nature of truth' (OWA, 52). In Heidegger's 'Origin' lectures, the work of the artwork is a doubly reflective relation to that which is: next to the presentation of the bare but remarkable fact that it, the work, is (rather than is not) is that it establishes the clearing that goes beyond any particular being— such as the peasant shoes—that is. The painting works as a reflective relation to relations of presentation because unlike the degraded conception of truth as correctness, it attends to that which this conception presupposes as merely given, namely, the 'there is' [*es gibt*] of the thing. The artwork 'presents' the shift from what-a-being-is to that-it-is, and in doing so discloses truth as *aletheia*.

Nancy criticises Heidegger's description of the work of the artwork: although he reiterates the Heideggerian perspective on the arts as a disclosing, he argues that that which art discloses is not the 'that it is,' but the 'plural touching of the singular origin' (BSP, 14). His emphasis lies not on a general 'givenness,' but on the dispersed, unexchangeable moments of the emergence of sense (BSP, 75). The significance of this emphasis is the support it lends to two further claims that Nancy makes against Heidegger: (1) that Heidegger's emphasis on the givenness of the thing diminishes the intimate relation between 'making' or praxis and affectability, and (2) that Heidegger's thought is structured by a 'desire for the exception.' Nancy uses an operationalised conception of the artwork to deal with these shortcomings.

1. The salient feature of Nancy's approach to the artwork—the foregrounding of the *process* of the 'making' rather than the givenness of the thing—emphasises the instant in such a way that the mode of the 'coming to presence' or the element of the 'making' and thus the modality of technique is foremost.[38] Sense, insofar as it is posed as a question in the arts, thus becomes, at each moment of its posing, and in stark contrast to Heidegger, a question of technicity (TM, 25–27). This, as Heidegger's deliberate ambiguity on the relation of art to technicity in his technology essay anticipates, implodes the category of the arts, or what is perhaps the same thing, the ability of 'art' as a single term to act as a counter-image to the technological. Nancy emphasises the 'making' of the arts for the same reason as he describes technology as praxis—to underline the affectability of art and technics and also to indicate thus the locus and level of analysis of the significance of these for an ontological discourse. Affectability is not just a feature of sense making in art, but of sense making in general.

2. When Nancy, against Heidegger's order of ontological exposition, describes the 'rudimentary ontological attestation' of the 'with,' he phrases it in the terms used by Heidegger in the 'Origin of the Work of Art,' but he deploys this description for a critique of the 'desire for the exception' which, in Heidegger, 'presupposes disdain for the ordinary' (BSP, 9–10). When Heidegger claims that the work of the artwork shows the ordinary to be exceptional, Nancy extends this claim to argue, on the basis of the 'rudimentary ontological attestation' of the 'with,' that the ordinary 'is always exceptional' (BSP, 10). The criticism Nancy makes of Heidegger concerns the double movement whereby

Heidegger affirms that the meaning of Being must start from everydayness, but 'then begin[s] by neglecting the general differentiation of the everyday, its constantly renewed rupture, its intimate discord, its polymorphy and its polyphony, its relief and its variety. A "day" is not simply a unit for counting; it is the turning of the world—each time singular' (BSP, 9). This critique of the Heideggerian 'everyday' as 'undifferentiated, . . . anonymous, . . . and statistical' and the call for the 'rudimentary ontological attestation' of the *difference* at the origin of singularities is clearly an extension of Heidegger's thesis concerning the work of the artwork in the 'Origin' essay to 'everyday experience'—the latter now defined as 'the exposing of the singularity according to which existence exists, irreducibly and primarily' (BSP, 9). As an ontological attestation that concerns 'all beings' the features that Nancy identified first in the art work extend everywhere: ' "Nature" is also "strange," and we exist there; we exist *in* it in the mode of a constantly renewed singularity, whether the singularity of the diversity and disparity of our senses or that of the disconcerting profusion of nature's species or its various metamorphoses into "technology." Then again, we say "strange," "odd," "curious," "disconcerting" *about* all of being' (BSP, 9–10). Nancy develops Heidegger's claim that the work of the artwork shows the ordinary to be exceptional, to state that the ordinary 'is always exceptional'; and the artwork essay is thus deployed by Nancy for the purpose of a genetic accounting of the coming-to-presence that is, on his view, a forgotten feature of beings in general. This thesis is, for Nancy, like Heidegger's claims about the artwork, primarily a claim about the forgotten origins of sense in general.

Despite Nancy's frequent criticisms of the use of 'art' as if it had a homogeneous, static, interior meaning and significance, 'art' is an indispensable quarry for Nancy's ontology.

Neither of the two trajectories from which Nancy's thinking on presentation developed, capital and Western philosophy, were, as we saw, able to articulate and defend the conception of affectability required by Nancy's ontology. Nancy's dependence on 'art' for this purpose can be qualified here in terms of its relationship to the place of art in Heidegger's thought. Unlike in Heidegger's thinking, in Nancy's thought ordinary things *are* extraordinary and they are not in need of 'sublime figures' to show this. But, at the same time, it is the expression and experience of the arts that enable Nancy, as they did Heidegger, to argue for the general rule of the extraordinary and provide him with the conceptual tools and exemplary vehicle of articulation for his ontology of the praxis of sense making.

Heidegger, as we saw, was only able to identify and criticise the totalising effects of the *Gestell* from the vantage point of aesthetic art; Nancy, conversely, arrives at the point where art no longer offers an authentic critical perspective on capital *as a result* of its own privileged unfolding of the forgotten genesis of sense. 'Art' is an operational term used to provide a genetic account of the general picture he gives of sense as fractal coming-to-presence. But just as their genetic role means that the arts, plural, disclose a general ontology rather than properties peculiar to 'art,' it also means that the arts are 'touched' by the ontology they disclose. The history of art becomes doubled in much the same way as Nancy had described the effect on the history of philosophy of the moment when, with Nietzsche, it describes itself as the history of metaphysics. Nancy argues that the opening that commences with Nietzsche's account of nihilism also transforms the history of art into 'history in a radical sense, that is, not progress but passage, succession, appearance, disappearance, event' (TM, 87). The meaning that is attached to art in our time as a degradation or loss of an earlier sublime practice is thus contested by Nancy, who insists that art not be measured by a 'common standard' but according to the principles that I have argued here characterise his thought as an operationalised use of the artwork—as each time a singular event in which the genesis of sense is presented[39]—'art,' like, we might add, any other 'region' of being, 'can no longer be understood or received according to the schemas that once belonged to it' (TM, 84). Hence, following Heidegger's call for a post-aesthetic conception of the arts, Nancy attempts to think the withdrawal of sense *in* art, but without the gesture organising Heidegger's discussion of the artwork that reinstalls, in the withdrawal of the *physis,* a term that is able to withdraw from appearance and relation.

Two important, albeit discordant, themes have emerged from this discussion of Nancy's relation to Heidegger on the topic of the artwork. These themes substantially develop the implications of Nancy's use of

Heidegger's 'Origin' lectures and show that Heidegger's order of ontological exposition is merely one instance of a more general tendency to privilege
an authentic point of origin. On the one hand, Nancy, unlike Heidegger,
does not credit the epoch of technology/capital with the capacity to exhaust the field of presentations or, by implication, to render the artwork
impotent. It is because of the expanded role of affect in Nancy's thinking
that this crucial point of distinction from the Heideggerian project is possible. The operations of capital are themselves described in the vocabulary
of co-appearing, and it is the forgetting in Heidegger of the fact that 'we'
are the technological that allows him to depict it, on Nancy's reading, in
negative terms as an alienation of a more authentic mode of being. In this
respect Nancy's description of a continuity between nature and the technological as different moments and points of contact in co-appearing needs
to be seen as a riposte to the order of ontological exposition in Heidegger
that separates an authentic moment (the withdrawal of the *physis*) from its
fall (into the suppression of *poiesis* in the *Gestell*). On the other hand, Heidegger deliberately cultivates an ambiguity around the conclusion his account of the technological *Gestell* leads us inexorably toward; namely, with
the prevailing schematisation of experience in the epoch of the *Gestell* art
loses its status as an exceptional mode of presentation. The reasons for
Heidegger's attempt to avoid stating this conclusion seem to be the following: Heidegger needs 'art' both as the vantage point from which to disclose
the encroaching claims of the *Gestell* and because he is unwilling to entirely
give up the possibility of an authentic counter to the alienation of the technological epoch. Here again, Nancy parts company with Heidegger. For
Nancy, the epoch of techno-capital needs to be thought in a way that
avoids splitting off from it an authentic counter-image able to oppose it.
The post-Marxist discourse of social criticism in general depends on this
split. It is because of his insistence on co-appearing that 'art' is no homogeneous category of meaning or, correlatively a term invested with 'authentic,' critical value.

Nancy's critical departure from Heidegger on these points throws into
relief how his approach to the topic of presentation differs from the other
figures considered in this book. Kant viewed presentation as a technical
problem. Beautiful forms in nature stood in for ideas that were otherwise
absent from the sensible world. Heidegger too retained a structure of 'referential ideality' in his use of art as an authentic counter-term to the *Gestell*

or in the structuring role his references to the Greek origins of Western philosophy played in his thought. Like Lacoue-Labarthe, Nancy sees these orientating structures of meaning as the source of Heidegger's failure to grapple with the problem of presentation. In Nancy's ontology art is characterised as the 'presentation of presentation.' It is in art that the staging of sense occurs. But aside from modelling the genesis of sense, artworks are used by Nancy to make the point that there is no presentable idea (Kant), or withdrawn point of origin (Heidegger) shadowing presentation. Instead, in the paradigmatic cases of the arts, technique is given the 'weight' of sense itself.

# Conclusion: The Path of Presentation

In this study I have tried to foreground the dualist framework that places aesthetic presentation in the role of a type of co-articulation of ideas and sensible forms in Kant's thinking. This way of defining presentation in Kant gives historical generality to this concept and allows us to consider Heidegger, Lacoue-Labarthe, and Nancy as thinking through the breakdown of the metaphysical coordination of ideas and sensible forms in our era. The theme of exhaustion or crisis of meaning or meaningful experience may be taken up in this perspective, as indeed Nancy explicitly does.

This identification and thinking through of the unravelling of the coherence of ideas and material forms ultimately alters the definition and the stakes of 'presentation' in these thinkers. In particular, presentation no longer refers as it did in Kant to the sensibilisation of ideas but to the problem of thinking the meaning-depth, as it were, of sensible experience without the scaffolding of ideas, without what Nancy terms 'ideal referentiality.' This means that the stakes of presentation are reorientated from the problem of a coordination of sensory forms and intelligible ideas to the task of articulating the ground (or, as Heidegger puts it, the 'giving') of the experience of meaning within the horizon of a more or less rigorous immanence, without being reductive.

From its position in Kant as a technically posed problem of orientative coordination of the intelligible and the sensible, the topic of presentation becomes from Heidegger onward an ontologically posed problem of an originary experience, which being simultaneously reflective, is constitutive of the duality of the intelligible and the sensible. This reflective experience, which philosophy has to articulate, is for all these thinkers most fully 'presented' in the aesthetic register and bears the marks of the tools, resources, and place of its elaboration. In the way that these writers scrutinise art or 'literature' as the 'originary' site of experience of meaning, or in Nancy's terms 'praxis of sense,' their reflection on the topic of presentation also engages in an aesthetic steering of philosophy.

Perhaps, to extrapolate a little from Nancy's account, this philosophical treatment of the theme of presentation may be formulated in terms accessible to the common understanding. Put in such terms the problem of presentation may be phrased as the problem of seeing in existence fundamental or orientating meanings. In this context we might ask whether this theme, that we have followed here as a certain way of doing philosophy after Kant, may also operate as a general feature of any norm-orientated behaviour. Are behaviours that are structured by internally imposed or sanctioned rules of meaning (and not by external laws) also aesthetically formed? Do the attempts to revitalise everyday secular life by finding orientating meanings in revolutionary political ideologies, or by finding existential satisfaction in alternative lifestyle practices, constitute other contexts in which this theme of finding in material life more than merely material representations can be identified and reflected upon? If so, what would be the consequences of such reflection for the claims of these secular 'religions'?[1]

Alternatively, and to return once more to the context of aesthetics in which this study has pursued its topic, we may ask whether the problem of 'presentation,' as the pattern of finding meaning in sensible forms, has continuing relevance in contemporary theory. Nancy states that he uses the word 'presentation' 'in order to go elsewhere, towards other words' (G, 57), and in this respect he raises a question that is crucial for the central claims of this study: are the modes and exigencies that determine this problem after Kant, as the aesthetic orientation that allows the pursuit of a radical thought or a 'first philosophy,' approaching some kind of end or transformation? We have already seen how the schematic definition of presentation as the coherence of ideas and sensible forms allows us to point out and critically assess the intimacy between the concept of 'presentation' as it is defined by Kant and the role 'art' is given in modern philosophy as a vehicle of critique: the problematic of presentation subtends the hermeneutics of the material representations of art in the Romantic and post-Romantic aesthetics, and gives access to a critical understanding of the utopian dimension of the artwork. It is here too, I think, that we can locate the ongoing pertinence of the topic of presentation for understanding some of the main themes and approaches in contemporary critical theory.[2]

Such schematic uses of this topic need to be distinguished, however, from the status that 'presentation' has as a vehicle for the radicalisation of thought in the writing of Heidegger, Lacoue-Labarthe, and Nancy. The way these thinkers develop a particular understanding of the concept of aesthetic presentation in terms of originary experience gives the question of the ongoing significance of the topic of presentation a distinct inflection. Would it be possible, we may ask, to adopt the radical terms in which these thinkers approach ontology without the aesthetic orientation that they derive from the originally Kantian determination of presentation? Is writing a 'first philosophy' or shaping the questions of 'being' or 'mimesis' into the fundamental positions that these thinkers do possible without aesthetic resources? Finally, if one were to follow the aesthetic path on which presentation is shaped into a fundamental orientation, could one ever reach a point of resolution in which it would be possible 'to go elsewhere, towards other words'?

The use of the problem of presentation to steer philosophy in an aesthetic direction may fall into the category of what sociologists of institutions call 'path dependency.'[3] The path of aesthetic presentation, which these thinkers shape and follow, engenders constraints that would make it difficult to pursue the fundamental orientation they develop, or the questions that they formulate, on any other path. On the path that they follow, which obscures all others, there is no end to the problem of presentation. But this is not to say that no other paths are open to philosophy.

# Notes

INTRODUCTION

1. Immanuel Kant, *Critique of Judgment,* trans. Werner S. Pluhar (Indianapolis: Hackett, 1987). Hereafter cited as CJ.

2. Martin Heidegger, 'Plato's Doctrine of Truth,' in *Pathmarks,* ed. William McNeill (Cambridge, UK: Cambridge University Press, 1998), 164.

3. Incidentally, this means that the doctrine of creation is not amenable to this treatment, that is, in terms of presentation, as Nicolas of Cusa understood. Bruno's rejection of divine personhood and 'revelation' in favour of God's impersonality and manifestation signals a stepping out of Christianity by treating the world not as a creation any more but in fact as the manifestation of God. See Blumenberg's discussion of the 'index' of ideas in Plato and his discussion of Nicholas of Cusa in *The Legitimacy of the Modern Age,* trans. Robert M. Wallace (Cambridge, MA: MIT Press, 1993), 71–72 and 483–595.

4. Martin Heidegger, 'The Age of the World Picture,' in *The Question Concerning Technology and Other Essays,* trans. W. Lovitt (New York: Harper and Row, 1977), 115–55.

5. Theodor Adorno, *Aesthetic Theory,* trans. R. Hullot-Kentor (Minneapolis: University of Minnesota Press, 1997), 61.

6. Jean-François Lyotard, 'The Sublime and the Avant-Garde,' in *The Lyotard Reader,* ed. Andrew Benjamin (Cambridge, MA, and Oxford, UK: Basil Blackwell, 1989), 196–211.

7. Jacques Derrida, *Acts of Literature,* ed. Derek Attridge (New York and London: Routledge, 1992), 38.

8. Karl Heinz Böhrer, *Suddenness: On the Moment of Aesthetic Appearance,* trans. Ruth Crowley (New York: Columbia University Press, 1994).

9. Hans Robert Jauss, 'The Idealist Embarrassment: Observations on Marxist Aesthetics,' in *New Literary History,* Vol. 7 (1975–1976), 197.

10. See on this point the discussion by Bernard Bourgeois in his *Philosophie et droits de l'homme: de Kant à Marx* (Paris: PUF, 1990), 124–27.

11. Jürgen Habermas, *Between Facts and Norms: Contributions to a Discourse*

*Theory of Law and Democracy,* trans. W. Rehg (Cambridge, MA: MIT Press, 1996), Appendix 1: 'Popular Sovereignty as Procedure,' 490, his italics.

12. In Derrida the question of presentation is also a central topic, but, despite his influence on Lacoue-Labarthe and Nancy, the approach he takes to it is distinct from these thinkers. Derrida approaches this topic in terms that are closer to Kant's original formulation of the problem of presentation. Rather than a radicalisation of Heidegger's project of thinking in the direction of a reflection on the presentation of meaning (Nancy) or as an account of the necessary primacy of presentation over the terms it presents (in art for Lacoue-Labarthe or ontological relations for Heidegger), the theme of the trace in Derrida can, I think, be understood as an adaptation of the Kantian phrasing of the problem of presentation as the necessary dehiscence between ideas and material forms. In this respect, Derrida may be contrasted with the ontological inspiration behind Nancy's writing, no less than the focus on the arts that emerges from Lacoue-Labarthe's reworking of Heidegger. Indeed, to the extent that there are direct points of connection between Kant and Derrida they seem to me to lie exclusively in their shared approach and formulation of the problem of presentation. Derrida's painstaking descriptions of aporetic logics, which he argues are formulated with peculiar force in the arts, have an intimate relation to the Kantian phrasing of the problem of presentation as an irresolvable relation between sensible forms and ideas. Aside from the fact that Derrida's thought, unlike the French thinkers treated in this study, has been the topic of intense scholarly interest and debate, the main feature of Derrida's work that has kept me from including him in this study is that he does not share the particular understanding of the historical coordinates that frames the treatment of the topic of presentation in Lacoue-Labarthe and Nancy's work. I have discussed Derrida's thought in relation to this topic elsewhere: see my 'Historical Undecidability: The Kantian Background to Derrida's Politics,' in *International Journal of Philosophical Studies* 12, no. 4 (December 2004) and 'Errant Beauty: Derrida and Kant on Aesthetic Presentation,' in *International Studies in Philosophy* 33, no. 1 (2001).

13. Lacoue-Labarthe writes: 'a historical necessity . . . commits metaphysics, in the process of completing itself, since Hegel, to (re)presenting itself (*sich darstellen*) in figures, as well as to representing (*vorstellen*) transcendence, from the perspective of the "subjective" determination of Being, as the form, figure, imprint, type of a *humanity.*' Philippe Lacoue-Labarthe, *Typography: Mimesis, Philosophy, Politics,* ed. Christopher Fynsk (Stanford, CA: Stanford University Press, 1998), 52.

14. Lacoue-Labarthe and Nancy, 'Scène,' in *Nouvelle revue de psychanalyse* 17 (1992): 73–98.

CHAPTER I

1. See Theodor Adorno, *Aesthetic Theory,* trans. R. Hullot-Kentor (Minneapolis: University of Minnesota Press, 1997), 10–14. These pages give a clear account of

his views on Kant's formulation of pure taste as a structural dislocation of interests, as well as his own concern to attach to this dislocation a critical perspective
on social relations.

2.  The specific relational structure of Kantian aesthetics has been emphasised
by Jean-Marie Schaeffer in his *Art of the Modern Age: Philosophy of Art from Kant
to Heidegger,* trans. Steven Rendall (Princeton, NJ: Princeton University Press,
2000). Schaeffer is concerned to differentiate 'the type of mental attitude' active
in Kant's theory of aesthetic judgment from the category of a 'type of objects,' 59.
Jacques Taminiaux also phrases the distinctive feature of Kant's aesthetics in terms
of its advocacy for 'an aesthetic attitude' rather than a theory of objects of fine art.
See his *Poetics, Speculation and Judgment: The Shadow of the Work of Art from
Kant to Phenomenology,* trans. and ed. Michael Gendre (Albany: State University
of New York Press, 1993), 57.

3.  Jay Bernstein glosses the different tendencies in Kant scholarship by stating
that 'continental' philosophy proceeds from the view that Kant's critical system
fails, whereas 'analytic' philosophy takes as given the distinctions that Kant attempts to establish between ethics, aesthetics, and epistemology. See his *The Fate
of Art: Aesthetic Alienation from Kant to Derrida and Adorno* (Cambridge, UK:
Polity Press, 1992).

4.  See for examples of an exclusive focus on aesthetic judgment *Essays in Kant's
Aesthetics,* ed. Ted Cohen and Paul Guyer (Chicago and London: University of
Chicago Press, 1982); Paul Guyer, *Kant and the Claims of Taste* (Cambridge and
London: Harvard University Press, 1989); and Mary McCloskey, *Kant's Aesthetic*
(Albany: State University of New York Press, 1987).

5.  One of the reasons the third *Critique* is considered in this selective fashion by some commentators is that the (supposed) aesthetic resolution to the bi-
furcation of nature and reason that it offers emerges in response to the first two
*Critiques* but, equally, is foreshadowed in neither of them. Hence the plausible
claim that aesthetics is a separate topic within Kant's thought which, prior to the
final *Critique,* had no place within transcendental idealism. We can cite against
this compartmentalised approach to the *Critique of Judgment* the significant tradition of scholarly interpretation that focuses on the genesis of the problems
of this critique in the Kantian philosophy and also places it in the broader historical context of the pantheist dispute. The most recent work in this tradition
that has included scholars such as James Meredith, Giorgio Tonelli, Gerhard
Lehmann, and Michel Souriau is John Zammito's *The Genesis of Kant's Critique
of Judgment* (Chicago and London: University of Chicago Press, 1992). The engagement by French philosophers with Kant's third *Critique,* discussed in note 6,
is missing from Zammito's otherwise extensive account of the literature on this
*Critique.*

6.  Kant writes, 'if the treatment of [taste] . . . has a transcendental aim, then
this critique fills a gap in the system of our cognitive powers, and hence opens up

a striking and—I think—most promising prospect [for] a complete system of all the mental powers' (CJ, 434).

The importance of this *Critique* in recent French philosophy is worth noting. Derrida, Deleuze, and Lyotard all concur with the view of German Idealism and Romanticism that Kant's aspiration to 'complete' his system fails, but their own use of this work does not revolve around this failure. Each identifies in this *Critique* a rich source of important philosophical topics. Both Derrida and Deleuze find in Kant's notion of reflective judgment a way of thinking singularity. Derrida is less generous than Deleuze in his view that Kant controls the indeterminacy proper to reflective judgment. See Derrida's *The Truth in Painting* in which he emphasises the way Kant frames his study of aesthetic, reflective judgment by the terms of his earlier inquiry into cognitive judgments. See *The Truth in Painting*, trans. Geoffrey Bennington and Ian McLeod (Chicago and London: Chicago University Press, 1987), 71 ff. In Deleuze's *Kant's Critical Philosophy: The Doctrine of the Faculties*, he argues that both reflective and determinative judgments 'involve . . . inventiveness' and thus attention to singularity. See *Kant's Critical Philosophy*, trans. Hugh Tomlinson and Barbara Habberjam (Minneapolis: University of Minnesota Press, 1990), 58. In his Kant book Deleuze gives the example of a doctor's diagnosis as an inventive judgment of this type. This example is at the core of his so-called critical and clinical project. See Deleuze's *Essays Critical and Clinical*, trans. Daniel W. Smith and Michael A. Greco (Minneapolis: University of Minnesota Press, 1997). In Deleuze and Guattari's *What Is Philosophy?* they argue that the final *Critique*, rather than a resolution of the dualism of its predecessors, marks a significant departure from the terms of the first and second *Critiques*. They write that the *Critique of Judgment* is 'an unrestrained work of old age which [Kant's] successors have still not caught up with: all the mind's faculties overcome their limits, the very limits that Kant had so carefully laid down in the works of his prime' (*What Is Philosophy?* [New York: Columbia University Press, 1994], 2). This reading relies, as does Deleuze's earlier interpretation of Kant, on inflating the significance of Kant's appendix on the sublime. Derrida's essay 'Economimesis' (trans. Richard Klein, in *Diacritics* 11[1981], 3–25) seems to me to be much closer to the valence Kant intends for the various parts of his final *Critique*. Rather than overcoming the limits of the faculties, the sublime is treated by Derrida as the apex of his metaphysics as, I think, Kant intends it to be read.

Although many of Lyotard's published works on the third *Critique* focus on the appendix on the sublime, he keeps in view the connections between this appendix and the other parts of the *Critique*. Lyotard's reading of Kant also focuses, as I intend to here, on the question of presentation. However, as will become apparent in my discussion of Lacoue-Labarthe in Chapter 5, Lyotard's formulation of the sublime in his use of Kant's conception of presentation to defend avant-garde painting seems to substantialise an absolute that is 'beyond' the conditions of presentation. For this reason, and despite the strong connections between

Lyotard and Kant on the topic of presentation, he does not have a more prominent place in this study. For evidence of the continuity for Lyotard's thinking of
the third *Critique* see his *Lessons on the Analytic of the Sublime* (Stanford, CA:
Stanford University Press, 1994) and *Discours, figure* (Paris: Klincksieck, 1971). For
his use of the sublime to analyse presentation in avant-garde painting, see his 'The
Sublime and the Avant-Garde,' ed. Andrew Benjamin, *The Lyotard Reader* (Cambridge, MA and Oxford, UK: Basil Blackwell, 1989), 196–211.

7. Lacoue-Labarthe and Nancy's *The Literary Absolute: The Theory of Literature in German Romanticism*, trans. Phillip Barnard and Cheryl Lester (Albany:
State University of New York Press, 1988) is often cited in projects on the 'history
of ideas' that take this verdict as a given. In later chapters I will argue that such a
use of this text seriously mistakes its agenda. Like Derrida's essay 'Economimesis,'
this text does not endorse the reading of Kant's philosophy as an inadequate
metaphysics but conducts a critique of the interpretation of the third *Critique* in
this way by calling on German Idealism and Romanticism. The force of the authors' critique needs to be brought out by an analysis of their other writings as
well as the use they make of Heidegger's lectures on Schelling, which also make
this criticism of Idealism and Romanticism. See my later discussion on these
points in Chapters 3, 5, and 6.

8. Other works that treat the topic of presentation as the core problem of the
*Critique of Judgment* and look, through this focus, at the scope of its influence in
subsequent literary and philosophical debate are Lacoue-Labarthe and Nancy's *The
Literary Absolute;* and, following the lead of this European reception of Kant, are
works by Martha B. Helfer, *The Retreat of Representation: The Concept of Darstellung in German Critical Discourse* (Albany: State University of New York Press,
1996) and Azade Seyhan, *Representation and Its Discontents: The Critical Legacy of
German Romanticism* (Berkeley and Los Angeles: University of California Press,
1992).

9. See Derrida's critique in *The Truth in Painting* of the false autonomy of
aesthetic judgment given Kant's use of the same frame developed in his account of
cognitive judgment for aesthetic judgment: quality, quantity, relation, and modality, 71 ff.

10. See Luc Ferry's account in his *Political Philosophy, Vol. 2, The System of
Philosophies of History*, trans. Franklin Philip (Chicago and London: University of
Chicago Press, 1992), 86–87.

11. Kant, *The Prologomena*, trans. P. Carus and J. W. Ellington (Indianapolis:
Hackett, 1985), 42–43: 'objective validity and necessary universal validity (for every-
body) are equivalent concepts' and the commentary of Markus: 'It is, however,
conspicuous that here (*Critique of Pure Reason*, B848) Kant treats intersubjective
communicability and the possibility of consensus only as the external (and pre-
sumptive) *mark* of objective validity, while in the above invoked quotations, from
*later* writings (i.e. *The Prologomena*) the two are stated to be synonymous, that is,

intersubjectivity is regarded as the constitutive, definitory [*sic*] characteristic of knowledge in general.' György Markus, 'Changing Images of Science,' *Thesis 11,* 33, 1992:51.

12. In his translation of the final *Critique,* Pluhar uses 'exhibition' to translate *Darstellung* and 'presentation' to translate *Vorstellung.* I have used the more conventional terminology of 'presentation' for *Darstellung* and 'representation' for *Vorstellung.* In my discussion of Kant I have adjusted all quotations from Pluhar's translation of the third *Critique* to conform to my own preference. I have signalled this amendment in the text by giving the German in brackets.

13. For a comprehensive study of the topic of judgment in Kant's first *Critique* see Béatrice Longuenesse's *Kant and the Capacity to Judge: Sensibility and Discursivity in the Transcendental Analytic of the 'Critique of Pure Reason,'* trans. Charles T. Wolfe (Princeton, NJ: Princeton University Press, 1998); and Klaus Reich's *The Completeness of Kant's Table of Judgments,* trans. Jane Kneller and Michael Losonsky (Stanford, CA: Stanford University Press, 1992).

14. The mark of 'pleasure' that Kant uses to differentiate cognitive from aesthetic judgments has been a topic of considerable interest given Kant's perplexing comment in the *Critique of Judgment* that there is an immemorial relation of pleasure to cognition (CJ, 27). See for commentary on the significance of this remark J. M. Bernstein's *The Fate of Art: Aesthetic Alienation from Kant to Derrida, and Adorno* (Cambridge, UK: Polity Press, 1992) and Peter Fenves's *Late Kant: Towards Another Law of the Earth* (New York and London: Routledge, 2003), 8–32.

15. Winfried Menninghaus gives a fascinating account of the significance of the disciplining of genius by taste in Kant's third *Critique.* He argues that in Kant's text 'genius gravitates toward nonsense' and needs to be restrained by taste, but that taste itself 'gravitates toward the grotesque' and thus has its own vices. He describes the thesis that the *Critique of Judgment* puts forward 'a free and harmoniously tuned interplay of the faculties' (a thesis notably put forward as Kant's 'romanticism' in Deleuze's *Kant's Critical Philosophy*–A.R.) as the 'chief fiction' of this *Critique.* Winfried Menninghaus, *In Praise of Nonsense: Kant and Bluebeard,* trans. Henry Pickford (Stanford, CA: Stanford University Press, 1999), 22–23.

16. Deleuze qualifies this 'indirect' but 'positive' relation, noting that it is achieved by 'reflection.' Deleuze, *Kant's Critical Philosophy,* 58.

17. Kant's first two *Critiques* establish a division between freedom and the sensible world. In the *Critique of Pure Reason* the task of the critical philosophy is to restrain reason from the illusory use that consists in confusing what it is possible to think with what may be known according to the sensible conditions of thought (Immanuel Kant, *Critique of Pure Reason,* trans. Werner S. Pluhar [Indianapolis: Hackett, 1996], 8). The risk of such a confusion of ideas and objects of possible experience is that a fabrication of reason may be confused for something that exists in the domain of experience. The *Critique of Practical Reason,* on the other

hand, locates a danger in the influence on moral action of circumstance. Here the sensible world and the subject's feelings do not provide a necessary orientation for ideas of reason, so much as threaten to lead it astray. Accordingly, the formalism of the moral law guards the possibility of a moral action in the world of sensibility, defining such action as a strict adherence to the principles of reason (*Critique of Practical Reason*, Third Edition, trans. Lewis White Beck [New York: Macmillan, 1993], 74). Whether it is reason's tendency to fanaticism—an error that follows the hubris of limitlessness—or the claim circumstances make upon it and constrain it under a false limitation, critical restraint in either case follows a juridical model. Accordingly, Kant's texts reinforce the sense of renunciation—of desires or of errant speculation—in the recurrent references to 'the court of reason', which legislates the proper use and safe extension of reason's ideas. Hence the 'revolution' that proceeds by pleas for moderation is fought on two fronts: against the illusions of a reason 'independent of all experience' and against the claim of circumstance on action. The project of the *Critique of Judgment* may be described as an attempt to mediate this split between experience and freedom through the faculty of judgment while, as we will see, retaining the emphasis on a renunciation of the false satisfactions of charm and merely illusory ideas.

18. *Critique of Pure Reason*, B207, n.67 and CJ, 328.

19. See Tzvetan Todorov's discussion of this distinction in his *Theories of the Symbol*, trans. Catherine Porter (Ithaca, NY: Cornell University Press, 1982), 206–208.

20. Derrida calls into question the source of Kant's example of the tulip, noting that this example is used by Saussure in a text often cited by Kant: 'So it's to do with a flower. Not just any flower: not the rose, not the sunflower, nor the broom-flower [*genêt*]—the tulip. But there is every reason for presuming that it does not come from nature. From another text, rather. The example seems arbitrary until we notice that a certain Saussure is often cited by Kant in the third *Critique*. Now this Monsieur de Saussure, "a man as witty as he is profound," says Kant in the great "General Remark concerning the Exposition of Reflexive Aesthetic Judgments," was the author of a *Journey in the Alps*. There we read something that Kant did not quote: "I found, in the woods above the hermitage, the wild tulip, which I had never seen before," ' *The Truth in Painting*, 85. Derrida here pokes fun, among other things, at Kant's assiduous attention to the details of travel writing but famous reluctance to leave the city limits of his native town of Konïgsberg.

21. See Rodolphe Gasché's *The Idea of Form: Rethinking Kant's Aesthetics* (Stanford, CA: Stanford University Press, 2003) for a reappraisal of form in relation to what he refers to as Kant's 'para-epistemological' task of ' "cognition in general." ' Gasché's book contests the interpretation of Kant's formalism as a concept severed 'from all questions of cognition,' 10.

22. See my 'Errant Beauty: Derrida and Kant on Aesthetic Presentation' for a detailed discussion of the cut from function that makes beauty purposeless, *International Studies in Philosophy* 33 no. 1 (2001): 87–104.

23. Immanuel Kant, *What Real Progress Has Metaphysics Made in Germany since the Time of Leibniz and Wolff?* trans. Ted Humphrey (New York: Abaris Books, 1983).

24. The intuition is connected with the concept in terms of a relation of form. Intuitive representations—whether schematic or symbolic—are presentations rather than characterizations. They designate concepts 'by accompanying sensible signs.' Such signs do not contain anything that is part of the intuition of the object. Instead they serve the subjective point of providing a means for reproducing concepts in accordance with the imagination's law of association. These signs are either visible (algebraic or mimetic) signs or words that *express* concepts (CJ, 227). The difference between the intuitive element that represents a concept and the discursive characterization of it lies in their relation to their object. Whereas the former constitutes an element in cognition in which our concepts are given an objective reality, the latter is merely a tool of the expression of these concepts. Hence for Kant, God, as we will see in the next chapter, can receive a positive characterization but only a negative presentation [*Darstellung*]. And in taste a particular sensible form presents but only indirectly (through reflection) our own freedom from determined ends.

25. Zammito disputes this emphasis, arguing that Kant's focus on nature is not indicative of hostility to art. *The Genesis of Kant's Critique of Judgment*, 132 ff. See also Deleuze, who examines the productions of genius as a site for the presentation of the ideas of reason, *Kant's Critical Philosophy: The Doctrine of the Faculties*. Against Zammito witness Kant's frequent criticisms of those products that issue from 'man' (flute playing) and his praise of the productions of nature (birdsong) (see CJ, 166 and 169). Although the moral issue of deception clouds Kant's discussion of these particular examples, it is clear that the context of the problem of aesthetic presentation as that of mediating the divide between nature and reason explains the special value natural beauty enjoys in this *Critique*. Nature's beauties are suitable vehicles for pure aesthetic judgments because, Kant alleges, there is no ascertainable intention behind their particular form.

26. As Niklas Luhmann does through the notion of the Kantian schema in *The Reality of the Mass Media*, trans. Kathleen Cross (Stanford, CA: Stanford University Press, 1996).

27. Cf. Kant's reference to 'ever advancing culture', CJ, 188. Kant is one of the first to explicitly articulate the discrepancy in meaning between civilisation and culture. The differentiation Kant makes in his popular writings associates civilisation with social propriety and decorum and culture with morality ('Idea for a Universal History' [1784], *Perpetual Peace and Other Essays on Politics, History and Morals*. trans. Ted Humphrey [Indianapolis: Hackett, 1983]). In the *Critique of Judgment* Kant differentiates between the evolving culture of skill, which is necessary for the realization of our ends but not sufficient to assist the will to choose and determine

its ends, and the higher culture of discipline. The latter is represented by the progress of the sciences and the arts and, in liberating us from the despotism of desires, is venerated by Kant in its ability to make us receptive to higher ends (CJ, §83). I will discuss this distinction in further detail in the next chapter. The noumenal and atemporal form of morality means that it cannot reside, contrary to the view Kant develops in 'Idea for a Universal History,' *in* high culture. For a discussion of the civilization/culture distinction in the eighteenth century see György Markus, 'Culture: The Making and the Make-Up of a Concept (An Essay in Historical Semantics)' *Dialectical Anthropology*, 18 (1993): 3–29; and Fernand Braudel, *On History*, trans. Sarah Matthews (Chicago: University of Chicago Press, 1980). See Part III, 'The History of Civilizations,' 177–217. For a critique of Kant's doctrine of taste as the assertion of the culture of the educated over the civilising practices of the court, see Pierre Bourdieu's *Distinction: A Social Critique of Pure Taste*, trans. Richard Nice (Cambridge, MA: Harvard University Press, 1984).

28. Jacques Derrida, *The Truth in Painting*, 35.

29. This is arguably also a feature of Kant's popular essays on politics. I will return to this point in the next chapter.

CHAPTER 2

1. Martin Heidegger, *Kant and the Problem of Metaphysics*, trans. Richard Taft (Bloomington and Indianapolis: Indiana University Press, 1997). Hereafter cited as KB.

2. Kant's *Anthropology from a Pragmatic Point of View*, trans. Victor Lyle Dowdell (Carbondale and Edwardsville: Southern Illinois University Press, 1978), which was only published in 1798 and thus after the publication of the three *Critiques*, was based on notes for lectures given on the topic of anthropology by Kant from at least 1772. However, these lectures were drawn from earlier research on topics such as physical geography begun as early as 1756. Thus in their genesis, development, and delivery these lectures span the precritical and critical periods of Kantian philosophy. See Frederick P. Van De Pitte's 'Introduction,' in *Anthropology from a Pragmatic Point of View*, xi–xxii, and Howard Caygill, *A Kant Dictionary* (Oxford, UK and Malden, MA: Blackwell, 1995), 73.

3. I comment on the usage of 'man' in Note 34. Before Heidegger, Nietzsche had noted the genesis of the critical philosophy in Kant's faith in man's moral vocation or reason. It is Heidegger, however, who provides the analysis of Kant's critical philosophy in terms of this 'faith.' After Heidegger, Foucault's translation and commentary on Kant's anthropology for his *these d'état* together with his late essay on Kant, 'What Is Enlightenment?' can be cited here: in his *Commentary* on Kant's *Anthropology*, Foucault asks, is there 'a certain *concrete* image of man that no philosophical elaboration has essentially altered, which perhaps subsists in the very heart of the *Critique* and is formulated, without any major modifications, in

the last of Kant's published texts?' For an interpretation of Foucault's own critical project in terms of the constant tension between a critical and anthropological perspective, see Béatrice Han's *Foucault's Critical Project: Between the Transcendental and the Historical*, trans. Edward Pile (Stanford, CA: Stanford University Press, 2002). The citation from Foucault's *Commentary* is quoted in Han, *Foucault's Critical Project*, 21. Foucault's introduction to his French translation of Kant's anthropology has not been published and Han's book provides the invaluable service of access to citations from it. For Nietzsche's criticisms of the formative faith in the moral idea in Kantian philosophy, see his *On the Genealogy of Morals*, trans. Walter Kaufmann (New York: Random House, 1969). See his 'Third Essay,' in particular sections 7–13.

4. For the argument that the critical philosophy has its genesis in the themes and topics of the precritical works, see Susan Meld-Shell, *The Embodiment of Reason: Kant on Spirit, Generation and Community* (Chicago: University of Chicago Press, 1996); Monique David-Ménard, 'Kant's "An Essay on the Maladies of the Mind" and *Observations on the Feeling of the Beautiful and the Sublime*,' trans. Alison Ross, ed. Penelope Deutscher. In *Hypatia* 15, no. 4 (Fall 2000): 82–98; and, in the same volume, Alison Ross, 'Introduction to Monique David-Ménard on Kant and Madness,' 77–82. It is worth comparing the approach to madness and the account taken of Kant's writing on anthropology in Winfried Menninghaus's *In Praise of Nonsense: Kant and Bluebeard*, trans. Henry Pickford (Stanford, CA: Stanford University Press, 1999) with the psychobiographical weight given to madness that nonetheless proceeds from an analysis of the text of Kant's writing, in David-Ménard's *La folie dans la raison pure: Kant, lecteur de Swedenburg* (Paris: Librairie Philosophique J. Vrin, 1990). For a clear treatment of the stakes of the anthropology within the *Critique of Practical Reason*, see Otfried Höffe, 'Kant, morale et anthropologie,' in *Philosophie politique: revue internationale de philosophie politique*, Vol. 2, *Kant* (Paris: Presses Universitaires de France, 1992), 143–59.

5. I will examine the place of the third *Critique* in Heidegger's thinking in detail in Chapters 3 and 4. Derrida's emphasis on the place of anthropology in this work is not unusual: amongst those who share this emphasis, but not the execution of Derrida's argument, we can cite Deleuze's *Kant's Critical Philosophy*, Otfried Höffe's *Immanuel Kant*, trans. Marshall Farrier (Albany: State University of New York Press, 1994), and Jean-Michel Muglioni's *La philosophie de l'histoire de Kant: qu'est-ce que l'homme?* (Paris: Presses Universitaires de France, 1993).

6. Jacques Derrida, *The Truth in Painting*, trans. Geoffrey Bennington and Ian McLeod (Chicago and London: Chicago University Press, 1987), 105. Derrida's analysis of the examples Kant gives in the first part of the third *Critique* to distinguish between 'free' and 'adherent' beauties concludes that Kant's choice of examples is 'unintelligible' without the pragmatic anthropology of the 'Critique of Teleological Judgment' (*The Truth in Painting*, 105). According to this anthropology the horse is an adherent beauty, as its form (unlike that of the flower in the

wild or crustaceans in the sea) is not able to be detached from its function for 'man.' Kant, according to Derrida, only justifies this otherwise opaque example of adherent beauty in §83 of the 'Critique of Teleological Judgment,' in which he explains the claim that man is 'the final end of nature.'

7. Kant, *Anthropology from a Pragmatic Point of View*, 4.

8. In both parts of the *Critique*, however, this question also operates in a way that compromises Kant's chosen approach to the problem of aesthetic presentation. Just as taste relied on the empirical elements of charm and history, so too what is given in the forms of human existence in the 'Teleology' precedes the 'a priori' principles that critique discloses as (logically prior) conditions of possibility for freedom. In the 'Teleology' as in the 'Aesthetics,' what is held in abeyance as 'regulative' and 'noumenal' is constantly presupposed in the forms of aesthetic presentation that are called on to present reason's ideas.

9. Catherine Chalier has recently put the dilemma this way: 'All people, [Kant] . . . asserts—accepting not the slightest discussion on this point—provided that they reflect without hedging, are well aware that the definition of morality lies in the purity of intention.

'Of course, the fundamental intention governing behavior almost always eludes the clear conscience, but that changes nothing. It hardly matters, Kant says, whether a person knows how to discern that intention. In spite of everything, it—and not the result obtained—is what constitutes the morality of the act. In every circumstance, only the person who acts with the pure intention of doing his duty, without giving in to his inclinations, and solely out of respect for what duty commands, can be deemed moral. Nevertheless, the examples offered in Kant's *Groundwork of the Metaphysics of Morals* exacerbate the difficulty. For how are we to know if the unhappy person preserves his life out of duty—hence out of morality—and not out of a secret inner hope that better days are ahead, hence out of self-interest? How are we to know if a person's love for his or her neighbor stems from pure good will and not from some inclination, that is, in Kant's vocabulary, from the *pathological?*' Catherine Chalier, *What Ought I to Do? Morality in Kant and Levinas*, trans. Jane Marie Todd (Ithaca, NY and London: Cornell University Press, 2002), 27–28. The categorical imperative, which submits an action to the test of the universalisability of its maxim and tries to address these difficulties, itself presupposes that an agent can dissect the fundamental intention governing their behaviour and, by this means, differentiate sublime from moral motivations. I will return to this point.

10. Kant, 'On the Proverb: That May Be True in Theory, But Is of No Practical Use,' *Perpetual Peace and Other Essays on Politics, History and Morals*, trans. Ted Humphrey (Indianapolis: Hackett, 1983), 61–93.

11. It is worth citing in this regard his argument in 'On the Proverb: That May Be True in Theory, But Is of No Practical Use' that violence and war are the forces that compel peoples to enter into civil constitutions and international organisations, 87–88.

12. On the topic of the practical knowledge of freedom, see Kant, *Critique of Practical Reason,* 3rd ed., trans. Lewis White Beck (New York: Macmillan, 1993), pp. 56 ff and 144. Hereafter cited as CPrR. See also the treatment of this topic in the context of man's final purpose in CJ, 345.

13. For Hans Blumenberg, Kant's postulate of immortality is a myth of a special type, the type that aims to bring myth to an end, to provide a supportive environment for man's definitive self-assertion on his own behalf, and for the attendant responsibility. See Hans Blumenberg, *Work on Myth,* trans. Robert Wallace (Cambridge, MA: MIT Press, 1990), 290–94. Blumenberg understands myth functionally: the work of myth is to counter the 'absolutism of reality,' that is, looked at from the other end, the helplessness of man in the face of the world due to his 'instinct deficiency.' This condition deprives him of his 'ecological niche.' Mythical stories and figures divide and personalise nature, thus parcelling and reducing its overwhelming power and rendering it appeasable ('The archaic division of powers also means that the competence of each of the gods in relation to human life is only partial,' 144). Both the 'absolutism of reality' and 'bringing myth to an end' are 'limiting cases' or 'limit concepts' that are only functionally describable (pp. 3–32; pp. 113–44). It seems that the service that 'final myths' provide is not primarily directed to taming hostile reality but is meant to render endurable the 'oppressiveness of contingency,' 293. The oppressiveness in question is indeed the same as the one the Kantian goodwill would experience in the world without the solace of God and immortality. In myth, aesthetic presentation comes in the aid of ethical conduct. Put in this context, can the satisfaction that the virtuous act provides be anything other than aesthetic pleasure, precisely in the sense that Kant understands this term?

14. The difficulties in this 'reconciliation' are carefully discussed by Véronique Zanetti, 'Teleology and the Freedom of the Self,' in *The Modern Subject: Conceptions of the Self in Classical German Philosophy,* ed. Karl Ameriks and Dieter Sturma (Albany: State University of New York Press, 1995), 47–65.

15. Kant describes as the 'only merit' of physico-teleology that it leads the mind 'in its contemplation of the world, onto the path of purposes, and through this to an *intelligent* author of the world' (CJ, 372).

16. We might add here that Kant is ambivalent about the utility of the concept of art for assisting cognitive ends in nature. To call nature an analogue of 'art,' Kant writes, is to 'say far too little' (CJ, 254). Nature 'organizes itself ' rather than being organised by a being apart from it. The analogy 'with our own causality in terms of purposes' (CJ, 255) is a 'remote' one, which allows us to explain the possibility of nature's forms, but is inadequate for the reciprocal relation between cause and effect in nature. Kant thus contrasts self-organising natural organisms with man-made objects. In the case of a watch, for instance, its parts do not produce reciprocity of cause and effect. Each part exists for the sake of the other, but

is not *in* the organised whole *through* the causation of another part. The arts that 'man' employs can only give things an external purpose. Natural beings, in contrast, carry an intrinsic purposiveness at the same time as they participate in a system of extrinsic purposes. Hence Kant favours the reflective judgment of intrinsic purposiveness over the idea of an external rational cause or 'art' which gives no autonomy to its object and may function descriptively for objects of human fabrication but is less adequate as an unqualified category of explanation for nature's forms (see CJ, 246 and 312).

This preference acts to qualify Kant's view that in order to 'adequately become familiar with' or even better 'explain' how organized beings are internally possible we need to regard them as the products intended by 'an intelligent being' (CJ, 283–284). The idea of a 'divine author' who 'lies beyond and above nature' is a merely regulative principle to 'guide us in judging the things in the world in a way appropriate to our human understanding' (CJ, §79, 302). It is an open question whether Kant is able to restrain teleology to a merely regulative device. The use of the teleological principle introduces a rhetorical chain that licenses a reflection on nature as a system of purposes *designed for* man. Hence, unlike Kant's qualified support for the utility of 'art' for the explanation of nature's forms, in the case of the thinking man's moral vocation, the concept of 'art' to synthesise the natural world is crucial. This reflective idea of 'man' as nature's intended end is not limited, but is rather inflated by the use of 'man' as the analogical principle best able to determine the idea of nature's cause. Just as taste was cast as the principle of mediation between forms of nature and ideas that Kant, as we saw, paradoxically assumed were *already* linked, so too the ideas only reflectively permitted in the 'Teleology' seem to overstep their limits as merely regulative principles and they do so on account of the requirements of the pragmatic anthropology that they were supposed to support.

17. Pierre Hassner has a comprehensive discussion of Kant's political thought from the perspective of the problem of history in his entry on 'Immanuel Kant' in *History of Political Philosophy,* Third Edition, ed. Leo Strauss and Joseph Cropsey (Chicago and London: Chicago University Press, 1987), pp. 581–622. See also, for the historical dimension of the problem of reason in Kant's philosophy, Yiarmiahu Yovel's *Kant and the Philosophy of History* (Princeton, NJ: Princeton University Press, 1980). Hassner states, 'Kant's political teaching may be summarized in a phrase: republican government and international organization' ('Immanuel Kant,' *History of Political Philosophy,* 581). In my view, the governmental organisation required both for a republic and an international community pivots on the formative role Kant derives from his pragmatic anthropology.

18. Immanuel Kant, *Critique of Judgment,* trans. Werner S. Pluhar (Indianapolis: Hackett, 1987), §65. In Kant's writing this teleological idea is given a political reference prior to the French Revolution and the political references in the *Critique of Judgment* to organic form. Kant's 1784 essay 'Idea for a Universal History'

prefigures the relation between organised forms and the task for the realisation of the purpose such organisation entails. In the case of practical reason the formality of the moral law abstracts from the claim of particular circumstances but depends nevertheless on the capacity of the subject to think maxims without contradiction *for particular possible ends of action.* Hence Kant argues that where calculative ends prevail over the peremptory voice of duty one is led down the path of self-disgust.

19. In addition to this reference from 'On the Proverb,' 87–88, see also Kant's discussion of war as 'sublime' in the *Critique of Judgment,* §28, Ak. 263, p. 122; and in terms of its politico-historical role in the essay 'To Perpetual Peace: A Philosophical Sketch' (*Perpetual Peace and Other Essays on Politics, History and Morals,* trans. Ted Humphrey [Indianapolis: Hackett, 1983], 107–45) under the category of unsociability, Fourth Thesis, 31–32.

20. Hence violence intervenes in the decadence of a leisure class to reinstall the moral quality of discipline (CJ, 122 and 320–21).

21. This historical perspective is nonetheless used for a reading of history that gives the moral perspective credibility. Kant reads historical events through the filter of the idea of progress and in this way finds support for the view that freedom is historically shaped. This reading, as I noted in my opening remarks to this chapter, feeds and encourages the moral perspective, and it does so by giving hope in the idea of progress a basis in anthropology. In the 1795 essay 'To Perpetual Peace: A Philosophical Sketch,' Kant writes: 'Now the republican constitution is the only one wholly compatible with the rights of men, but it is also the most difficult to establish and still harder to maintain, so much so that many contend that a republic must be a nation of *angels,* for men's self-seeking inclinations make them incapable of adhering to so sublime a form of government. But now nature comes to the aid of that revered but practically impotent general will, which is grounded in reason. Indeed, this aid comes directly from those self-seeking inclinations, and it is merely by organizing the nation well (which is certainly within man's capacities) that they are able to direct their power against one another, and one inclination is able to check or cancel the destructive tendencies of the others.' The influence of Rousseau's notion of the 'general will' is marked in these formulations, although in Kant's case the organisation of the nation is what establishes a system of checks against man's self-seeking nature or inclinations and the installation of this system does not require a divine lawmaker but is, rather, 'certainly within man's capacities.' 'To Perpetual Peace: A Philosophical Sketch,' 124.

22. The account given here should be qualified in the terms used by Ingeborg Maus in her careful discussion of the distinction between positive law and the categorical imperative, 'Liberties and Popular Sovereignty: On Jürgen Habermas's Reconstruction of the System of Rights.' In *Cardozo Law Review* 17 (1996): 825–82. Against the account Habermas gives of Kant, she explains that positive law directly and substantively regulates behaviour, whereas maxims do not directly obligate action but permit action indirectly through reference to the moral law; see 859–66.

23. CPrR, 128.

24. As Véronique Zanetti argues, the intervention of a third principle, as in Kant's use of the 'supersensible' to mediate mechanism and teleology, would have the effect of subordinating one term to the other and thus not resolving the dualism; but history, as I have indicated here, also installs a de facto subordination as it suggests a principle of development according to which the later term (freedom) is more refined.

25. Kant's synthetic approach to historical events can be contrasted with Foucault's call for the human sciences to put aside the use of history to shelter 'philosophical anthropology' (*de la pensée anthropologique*) and to instead think 'a population of dispersed events.' Michel Foucault, 'On the Archaeology of the Sciences: Response to the Epistemology Circle,' in *Aesthetics, Method, and Epistemology: Essential Works of Foucault 1954–1984*, Vol. 2, ed. James D. Faubion, trans. Robert Hurley et al. (New York: The New Press, 1998), 297–333. ('Continuous history is the correlate of consciousness: the guarantee that what escapes from it can be restored to it; the promise that it will some day be able to appropriate outright all those things which surround it and weigh down on it, to restore its mastery over them, and to find in them what really must be called—leaving the word all its overload of meaning—its home,' 301.)

26. Adherence to the moral law requires an endless progress as 'perfect fitness' to the moral law is 'holiness,' a perfection of which no rational being in the world of sense is capable (CPrR, 128).

27. CPrR, 150. See too *The Metaphysics of Morals,* trans. and ed. Mary Gregor (Cambridge, UK: Cambridge University Press, 1996) 6, no. 354, 123. Dieter Henrich refers to the idea able to promote practical ends as the 'moral image of the world.' See his *Aesthetic Judgment and the Moral Image of the World* (Stanford, CA: Stanford University Press, 1992), 24.

28. Kant argues that the greater need of cultivation for judgments of the sublime should not lead to the erroneous view that such judgments were 'initially produced by culture and then introduced to society by way of (say) mere convention. Rather, it has its foundation in human nature: in something that, along with common sense, we may require and demand of everyone, namely, the predisposition to the feeling for (practical) ideas, i.e., to moral feeling' (CJ, 125).

29. See CJ, §30, 141–43. Judgments of taste about the beautiful in nature require a deduction, which Kant glosses here as 'a legitimation of its pretension' to concern 'a liking . . . for the *form of the object*' (CJ, 141). This involvement of form means for Kant that the beautiful in nature prompts us to 'raise all sorts of questions about what causes this purposiveness in nature's forms, eg: How are we to explain why nature has so extravagantly spread beauty everywhere, even at the bottom of the ocean, where the human eye (for which, after all, this beauty is alone purposive) rarely penetrates?' (CJ, 142). Nature's beauty thus calls for a human audience, but the fact that it is frequently without one Kant's 'Teleology' re-

solves by the accent it places on man's use of nature. In the 'Critique of Teleological Judgment' Kant asserts that reason presupposes 'a personal value' for man by which 'his existence can be [a] final purpose.' He also cites moral interest as the probable basis for our attentiveness to the beauty and the purposes of nature (CJ, 350). This interest means that nature cannot be there simply for our enjoyment and admiration (CJ, 372). It is man's capacity to mould nature for his own uses that makes him 'consider all natural things beneficial' at the same time as it prohibits him from assuming 'a relative purpose of nature (directed to these uses). For man's own reason knows how to make things harmonize with the notions that were his own choice, notions to which even nature did not predestine him' (CJ, 246). Thus Kant replaces the valence given to nature as external to human interests in taste, with the active use to which 'man' puts nature in the 'Teleology.'

30. This explains why in the deduction of taste the liking for the beautiful in nature prompts us to 'raise all sorts of questions about what causes this purposiveness in nature's forms'; see note 28.

31. Horace Bénédict de Saussure was a Swiss geologist, geographer, botanist, and author of *Voyages dans les Alpes* (1779). See Pluhar's description in CJ, 124, n. 32.

32. Violence, in the form of war, is what elevates 'man' from mere animal existence and stimulates civilising processes. See 'To Perpetual Peace: A Philosophical Sketch,' 121 ff, and 'Idea for a Universal History with a Cosmopolitan Intent,' in *Perpetual Peace and Other Essays,* 29–41, Fourth Thesis.

33. 'Speculative Beginnings of Human History,' in *Perpetual Peace and Other Essays,* 49–60.

34. See Kant's *Observations on the Feeling of the Beautiful and the Sublime,* trans. J. T. Goldthwait (Berkeley: University of California Press, 1960) and his *Anthropology from a Pragmatic Point of View.* See especially 'The Mania of Domination' and 'The Character of Sex.' See also Sarah Kofman's excellent discussion of these themes in her 'The Economy of Respect: Kant and Respect for Women,' trans. Nicola Fischer, in *Feminist Interpretations of Immanuel Kant,* ed. Robin May Schott (University Park: Pennsylvania State University Press, 1997), 335–72. The role of women in Kant's philosophy does not alter substantially between the precritical and the critical writings. In each context, woman is charged with the responsibility (through her modesty) of instilling in man a moral capacity, a capacity that Kant consistently deems her incapable of developing herself. Women arguably function in Kant's thought as does the category of the species in his political reflections: namely, as anomalous to but responsible for the historical conditions for morality. The speculative historical dimension in Kant's popular writing makes use of the hierarchic economy of the sexes to finance the universalist moral perspective that his thought aspires to. In order to keep in view the significance of this aspect of Kant's thought I have tried to keep my discussion consistent with the gender specific language Kant uses throughout his texts.

35. The sublime is linked to the nascent moral category of refusal because it 'always . . . [has] reference to our *way of thinking,* i.e., to maxims directed to providing the intellectual (side in us) and our rational ideas with supremacy over sensibility' (CJ, 134–35). It is reason's 'dominance over sensibility' in the sublime that links it to the 'law-governed *task*' of morality and elevates it above the *play* of the beautiful (CJ, 128). It is this close proximity to the moral task that makes the sublime, considered within the moral problematic of the third *Critique* and, to some extent, against Kant's own stated views on this topic, more significant than the beautiful. In his appendix Kant includes the 'peasant' in the category of those without moral feeling (CJ, 124).

36. At the same time, the themes treated in Kant's appendix on the sublime underline some of the key problems that the path of sensory refusal raises for the resolution of Kantian dualism; many of these problems concern the irreconcilable differences in the approach to the topic of presentation in Kant's discussion of taste and teleology. One of the consequences of the definition of pragmatic anthropology in the 'Critique of Teleological Judgment,' not in the terms of the definition given of practical reason in the second *Critique,* but as the way that 'man' puts nature to 'use,' is that 'man's' ends are confirmed in nature by whatever way (even to nonmoral ends) that 'man' uses nature. The delicate problem in the deduction of taste of how nature can 'independently' confirm 'man's' moral ends is overrun in the 'Critique of Teleological Judgment' for the problem of how to distinguish man's capacity to mould nature for his own uses from the assumption of 'a relative purpose of nature (directed to these uses)' (CJ, 246).

37. Both the savage's esteem and the spectator's respect are spectatorial, and thus aesthetic rather than moral judgments. A moral judgment inflects the habit of judging to one's own acts.

38. This perspective on moral education is used for instance in his appendix on the sublime. Aesthetic judgments of the sublime are considered by Kant—as in the case of the debate over the statesman and the general—as useful vehicles for the cultivation of an interest in morals (CJ, 122).

39. It is worth noting here that Kant arrogates to the philosopher the final say on whether or not an act is moral: 'If one asks, however, what pure morality really is, by which, as the touchstone, the moral import of each action must be tested, I must confess that only philosophers can put the decision on this question in doubt' (CPrR, 161). The incorporation of examples as educational devices for those who do not know 'what pure morality really is' conforms well to Michèle le Doeuff's discussion of what she calls the 'philosophical imaginary' (*The Philosophical Imaginary,* trans. Colin Gordon [Stanford, CA: Stanford University Press, 1989]). The integral place of images to the articulation of philosophical concepts is disavowed by the projection of such images onto an Other, or series of others. This disavowal denies the image 'the status of an element within philosophical work' by the practice of an inclusive exclusion of images, 7. She schematises 'two

possible *alibis*' [her emphasis] for the presence in philosophical texts of 'non-philosophical' images. The 'occurrence of a discourse in images can be despatched either upstream or downstream,' 6. In the upstream version the presence of images is explained as 'the resurgence of a primitive soul, of archaic or infantile thought, of an uneducated or ineducable part of the mind. Paradigms of this projected Other are the child (in that we have all been one, before becoming . . . a man!), nursery stories, the people (irrational by nature), old wives' tales, folklore, etc.,' 6. This version seeks to 'maximize . . . the image's heterogeneity.' In contrast, in the downstream version, which Kant arguably uses in the cited examples from the CPrR, 'imagery is seen more in terms of an adaptation to the intended recipient of a discourse. Imagery speaks directly, with intuitive clarity, to a destined interlocutor who is still uncultivated by concepts and ignorant of philosophy, or at any rate of this philosophy. The image is a gangway, a mediation between two theoretical situations: the speaker's and the recipient's,' 7. In this 'downstream' variant the image is absorbed 'into the conceptualised problematic, its meaning being considered as congruent with the theoretical results which it simply translates or illustrates. A dross coming from elsewhere . . . serviceable to the reader's deficient culture,' 7.

40. 'If the law of morals and the image of holiness and virtue are to exert any influence at all on our minds, they can do so only in so far as they are laid to heart in their purity as drives unmixed with any view to welfare, because it is in suffering that they most notably show themselves' (CPrR, 162).

41. On the topic of suffering versus moral motive see CPrR, 132, and compare with the discussion of the distinction between affect and passion in the *Critique of Judgment*. Passions are 'persistent and deliberate' in their impediment to following principles and can 'never be called sublime' (CJ, 132, n. 39).

42. This instance is given an historical illustration by Kant. The quoted passage continues: 'Juvenal describes such an example in a climax which makes the reader vividly feel the power of the drive which lies in the pure law of duty as duty: "Be a stout soldier, a faithful guardian, and an incorruptible judge; if summoned to bear witness in some dubious and uncertain cause, though Phalaris himself should bring up his bull and dictate to you a perjury, count it the greatest of all sins to prefer life to honor, and to lose, for the sake of living, all that makes life worth living"' (CPrR, 164–65). Kant refers here to the tyrant of Agrigentum who burned his victims to death in a specially constructed brass ox (CPrR, 165, n. 1).

43. Kant, who earlier in the second *Critique* describes acts in terms of 'clues' that only 'suggest' the complexion of the underlying motives (CPrR, 89), meets this difficulty by characterising for us the evidence that differentiates an act driven by nonmoral motivations from those faithful only to 'esteem for duty' (CPrR, 163).

44. 'Now of all arguments there are none which excite more ready participation by those who are otherwise soon bored with all subtle thinking, or which are

more likely to bring a certain liveliness into the company, than one about the moral worth of this or that action from which the character of some person is to be made out. Those who otherwise find everything which is subtle and minute in theoretical questions dry and vexing soon take part when it is a question of the moral import of a good or bad act that is recounted; and they are exacting, meticulous, and subtle in excogitating everything which lessens or even casts suspicion on the purity of intention and thus on the degree of virtue to an extent we do not expect of them on any other subject of speculation' (CPrR, 159).

45. I have not included in this list the role human vices play in establishing the republican constitutions that regulate them, because it is clear that the idea of historical progress in political constitutions is distinct from those examples that concern the moral idea.

46. These are the terms used by Heidegger in 'The Age of the World Picture' to define humanism: 'Humanism, therefore, in the more strict historiographical sense, is nothing but a moral-aesthetic anthropology.' In the same text he goes on to explain 'anthropology' in terms germane to Kant's systematisation of nature under the idea of an art for 'man's' 'final ends': as 'that philosophical interpretation of man which explains and evaluates whatever is, in its entirety, from the standpoint of man and in relation to man' (AWP, Appendix 10, 133).

47. The impasse of the moral problematic of aesthetic presentation is the following: a form may be given for adherence to a rule, but the motive for this adherence cannot take a form. In this light, moral education is indispensable for Kant because it forms the signs of an internal disposition by reference to the evidence of external compliance.

CHAPTER 3

1. Martin Heidegger, *Nietzsche: Volumes I and II, The Will to Power as Art, The Eternal Recurrence of the Same,* trans. David Farrell Krell (San Francisco: Harper and Row, 1979), 100–111.

2. In 'The Word of Nietzsche: "God Is Dead" ' Heidegger describes reason as 'the most stiff-necked adversary of thought,' in *The Question Concerning Technology and Other Essays,* trans. W. Lovitt (New York: Harper and Row, 1977), 112.

3. The 'persistent confusion' of beings and being 'must be considered an event and not a mere mistake.' Martin Heidegger, 'Introduction to "What Is Metaphysics?" ' in *Pathmarks,* ed. William McNeill (Cambridge, UK: Cambridge University Press, 1998), 281.

4. This quoted expression is used by Heidegger in his 1936 Schelling lectures, later published as *Schelling's Treatise on the Essence of Human Freedom,* trans. Joan Stambaugh (Athens: Ohio University Press, 1985), 11 (hereafter cited as SB), but describes, I believe, the general terms for his inquiry into the ground of our history in which he hopes to disclose 'our simple relations' to 'what is.' In 'The Age

of the World Picture' (hereafter cited as AWP), in *The Question Concerning Technology*, Heidegger argues that the current world view needs and uses philosophical erudition but it does not require philosophy 'since, as world view, it has already taken over a particular interpretation and structuring of whatever is' (AWP, 140).

5. Heidegger, 'The Way to Language,' in *On the Way to Language*, trans. Joan Stambaugh (San Francisco: Harper and Row, 1982), 127.

6. Heidegger, *Schelling's Treatise on the Essence of Human Freedom*, 75–76; 'Letter on "Humanism"' in *Pathmarks*, 250.

7. Heidegger notes that this 'end of philosophy' is also the 'transition to another beginning' for 'thinking' in Martin Heidegger, *The End of Philosophy*, trans. Joan Stambaugh (London: Souvenir Press, 1975), 96.

8. Otto Pöggeler, *Martin Heidegger's Path of Thinking*, trans. Daniel Magurshak and Sigmund Barber (Atlantic Highlands, NJ: Humanities Press International, 1987), 2, his italics.

9. Jean Grondin, 'Prolegomena to an Understanding of Heidegger's Turn,' trans. Gail Soffer, *Heidegger and the Political* (Graduate Faculty Philosophy Journal, New School for Social Research) 14, nos. 1, 2, and 5 (1991): 95.

10. Grondin, 'Prolegomena to an Understanding of Heidegger's Turn,' his italics, 86.

11. Ibid., 92.

12. Joan Stambaugh also confirms the precepts of this thesis of continuity. See, among other places, the 'Introduction' to her translation of Heidegger's "Time and Being' in *On Time and Being* (New York: Harper and Row, 1972): 'the road from *Being and Time* to "Time and Being" is too subtle and too complex to speak of a mere reversal of the concepts of Being and time. For in the later lecture these "concepts" have undergone a profound change without, however, relinquishing their initial fundamental intention,' vii.

13. Heidegger's lecture 'The End of Philosophy' is instructive on this topic. *The End of Philosophy*, trans. Joan Stambaugh (London: Souvenir Press, 1975). See too 'Time and Being,' in which Heidegger acknowledges the extent of the revision of the project of *Being and Time* but describes it as a 'repeating' of the 'whole analytic of Dasein' 'in a completely different way' in *On Time and Being*, 32. Other notable discussions of this topic in Heidegger occur in his 'Letter on "Humanism"' and the lecture 'What Is Metaphysics?' in *Pathmarks*, 91, 277.

14. Martin Heidegger, 'The Origin of the Work of Art' in *Poetry, Language, Thought*, trans. Albert Hofstadter (New York: Harper and Row, 1971) 17–78. Hereafter cited as OWA.

15. In his 1949 'Introduction to "What Is Metaphysics,"' Heidegger writes, 'In fact, the attempt to recall the truth of Being, as a going back into the ground of metaphysics, has already left the realm of all ontology with its very first step' (*Pathmarks*, 289).

16. Jacques Derrida has drawn attention to the aporia of epochal thinking. In an essay on Foucault he writes: 'the transcendental condition of a series is also, paradoxically, a part of that series, creating aporias for the constitution of any set or whole [*ensemble*], particularly, of any historical configuration (age, *episteme*, paradigm, *themata*, epoch, and so on). These aporias are anything but accidental impasses that one should try to force at all cost into received theoretical models. The putting to the test of these aporias is also the chance of thinking.' Jacques Derrida, 'To Do Justice To Freud: The History of Madness in the Age of Pyschoanalysis,' in *Foucault and His Interlocutors*, ed. Arnold I. Davidson (Chicago and London: University of Chicago Press, 1997), 65.

17. This is clearly an interpretation Heidegger would disagree with. In his 'Letter on "Humanism"' he makes a number of points that consolidate the claims by his influential interpreters that his thinking needs to be understood in terms of the continuity of a 'path.' Accordingly, his discussion of *Being and Time* in this essay refers among other topics to the distinction between the discussion of human experience in its temporal mode of existence (*Dasein*) and anthropology. This claim regarding the distance marked by *Being and Time* to any anthropology is also made explicitly in 'What is Metaphysics?,' *Pathmarks*, and the 1941 lectures on Schelling published as an appendix to *Schelling's Treatise on the Essence of Human Freedom*, trans. Joan Stambaugh (Athens: Ohio University Press, 1985), 187.

18. See 'What Is Metaphysics?,' 'Postscript to What Is Metaphysics?' and 'Letter on "Humanism"' in *Pathmarks*, ed. William McNeill, (Cambridge, UK: Cambridge University Press, 1998), 82–97, 231–77.

19. Heidegger uses '*es gibt*' to avoid the locution 'being is': ' "is" is commonly said of some thing that is. We call such a thing a being. But being "is" precisely not "a being."' *What Is Called Thinking*, trans. J. Glenn Gray (New York: Harper and Row, 1968), 255. Hereafter cited as WIT.

20. OWA, 32.

21. I will discuss some of the representative approaches to this topic in the next chapter. Krzysztof Ziarek's work on Heidegger is exemplary of the reflection on the relation of art and technology that I have in mind here.

22. After *Being and Time* Heidegger leaves behind the phenomenological *method*, understood in broad terms as the reduction of experience to its constitutive features, but retains the phenomenological *attitude* with its emphasis on the primacy of a noncalculative experience as the ground of philosophical investigation.

23. Joan Stambaugh's introductions to her translations of Heidegger's *The End of Philosophy* (London: Souvenir Press, 1975), *Identity and Difference* (New York: Harper and Row, 1969), and *On Time and Being* (New York: Harper and Row, 1972), each give succinct accounts of the relevance of the original project of *Being and Time* for his later writings.

24. KB, xvii.

25. KB, 150–51.

26. Christopher Fynsk has argued that Heidegger often refused 'certain dimensions of the thought of those to whom he turns in his interpretative encounters.' He notes, in particular, that 'Heidegger failed to recognize in his *Kantbuch* (and, in some ways, throughout his career) just how unsettling his meditation on the finitude of Being and of thought might be. He points to this fact himself when he remarks much later (in 1956) that he has been unable to find a satisfactory answer to the problem of finitude.' Fynsk refers here to Heidegger's 1956 'Addendum' to 'The Origin of the Work of Art.' Christopher Fynsk, *Heidegger: Thought and Historicity* (Ithaca, NY and London: Cornell University Press, 1986), 17.

27. KB, 24–25.

28. Both Pöggeler and Grondin have raised the question of Kant's significance for Heidegger. Pöggeler is explicit in denying Kant a positive role in the 'path' of Heidegger's thinking (Otto Pöggeler, *Martin Heidegger's Path of Thinking*, 167–69). Grondin provides a more generous appraisal of Kant's significance, noting that in the period of the *Kehre* (i.e., around 1928 when the term first appears in his work) Heidegger thought 'above all' about Kant (Jean Grondin, *Le tournant dans la pensée de Martin Heidegger,* Paris: PUF, 1987, 125). However, Grondin, like Pöggeler, treats the status of finitude in Kant without linking it to the definitive problem of presentation that, I believe, explains Kant's full significance for Heidegger.

29. Heidegger mentions that the third *Critique* reworks the transcendental imagination but does not expand on this point: KB, §31 [161–62], 113.

30. The other significant works between the Kant book and the lectures on Schelling are Heidegger's *The Fundamental Concepts of Metaphysics: World, Finitude, Solitude,* trans. W. McNeill and N. Walker (Bloomington and Indianapolis: Indiana University Press, 1995), hereafter cited as FCM, and 'What Is Metaphysics?' in *Pathmarks,* 82–97. Both link Kantian philosophising to the questioning of the Greeks.

31. There are many references of this type by Heidegger. Among them is his reference to Kant in FCM as 'for the first time' (FCM, 45), bringing a halt to the integration of ancient philosophy into dogma and establishing again a 'proper questioning.' It is this quality in Kant that requires us to free ourselves from the nineteenth-century interpretation of Kant and get at 'Kantian philosophising' (FCM, 45).

32. This repetition has the force of a double reading: Heidegger drags Kant's 'unspoken "presuppositions"' (such as finitude) to 'the character of decisive problems' rather than bland statements of fact (KB, 153).

33. In his lectures on Schelling Heidegger credits Kant with returning to the 'fundamental meaning of the primary philosophical concepts of the

Greeks' (SB, 37). In the Kant book Heidegger testifies to this philosophising attunement in his description of Kant's *Critique of Pure Reason* as the 'first express ground-laying for metaphysics' (KB, 191) in which Kant pursues an ontology that seeks 'a theory of Being in general, without assuming Objects which were given' (KB, 196). This attribution of a 'fundamental ontology' to Kant depends on the hermeneutics crucial to Heidegger's later works where he questions what has not been said instead of 'writing in a fixed way about what Kant said' (KB, 175). It is this distinction between what has and has not been said in Kant's texts that also introduces the qualification to the compliment regarding Kant's 'authentic philosophising' (KB, 150): for Kant returned 'back to the fundamental meaning of the primary philosophical concepts of the Greeks' but did so unreflectively, or as Heidegger puts it in another text, 'with the certainty of a sleepwalker [or] better, by dint of the genuine philosophical instinctive relationship' (SB, 37).

34. Amongst the different terms used by Heidegger to describe the topography of the modern philosophical understanding of being, three have particular significance for his approach to the topic of presentation: 'system' (names all beings as being), 'will' (resentment against time and its irreversibility), and the 'absolute.' Each of these terms is related to grounding, but in the last case this is so to a greater extent.

35. Although I will treat these couples together for my purposes here, it is important to note that they are not equivalent for Heidegger (see his book *The End of Philosophy*).

36. Martin Heidegger, 'Metaphysics as History of Being,' in *The End of Philosophy,* trans. Joan Stambaugh (London: Souvenir Press, 1975), 11.

37. Martin Heidegger, 'The Turning,' in *The Question Concerning Technology and Other Essays,* trans. W. Lovitt (New York: Harper and Row, 1977), 36–53.

38. Martin Heidegger, *An Introduction to Metaphysics,* trans. R. Manheim (New Haven, CT: Yale University Press, 1959), 194. Hereafter cited as IM.

39. Heidegger's commentary on Plato in 'Plato's Doctrine of Truth,' *Pathmarks,* 155–83, deals with a similar collection of themes: 'the things that are visible in the daylight outside the cave, where sight is free to look at everything, are a concrete illustration of the "ideas." According to Plato, if people did not have these "ideas" in view, that is to say, the respective "appearance" of things—living beings, humans, numbers, gods—they would never be able to perceive this or that as a house, as a tree, as a god. Usually they think they see this house and that tree directly, and the same with every being. Generally they never suspect that it is always and only in the light of the "ideas" that they see everything that passes so easily and familiarly for the "real." According to Plato, what they presume to be exclusively and properly the real—what they can immediately see, hear, grasp, compute—always remains a mere adumbration of the idea, and consequently a shadow.'

40. It is worth recalling that the discussion of this topic in Lacoue-Labarthe and Nancy's *The Literary Absolute* draws on the terms developed in Heidegger's Schelling book. I will discuss this point in further detail in Chapter 5. Tzvetan Todorov also discusses the heuristic feature of the Kantian ideas in his *Theories of the Symbol*, trans. Catherine Porter (Ithaca, NY: Cornell University Press, 1982) 206–208.

41. He also makes occasional references to Leibniz in this respect: SB, 34, and in 'The Word of Nietzsche: "God Is Dead," ' in *The Question Concerning Technology and Other Essays*, trans. W. Lovitt (New York: Harper and Row, 1977), 90.

42. AWP, 140. Here again Heidegger contrasts the ineffectual form of 'mere Cartesian Scholasticism' which is unable to 'shape modern times' with the metaphysics that 'begins the completion and consummation' of the West in Descartes. See also Jacques Taminiaux's discussion of Heidegger's reading of Descartes in which he emphasises the connections in 'Heidegger's eyes' between Nietzsche and Descartes, 'On a double reading of Descartes,' *Heidegger and the Project of Fundamental Ontology*, trans. and ed. Michael Gendre (Albany: State University of New York Press, 1991), 161–75, 166.

43. Heidegger, 'The Word of Nietzsche: "God Is Dead," ' in *The Question Concerning Technology and Other Essays*, 112.

44. See Heidegger's discussion of how the apparent simplicity of Nietzsche's renunciation of system is disingenuous (SB, 24).

45. Heidegger, 'The Word of Nietzsche: "God Is Dead," ' in *The Question Concerning Technology and Other Essays*, 84.

46. Heidegger consistently makes the point in the works of the early 1930s as well as in his Kant book that it is in Kant that one finds 'authentic philosophising.' This compliment distinguishes Kant from all the moderns, including Nietzsche, who confirms the core of modern representation as a willing. See, for instance, KB, 150.

47. For Heidegger, we can say the anthropology from which he increasingly distances himself after *Being and Time* is a mirror reversal of the anthropological turn in Kant. Heidegger's Kant book, further, documents this latter turn as an intimate feature of Kant's faith in reason through which his insight into the priority of presentation over reason's ideas is suppressed (KB, 118). Kant does not critique reason's ideas but assumes them as given (SB, 38). This criticism of Kant develops the complaint against Kant in Heidegger's Kant book: the role of the understanding in the schematism does not just usurp the imagination and ground time in the subject, but in so doing the schematism provides superficial and easy answers to the question of how beings are given. In Kant's description of the categorical structure of experience he presupposes the forming structure of the categories and provides in advance, as it were, the answer to the question of fundamental ontology. All of this indicates that within his account of modern metaphysics on the

question of presentation, Heidegger is profoundly ambiguous in the exceptional status he attributes to Kant. The attempt to exhaust the intelligibility of being as if it were a 'ground' or 'thing' at the disposal of human calculation which defines modern metaphysics is an impulse one may detect in Kant. On the other hand, if, as Heidegger suggests, Kant is to be distinguished from the process of the completion of this impulse in the German Idealists, what importance can we attach to the evidence of Kant's reticence in the A version of the *Critique of Pure Reason* towards the project for the intelligibility of being?

48. I have already mentioned the comments of Pöggeler, Grondin, and Stambaugh on this topic. There are many commentators who share this emphasis on the constancy of Heidegger's thinking. It is worth mentioning in this context Reiner Schürmann's examination of the concept of the turning in relation to the question 'what is to be done?' in his *Heidegger on Being and Acting: From Principles to Anarchy,* trans. Christine-Marie Gros (Bloomington and Indianapolis: Indiana University Press, 1987), 32.

49. See Dominique Janicaud's discussion of Heidegger's destinal historicism in *The Shadow of That Thought: Heidegger and the Question of Politics,* trans. Michael Gendre (Evanston, IL: Northwestern University Press, 1996), 69–81: 'One of the most remarkable paradoxes of the Heideggerian reinterpretation of Western history as the history of Being is that, while pretending not to be Hegelian (because it does not recognize anything like a transcendent rational necessity), this reinterpretation ends up admitting necessity or a destinal "inevitability." And this necessity is just as intractable as the judgment from the tribunal of Universal Reason,' 75.

50. See also his remarks on Plato's *eidos*, which adopts this same perspective, in 'Plato's Doctrine of Truth,' *Pathmarks*.

51. David Farrell Krell's book *Intimations of Mortality: Time, Truth, and Finitude in Heidegger's Thinking of Being* (University Park and London: Pennsylvania State University Press, 1986) argues 'that a single *Grunderfahrung* or "fundamental experience" underlies Heidegger's work from *Being and Time* through all the later writings' (ix). Krell thus uses the concept of experience to testify to the constancy of Heidegger's thinking. I would like to differentiate the perspectives of a fundamental experience that 'grips' the thinker in texts like FCM from the references to undergoing an experience with language [*mit der Sprache eine Erfahrung machen*] in essays like 'The Nature of Language,' in *On the Way to Language,* 57.

52. This position was most strikingly formulated in FCM. It is this existential feature of Heidegger's thinking that drew students to his lecture courses. I will discuss FCM in the context of my discussion of Lacoue-Labarthe's critique of Heidegger's politics in Chapter 5.

53. What Heidegger describes as a comportment of *Gelassenheit.* See his *Discourse on Thinking: A Translation of Gelassenheit,* trans. John M. Anderson and E. Hans Freund (San Francisco: Harper and Row, 1966), 54–55.

CHAPTER 4

1. In *The Fate of Art: Aesthetic Alienation from Kant to Derrida and Adorno* (Cambridge, UK: Polity Press, 1992), Jay Bernstein emphasises that Heidegger's comments on technology and *poiesis* are ambiguous. For Bernstein, Heidegger's claim that *Gestell* 'drives out' and 'blocks *poiesis*' could mean either that *Gestell* 'as a mode of revealing is the only one such whose very nature itself involves a refusal of *poiesis*' or 'that because in its nature *Gestell* drives out *poiesis* it therefore, literally, banishes all other modes of revealing into non-existence' (Bernstein, *The Fate of Art*, 113). This distinction is crucial for understanding the link between art and technology in this essay because in the first case 'questioning would probe the way the centre holds sway' but in the second case it would only be possible to decentre the *Gestell* 'from the centre alone' and 'questioning would have to focus on how that decentring could take place' (Bernstein, *The Fate of Art*, 113–14). I will return to the ambiguous position Heidegger reserves for art in this essay in more detail in section 3 of this chapter.

2. Gianni Vattimo uses these terms in *The End of Modernity*, and they are echoed in Ziarek's *The Historicity of Experience*. For both Vattimo and Ziarek, Kant is the ghost behind the extra-aesthetical significance that art claims in Heidegger. Kant's conception of disinterested contemplation cuts art off from its ontological roots to define it 'as lacking any practical or cognitive points of reference' in its exclusive tie 'to a specific stance assumed by the observer' (Gianni Vattimo, *The End of Modernity: Nihilism and Hermeneutics in Post-modern Culture*, trans. Jon R. Snyder [Cambridge, UK: Polity Press, 1988], 122; see also Krzysztof Ziarek, *The Historicity of Experience: Modernity, the Avant-Garde and the Event* [Evanston, IL: Northwestern University Press, 2001], 88). Although one of the central themes in Kant's account of aesthetic judgment is that pure taste is exercised against the instrumentalism of use, whether of the cognitive interest that would determine an object's form according to its function or the more venal interests of personal ends, this potential affinity with Heidegger is lost precisely because Vattimo and Ziarek interpret Kant's doctrine of aesthetic disinterest as cutting off the ontological root that would allow this critique of instrumentalism to work outside the quarantined and therefore impotent 'cultural field.' In this regard, these authors do not just claim a continuous role for the art of criticism within the economy of Heidegger's thinking but exemplify the posture that, since Schiller's interpretation of Kant, sees the arts as the bearer of extra-aesthetical, political significance. This negative interpretation of Kant's influence on Heidegger can be contrasted with Heidegger's own positive account of the Kantian conception of aesthetic disinterest in his Nietzsche lectures (Martin Heidegger, *Nietzsche: Volumes I and II, The Will to Power as Art, The Eternal Recurrence of the Same*, trans. David Farrell Krell [San Francisco: Harper and Row, 1979], 110–11).

3. Krzysztof Ziarek, 'After Aesthetics: Heidegger and Benjamin on Art and Experience' *Philosophy Today*, 41, no. 1 (Spring 1997): 200.

4. Ibid., 201.

5. Ibid.

6. Ibid.

7. Ibid., 202.

8. Krzysztof Ziarek, 'Powers to Be: Art and Technology in Heidegger and Foucault,' *Research in Phenomenology,* 28 (1998): 179. See also for this use of the metaphor of the mirror to describe the relation between technology and art, Ziarek, 'After Aesthetics: Heidegger and Benjamin on Art and Experience,' 201: 'To the extent that it is poetic, a *poiesis,* art brings forth the obverse side of experience and its technological regimentation; it discloses the tain of the representational mirror, the other side of the metaphysical *Historie*–its "poetic" *Geschichte.*'

9. Kathleen Wright, 'The Place of the Work of Art in the Age of Technology,' *Southern Journal of Philosophy* 22, no. 1 (Spring 1984): 599.

10. Ibid., 580.

11. Miguel de Beistegui, *Thinking with Heidegger: Displacements* (Bloomington and Indianapolis: Indiana University Press, 2003), 154.

12. Ibid., 154

13. Ibid., 159

14. Ibid., 155 and 160.

15. Ibid., 159 and 167.

16. We can also cite here Bernard Stiegler's interpretation of art as the counter to technics in Heidegger's thinking of technology in his *Technics and Time, 1: The Fault of Epimetheus,* trans. Richard Beardsworth and George Collins (Stanford, CA: Stanford University Press, 1998), 9; and Giorgio Agamben's Heideggerian-styled critique of the fate of art under the aesthetic regime which calls for an exit from 'the swamp of aesthetics and technics' by post-aesthetic work. Giorgio Agamben, *The Man Without Content,* trans. Georgia Albert (Stanford, CA: Stanford University Press, 1999), 66–67.

17. Beistegui, *Thinking with Heidegger: Displacements,* 152–60 and Wright, 'The Place of the Work of Art in the Age of Technology,' 579ff. See also Heidegger's 'Origin of the Work of Art' in *Poetry, Language, Thought,* trans. Albert Hofstadter (New York: Harper and Row, 1971), 41–43, for the discussion of place in the case of the Greek temple. In contrast, Michel Haar's reading of Heidegger's account of technology and art retains their epochal distinction. On the one hand, Haar, like Vattimo and Ziarek, emphasises that Heidegger saves poetry from the contained position it has in formalist and materialist aesthetics (Michael Haar, *The Song of the Earth: Heidegger and the Grounds of the History of Being,* trans. Reginald Lilly [Bloomington and Indianapolis: Indiana University Press, 1993], 112), but on the other, he does not go on to name, as Wright has, poetry *as* the 'saving power' for the technological *Gestell,* but describes this 'saving power' in the nonart terms of appropriation (Haar, *The Song of the Earth: Heidegger and the Grounds of the History of Being,* 89). Dominique Janicaud is sceptical of Heidegger's homogenised

view of technological relations. Although he cites Heidegger's description of world in his 'Origin' essay to show the perforation points Heidegger's own thought gives for the *Gestell,* he also cites the event of appropriation in this regard (Dominique Janicaud, *Powers of the Rational: Science, Technology and the Future of Thought,* trans. Peg Birmingham and Elizabeth Birmingham [Bloomington and Indianapolis: Indiana University Press, 1994], 184). See also Robert Bernasconi's interpretation of the essay on technology as a continuation of 'The Origin of the Work of Art' lectures. Bernasconi, like Ziarek, emphasises the motive for Heidegger's turn to art for the meditation on technology in the technology essay as the 'proximity' or 'co-belonging' between art and technology, but also sustains the modal relation Heidegger takes to art's place that I will be emphasising here. See his 'The Greatness of the Work of Art,' 115; and for a critical inflection of the topic of place in the age of technology, 'The fate of the distinction between praxis and poiesis,' 16–17, both in Robert Bernasconi, *Heidegger in Question: The Art of Existing* (Atlantic Highlands, NJ: Humanities Press, 1993).

18. Martin Heidegger, *Identity and Difference,* trans. Joan Stambaugh (New York: Harper and Row, 1969), 38.

19. Heidegger praises Schelling in his Schelling lectures for placing the relation over entities, but the call he makes there for 'another beginning' is answered not in philosophy but in the thinking of technology. The references to technology in his late essays indicate that it is in technology that this epochal shift becomes possible. See his discussion of relationality in 'The Principle of Identity' in Heidegger, *Identity and Difference,* 23–42. See also Janicaud's discussion of these points in 'Heideggeriana,' in Dominique Janicaud and Jean-François Mattéi, *Heidegger from Metaphysics to Thought,* trans. Michael Gendre (Albany: State University of New York Press, 1995), 18–19.

20. See Bernasconi's systematic account of the different versions of this essay: 'The Greatness of the Work of Art' in *Heidegger in Question: The Art of Existing,* 99–117.

21. Martin Heidegger, 'Origin of the Work of Art' in *Poetry, Language, Thought,* trans. Albert Hofstadter (New York: Harper and Row, 1971), 24. Hereafter cited as OWA.

22. The 'translation of Greek names into Latin is in no way the innocent process it is considered to this day. Beneath the seemingly literal and thus faithful translation there is concealed, rather, a *trans*lation of Greek experience into a different way of thinking. *Roman thought takes over the Greek words without a corresponding, equally authentic experience of what they say, without the Greek word.* The rootlessness of Western thought begins with this translation' (OWA, 23, Heidegger's emphasis).

23. The exact quote here reads: 'all immediate experience of beings' (OWA, 31).

24. This essay contains a constant dialogue with his discussion of aesthetics in his Nietzsche lectures of the 1930s and particularly his defence of Kant in those

lectures. Hence he asks whether this 'most difficult of tasks' is so difficult because it is 'the opposite of the indifference that simply turns its back upon the being itself in favor of an unexamined concept of being? We ought to turn toward the being, think about it in regard to its being, but by means of this thinking at the same time let it rest upon itself in its very own being' (OWA, 31). It is this difficult task, misunderstood by Nietzsche and Schopenhaeur as 'indifference,' that Heidegger finds in the Kantian doctrine of aesthetic disinterest.

25. The critique of the status of the artwork as a mere 'example' in Heidegger is a common complaint in recent works on aesthetics; see, for instance, Andrew Benjamin's *Disclosing Spaces: On Painting* (Manchester, UK: Clinamen Press, 2004), 36, n.3, and Lacoue-Labarthe's comments on exemplification in *Heidegger, Art and Politics*. A sustained critique of Heidegger's treatment of artworks as subordinate avenues for the exemplification of philosophical theses is given in Jean-Marie Schaeffer's *Art of the Modern Age: Philosophy of Art from Kant to Heidegger*, trans. Steven Randall (Princeton, NJ: Princeton University Press, 2000): 'Instead of analysing the poem as it presents itself and instead of asking the questions its semantic structure makes it possible to ask, Heidegger postulates as a prior principle that it coincides with an overall structure of interpretation capable of bringing to light a coherent conception. He does not analyse the poem as it is, but as it would be if it were a successful transposition of the overall interpretation he proposes: "The text used for the present commentaries is based, after being revised in accord with the handwritten drafts, on the explication that we shall attempt," ' 270.

26. OWA, 36. He continues: 'This entity emerges into the unconcealedness of its being. The Greeks called the unconcealedness of beings *aletheia*. We say 'truth' and think little enough in using this word. If there occurs in the work a disclosure of a particular being, disclosing what and how it is, then there is here an occurring, a happening of truth at work' (OWA, 36).

27. OWA, 41. 'Refusal' may be understood as the structural way for things to be present such that their being is not fully exhausted in the way we relate to them; and 'dissembling' as when refusal is not given as a feature of the relation to what is, but in the epochal terms of dissemblance.

28. The quality of luminosity in the artwork underlines this interplay of concealing/unconcealing: 'Color shines and wants only to shine. When we analyse it in rational terms by measuring its wavelengths, it is gone' (OWA, 47).

29. 'Science is not an original happening of truth, but always the cultivation of a domain of truth already opened, specifically by apprehending and confirming that which shows itself to be possibly and necessarily correct within that field. When and insofar as a science passes beyond correctness and goes on to a truth, which means that it arrives at the essential disclosure of what is as such, it is philosophy' (OWA, 62).

30. Heidegger indeed moves from thinking *aletheia* in 'the Greek way' as unconcealing to think 'above and beyond' the Greeks *aletheia* as the opening of

self-concealing (Martin Heidegger, *On Time and Being,* trans. Joan Stambaugh [New York: Harper and Row, 1972], 71).

31. There are also two examples of poetry used by Heidegger to defeat the conception of art as an accurate depiction of a given thing, Hölderlin's hymn 'The Rhine' and C. F. Meyer's poem 'Roman Fountain' (OWA, 37). We will return to the example of the Hölderlin hymn in the next section.

32. In his Nietzsche lectures Heidegger follows Hegel's verdict that modern art is the decline of great art. By this we are not to understand that Hegel denied 'the possibility that also in the future individual works of art would originate and be esteemed. The fact of such individual works, which exist as works only for the enjoyment of a few sectors of the population, does not speak against Hegel but for him. It is proof that art has lost its power to be the absolute, has lost its absolute power' (*Nietzsche,* 85). In this respect Heidegger's criticisms of Wagner's project of a 'collective work of art' are instructive; see *Nietzsche,* 85 ff.

33. Martin Heidegger, 'The Question Concerning Technology,' in *The Question Concerning Technology and Other Essays,* trans. W. Lovitt (New York: Harper and Row, 1977), 14. Hereafter cited as QCT.

34. QCT, 11. In this account I compress the complicated approach that Heidegger takes to setting out how *Gestell* is a *poiesis.* First of all Heidegger emphasises how technology is not a bringing-forth but a challenging (QCT, 14); then he qualifies that both *Gestell* and *poiesis* are forms of unconcealing (QCT, 21); that both have the character of destining (QCT, 29); and finally, that *Gestell* 'has its origin as a destining in bringing-forth. But at the same time Enframing, in a way characteristic of a destining, blocks *poiesis*' (QCT, 30). One of the important points of interrelation between this essay and the 'Origin' essay is the theme of truth as concealing/unconcealing. It is a striking feature of the essay on technology that the ordering-revealing threatens being with oblivion because it drives out the concealing action of the earth. The gesture to the 'saving power' of art as the intensifying mystery that counters the revealing of technology is not supported by the necessary account of how art plays, or can *continue* to play, this role. The epochal conception of being in Heidegger requires that we look elsewhere than art for a 'saving power.'

35. In this respect Heidegger takes the claims of technology more seriously than many of the advocates of the radicalism of the revolution in the hard sciences in the twentieth century. Bachelard's polemic against phenomenology as an 'epistemological obstacle' for the understanding of contemporary scientific practice rests on the fact that the 'object' of science is no longer a given but a product of scientific procedures and experimentation. The primacy Bachelard gives to experimentation over the 'given' is affirmed by Heidegger as the general principle under which the technological *Gestell* operates. Heidegger attaches to this insight the question as to why the scientific revolution and the techno-scientific *Gestell* installed by it happened only in the West. It is this question that allows Heideg-

ger to deepen Bachelard's defence of scientific practice against the philosophical movements, particularly phenomenology, which are unable to understand the constructed nature of the new scientific objects. Heidegger links his account of technology to a specifically historical reflection in which being is understood as a destining. This reflection is guided by his thinking of the event (*Ereignis*) which, to say the least, tries to think the radical contingency of history with its having the character of a destining, a path that is compelled by the historical occurrence of the question of being. This destining does not mean 'the inevitableness of an unalterable course' (QCT, 25), where technology would be 'the fate of our age.' Rather the essence of technology 'starts man upon the way of that revealing through which the real everywhere, more or less distinctly, becomes standing-reserve,' (QCT, 24) but this destining (which is the relation of presentation in which the 'real everywhere' is reduced to standing-reserve) is also an 'open space,' which calls for a reflective relation to this relation of presentation (QCT, 25–26). In stark contrast to Bachelard, then, Heidegger reintroduces the history of philosophy as an explanatory guide for the revolution that, as he concurs with Bachelard, substitutes for classical notions of a given order of experience radically new relations of presentation. These relations are historicised as contingent, singular forms of presentation that are also the historical outcome of a particular destining of being. It is this aspect of Heidegger's thinking which reserves a fundamental and crucial place for the task of a rigorous rethinking of the history of philosophy, and especially the original distortion of metaphysics with the Greeks. In this context, interpreting Heidegger's later texts as if they were poetry suppresses precisely this thread that, in Pöggeler's words, connects 'Heidegger to time-based philosophical issues' (Otto Pöggeler, *The Paths of Heidegger's Life and Thought,* trans. John Bailiff [Atlantic Highlands, NJ: Humanities Press, 1997], 113).

36. It is important to note the complex threads involved in Heidegger's remarks on technology. The description of technology as a Janus-head allows him to keep in play the side of technology as a challenging-revealing (according to which '*poiesis*' also embraces technological revealing as bringing-forth) with the side that adopts a 'mere ordering relation' to what is. The double-sided nature of the account of technology allows Heidegger to use the impetus of the threat of mere ordering to argue for the reflective relation to technological relations.

37. Heidegger, *Identity and Difference,* 49.

38. Ibid., 51.

39. Ibid., 51–52, his emphasis.

40. Ibid., 72.

41. Ibid., 37.

42. Ibid.

43. 'The forester who, in the wood, measures the felled timber and to all appearances walks the same forest path in the same way as did his grandfather is today commanded by profit-making in the lumber industry, whether he knows it or

not. He is made subordinate to the orderability of cellulose, which for its part is challenged forth by the need for paper, which is then delivered to newspapers and illustrated magazines. The latter, in their turn, set public opinion to swallowing what is printed, so that a set configuration of opinion becomes available on demand' (QCT, 18).

44. Heidegger, *On Time and Being,* 53.

45. As Jay Bernstein comments, this use of Hölderlin's poem is an aesthetic use of art: 'Of course, Heidegger can read a poet like Hölderlin and find in him a *representation* of the contrast between an age in which the gods were still active and our age in which they have fled, a contrast between a dwelling place and abstract space, between unconcealment and truth, but in so far as these or analogous accounts are offered art remains aesthetic: an imaginative projection of other possibilities of thinking experience' (Bernstein, *The Fate of Art,* 115, his emphasis). Bernstein is critical of what he calls Heidegger's 'agnosticism' regarding art's critical capacity. This criticism is motivated by the loss entailed by Heidegger's departure from the earlier extra-aesthetical work of the artwork in the 'Origin' essay. In effect, Bernstein wishes to sustain art in the role of an interrogative alternative to technical, progressive culture. To make up the gap between this work of the artwork and Heidegger's later account of technology, he turns away from Heidegger to Adorno. My argument here endorses Bernstein's interpretation of the place of art in Heidegger. However, unlike Bernstein, I hope to show that when art is given the role of a counterforce to technical, progressive culture, it is thereby overburdened. In the context of interpretation that substitutes Heidegger's agnosticism for faith in art, it is worth recalling how Heidegger identifies in Nietzsche the pursuit of art as a countermovement to nihilism (*Nietzsche,* 90) and saw in this pursuit the fallacy of a commitment to 'values.' Given the complexity of Heidegger's relation to Nietzsche and his own desire for a 'new beginning,' that is, the very beginning Nietzsche was unable to provide, defenders of the thesis of art's exceptionalism in Heidegger need to show why he would uncritically return to this past project.

46. Heidegger had hoped to fulfil this project in a new addition to the 'Origin' essay in which the works of Paul Klee were to be discussed. For an account of the sources of this uncompleted addition, see Otto Pöggeler's *The Paths of Heidegger's Life and Thought,* trans. John Bailiff (Atlantic Highlands, NJ: Humanities Press International, 1997), 208–9.

47. There is much that could be said concerning Heidegger's understanding of technology and its relation to movements critical of the classical philosophy of science. Where he stands out from the innovative approach to the philosophy of science taken by thinkers such as Gaston Bachelard is that these exponents of a radical new break in the practice and conceptual basis of twentieth-century science would be seen by Heidegger to forget the groundlessness of any science. Hence even while Heidegger does understand the fundamental alteration that twentieth-century mathematical physics makes to the category of the equipmen-

tal, he remains contemptuous (if this is not too strong a word) of the failure of scientific practice to understand the *Ab-grund,* our failure to reckon with the earth. Heidegger's polarity of world and earth is used to emphasise that we ultimately have no hold on things; that the way we present things does not hold onto their brute 'thereness.' It is outside the scope of this chapter to explore in what respect the 'fourfold' comes to replace the world-earth schema as the context of truth happening.

48. Heidegger, *Identity and Difference,* 38: 'The appropriation appropriates man and Being to their essential togetherness. In the frame, we glimpse a first, oppressing flash of the appropriation. The frame constitutes the active nature of the modern world of technology. In the frame we witness a *belonging* together of man and Being in which the letting belong first determines the manner of the "together" and its unity.' For this reason commentators like Pöggeler argue that the 'other beginning' Heidegger had sought in his own rethinking of the history of philosophy is now provided by technology. See Pöggeler, *The Paths of Heidegger's Life and Thought,* 109. He writes of this aspiration: 'In their way, the expectations that Heidegger aroused and gave voice to are as dead today as the deluded enthusiasms of 1968, which Heidegger contemptuously dismissed as crazed' (Pöggeler, *The Paths of Heidegger's Life and Thought,* 110).

49. The question that Heidegger's account of the *Gestell* raises can be put in the terms of the historical and experiential approaches to the question of being that I broached in the previous chapter; historically, the *Gestell* places art in a constellation of relations of presentation that is past, but it also asks how the articulation of the experience of technology is enabling for a saying of being.

50. Martin Heidegger, 'Technik und Kunst–Ge-stell,' in *Kunst und Technik,* ed. Walter Bienel and Fredrich-Wilhelm von Herrmann (Frankfurt: Klostermann, 1989), xiii–xiv.

51. Cf: Heidegger's characterisation of man's natural affinity to metaphysics in his *The Fundamental Concepts of Metaphysics: World, Finitude, Solitude,* trans. W. McNeill and N. Walker (Bloomington and Indianapolis: Indiana University Press, 1995). The precise terms of this rethinking of the question of Being as a problem of presentation can be followed, as I argued in the previous chapter, in Heidegger's Kant and Schelling books where Kant is praised for identifying the problem of thinking sensible intuition but also criticised for tying this problem to the presentation of ideas of reason. In his Schelling book, Heidegger criticises German Idealism and Romanticism for having suppressed the problem of presentation by subordinating sensible forms to the presentation of the pre-given absolute (Martin Heidegger, *Schelling's Treatise on the Essence of Human Freedom,* trans. Joan Stambaugh [Athens: Ohio University Press, 1985], 35). The historicisation of the question of the meaning of being needs to be seen in Heidegger's thinking as the attempt to think present things without the ground of an absolute (as in idealism) or ideas of reason (as in Kant).

52. Martin Heidegger, *What Is Called Thinking?*, trans. J. Glenn Gray (New York: Harper and Row, 1968). Cited as WIT.

53. Martin Heidegger, 'Plato's Doctrine of Truth,' in *Pathmarks,* ed. William McNeill (Cambridge, UK: Cambridge University Press, 1998), 154.

CHAPTER 5

1. Jacques Derrida, 'Introduction: Desistance,' in Philippe Lacoue-Labarthe, *Typography: Mimesis, Philosophy, Politics,* ed. Christopher Fynsk (Stanford, CA: Stanford University Press, 1998), 2, his emphasis.

2. Ibid., 3.

3. Ibid.

4. Let me just cite a few examples of this: In a recent interview with Philippe Lacoue-Labarthe, Peter Hallward touches a raw nerve when he asks, 'What does being Heideggerian mean to you today?' and later, Why did you 'decide to remain faithful to [Heidegger], up to a point?' (Philippe Lacoue-Labarthe and Peter Hallward, 'Stagings of Mimesis: An Interview,' *Angelaki: Journal of the Theoretical Humanities* 8, no. 2 [August 2003]: 57–72, 65 and 66). It is telling that Lacoue-Labarthe not only remarks in his response to Hallward that Walter Benjamin is an equal influence on his writing, and we may add one about whom he has none of the ambivalence that propels his frequent criticisms of Heidegger but also notes that 'Heideggerians' in France practice a religious devotion to Heidegger's writing that he finds repellant. 'Stagings of Mimesis: An Interview,' 65. Similarly, Lyotard accuses Lacoue-Labarthe of being too close to Heidegger to criticise his political involvement with National Socialism. See Jean-François Lyotard, *Heidegger and 'the jews,'* trans. Andreas Michel and Mark Roberts (Minneapolis and London: University of Minnesota Press, 1997). See also Simon Critchley's comments on Lacoue-Labarthe in *The Ethics of Deconstruction: Derrida and Levinas* (Oxford, UK: Blackwell, 1992), 203, and the more sympathetic remarks by Joan Brandt in *Geopoetics: The Politics of Mimesis in Poststructuralist French Poetry and Theory* (Stanford, CA: Stanford University Press, 1997), 195.

5. Derrida, 'Introduction: Desistance,' 7.

6. The quotes in this passage are all from Lacoue-Labarthe's interview with Peter Hallward in 'Stagings of Mimesis: An Interview,' 66.

7. Derrida, 'Introduction: Desistance,' 8.

8. Ibid., 21.

9. Ibid., 20–21. Despite Derrida's reticence here it is interesting that Lacoue-Labarthe tends to elide Heidegger's insight that the metaphysics of subjectivity is only modern metaphysics. Metaphysics from Plato to Descartes is not one of subjectivity in the standard sense: it does rely on the *subjectum* but not on a *subjectum* understood as the conscious subject.

10. Lacoue-Labarthe describes his difference from Nancy in the following words: 'Nancy . . . is a true philosopher, even in his style, while I am just an essayist—that is the great difference between us,' Philippe Lacoue-Labarthe and Peter Hallward, 'Stagings of Mimesis: An Interview,' 66. The reference to his 'passion' and 'vocation' for literature is from the same interview, 57.

11. Philippe Lacoue-Labarthe and Jean-Luc Nancy, *The Literary Absolute: The Theory of Literature in German Romanticism,* trans. Phillip Barnard and Cheryl Lester (Albany: State University of New York Press, 1988), 5. Hereafter cited as LA. For the Jena Romantics, literature operates the actualisation of human moral destiny in the same way that figures actualise, rather than present, a prior idea of, the genre of the human in modern politics. See Lacoue-Labarthe and Nancy's 'Opening Address to the Centre for Philosophical Research on the Political' in *Retreating the Political,* ed. Simon Sparks (London and New York: Routledge, 1997), 107–22.

12. This definition is taken up by Nancy who, as we will see in the next chapter, criticises the Romantics for transposing the philosophical attempt to appropriate the generativity of sense into the operation of the *poiesis* of sense in literature; in Jean-Luc Nancy, *The Sense of the World,* trans. Jeffrey S. Librett (Minneapolis: University of Minnesota Press, 1997), 162–63.

13. Romantic criticism reconstitutes the 'efficacity' of 'the formative process' (LA, 111): 'it opposes to . . . an idealism of manifestation another idealism . . . : the idealism of production, of the conditions of production and of the exhibition of the conditions of production' (LA, 111). The conception of 'literature' in Romanticism can be described as dualistic. There is a *poiesis,* a forming relation to an origin, that is the act of criticism. It is worth noting the influence on these formulations of Heidegger's *Schelling's Treatise on the Essence of Human Freedom* and specifically the critique of a moulding of experience by ideas that he describes there. *The Literary Absolute,* which references a great deal of its discussion to this text of Heidegger's, can be understood as a reflection on and extension of the theses explored in his text under the theme of 'Idealism' to the terrain of 'Romanticism.'

14. Friedrich Nietzsche, *Twilight of the Idols,* in *The Portable Nietzsche,* trans. Walter Kaufmann (New York: Penguin Books, 1976), no. 38, 472. Lacoue-Labarthe is critical of Heidegger for citing some of Nietzsche's remarks on 'the problem of the actor' but of not properly analysing them. He reads this as evidence of Heidegger sharing with Nietzsche an 'underground residue of Platonism.' See Lacoue-Labarthe, *Musica Ficta (Figures of Wagner),* trans. Felicia McCarren (Stanford, CA: Stanford University Press, 1994, 110–11.

15. Lacoue-Labarthe, *Musica Ficta,* 103. Lacoue-Labarthe explains this contradiction in terms of Heidegger's position on key Platonic theses regarding the arts. In a passage in his 'Origin of the Work of Art' lectures, Heidegger defends Greek tragedy but does so by endorsing the Platonic intolerance towards theatre. Greek tragedy, according to Lacoue-Labarthe's rephrasing of the terms of its consecration in Heidegger, 'has nothing to do with theatrical performance and

production, with the *mise-en-scène*, with the presentation on stage' ('Stagings of Mimesis,' 57). Heidegger's dislike of theatre is fuelled by an aversion to mimesis which theatre is taken to embody, and his anti-Platonic approval of tragedy does not just reinforce the Platonic prejudice against theatre, but in doing so also unquestioningly follows the founding opposition between the sensible and the intelligible that his path of thinking nonetheless wishes to call into question. It is interesting that in these passages Lacoue-Labarthe draws attention less to the way that Heidegger sees in theatre 'the presentation on stage' than to the fear of mimetic impropriety that such 'presentation' entails. I will return to the relation between mimesis and presentation in Lacoue-Labarthe's analysis of Heidegger's politics later in this chapter. Suffice it to note here that Lacoue-Labarthe argues that in displacing 'truth' to the field of sensuous forms, Heidegger sustains the traditional privilege of intelligible or full meaning over forms of sensible presentation, or in the terminology of mimesis, a locus of authenticity against the false and derivative effects of merely sensory experience.

16. Philippe Lacoue-Labarthe, 'Oedipus as Figure,' *Radical Philosophy* 118 (March/April 2003): 12.

17. Philippe Lacoue-Labarthe, 'Typography,' in *Typography: Mimesis, Philosophy, Politics*, ed. Christopher Fynsk (Stanford, CA: Stanford University Press, 1998), 127. Hereafter cited as TYP.

18. Lacoue-Labarthe's treatment of mimesis may be compared with Deleuze's discussion of the same topic in his Appendix on 'Plato and the Simulacrum' in *The Logic of Sense*, trans. Mark Lester with Charles Stivale, ed. Constantin V. Boundas (New York: Columbia University Press, 1990). There are a number of similarities in their critique of the logic of derivation from model to copy; however, Deleuze rallies to 'simulacra' as the term able to destroy the world of models and copies and complete the unsuccessful (Kant) or incomplete (Nietzsche) reversals of Platonism in modern philosophy, 253–66. From Lacoue-Labarthe's perspective, any thinking that finishes with mimesis reintroduces it in some other guise. See in this respect Jacques Rancière's discussion of the conception of the literary operation at work in Deleuze's call for the destruction of the world of models and copies in *The Flesh of Words: The Politics of Writing*, trans. Charlotte Mandell (Stanford, CA: Stanford University Press, 2004), 159. I will analyse the significance of Lacoue-Labarthe's interest in intractable topics like mimesis and presentation later in this chapter.

19. A lot more could be said regarding the status of fictioning in Lacoue-Labarthe's writing. I would like to briefly draw attention in this note to the labile historical framework that works through his analysis of the proximity of 'fiction' and 'truth' in philosophy. Although Lacoue-Labarthe notes that one of the historical effects of modern aesthetics is the poeticisation of discourse such that 'from Nietzsche to Valéry' there is an awareness that perhaps philosophy is only an 'aes-

thetic phenomenon,' this awareness is preceded by the stylistic concern for beautiful presentation (such as the dramatic form of Plato's dialogues) or in the use of poetic resources such as examples for 'demonstrative rigour' in the classics. Fictioning is integrated into the system 'of the most "primitive" philosophical oppositions (sensuous/intelligible, dark/clear, indistinct/distinct, particular/universal, improper/proper, imaginary/real, veil/unveiling), etc.' Philippe Lacoue-Labarthe, 'The Unpresentable,' in *The Subject of Philosophy,* ed. and trans. Thomas Tresize (Minneapolis: University of Minnesota Press, 1993), 150–53. The fact that we may cite exceptions to this subordination of fictioning within the canon, as in Aristotle's defence of the speculative truths of tragedy, only reinforces the general point Lacoue-Labarthe wishes to make. The opposition between fiction or more specifically the figure and the evidence of truth has never entailed a simple exclusion of fictioning from truth. Rather, there is an unsurpassable integration of fictioning within the philosophical conception of truth, and the question of the relations between fictioning and philosophy concerns how this integration is managed. Lacoue-Labarthe seems to think that the management strategy adopted by metaphysics is that of a splitting of fiction between the functions of error and revelation. In Plato and Rousseau, for instance, a 'good' fiction (the mythologies, respectively, of the noble gods or of civic religion) is used as a path to truth as well as a device to strengthen it. The 'bad' fictions of dramatic tragedy (Plato) or theatre (Rousseau) are an obstacle to truth. The important historical displacement of this split between error and revelation occurs when aesthetics fuses fictioning with truth *as* a veiling. Heidegger's lectures on the 'Origin of the Work of Art' present 'truth' in just this way. See Lacoue-Labarthe's discussion on these points in 'The Unpresentable,' and 'Sublime Truth.' The latter is published in Courtine's *Of the Sublime: Presence in Question,* trans. Jeffrey S. Librett (Albany: State University of New York Press, 1993), 96. Le Doeuff identifies a similar splitting mechanism at work in the operation of what she terms 'the philosophical imaginary.' In her account the split between the 'good' (an image deployed for the benefit of the uneducated recipient of the discourse) and 'bad' (the dependence of an argument or concept on an image for its meaning) defines the practice of the inclusive ('bad') exclusion ('good') of images in philosophical discourse. See Michèle Le Doeuff, *The Philosophical Imaginary,* trans. Colin Gordon (Stanford, CA: Stanford University Press, 1989), 3.

20. Of course these formulations are close to many of the prominent themes in Derrida's writing. See my discussion of the salient points of Derrida's influence on Lacoue-Labarthe's writing in Note 22.

21. I draw here on Lacoue-Labarthe's coauthored book with Nancy: *The Title of the Letter: A Reading of Lacan,* trans. François Raffoul and David Pettigrew (Albany: State University of New York Press, 1992), 142–43. In this book, originally published in France in 1975, the authors signal their interest in Heidegger's more

rigorous destabilisation of the 'origin' of identity. It is interesting to note, then, that in his essay 'Typography,' also published in 1975, Lacoue-Labarthe includes Heidegger amongst a group of thinkers, including Plato, Rousseau, and Girard, who fail to think through the problem of mimesis and who overlook therefore the fictive constitution of 'identity.'

22. Derrida describes the important distinction between a mimesis at the level of products and one at the level of acts in his essay 'Economimesis,' trans. Richard Klein, *Diacritics* 11 (1981): 3–25. Lacoue-Labarthe cites this work in a number of his essays, including 'Typography,' 'Oedipus as Figure,' and 'Sublime Truth.' The mimesis of an act refers to the mimetic logic that binds human production to the production of a god. In the *Critique of Judgment* this binding occurs in Kant's description of the free productions of the genius, and it occurs alongside the injunction he places against the imitation in fine art of the products of nature. Derrida's account of this contradictory treatment of mimesis in Kant focuses on the role of 'analogy' in the third *Critique* as a rhetorical mark of distinction between 'man's' productions and those of 'God,' and by this means he places in view the consequences of the post-Kantian speculative collapse of the dualism that, in Kant, attempts to guard against the confusion of ideas with experience. Lacoue-Labarthe, I think, adapts the feature of Derrida's critique of production in speculative philosophy as a mimesis of divine acts that moulds experience by ideas to his topic of the 'figure.' The figure has an ontological status. It is an 'inverted or reversed' idea (Lacoue-Labarthe, 'Oedipus as Figure,' 8) which operates a schematised meaning. Thus he draws attention to the secondary status of the idea, which is primarily aesthetic, but also to the 'virile' conception of shaping or forming experience through ideas in the speculative response to Kant. For an examination of the significance of Derrida's essay for his reflection on political topics, see my 'Historical Undecidability: The Kantian Background to Derrida's Politics,' *International Journal of Philosophical Studies* 12, no. 4 (December 2004): 375–93.

23. Philippe Lacoue-Labarthe, *Poetry as Experience*, trans. Andrea Tarnowski (Stanford, CA: Stanford University Press, 1999), 8. Hereafter cited as PEX. See on this topic 'La panique politique' in *Retreating the Political*, 1–32.

24. Philippe Lacoue-Labarthe and Jean-Luc Nancy, 'The Nazi Myth,' *Critical Inquiry* (Winter 1990): 298.

25. Lacoue-Labarthe and Hallward, 'Stagings of Mimesis: An Interview,' 58.

26. Cf. Heidegger's comment in his essay 'Plato's Doctrine of Truth,' 172–82, that the idea forced Being into oblivion; see also his 'On the Question of Being,' 303, in which he describes the *Gestell*/figure of the worker, and 'The Letter on Humanism,' 259 and 265. Each essay is published in English translation in Heidegger, *Pathmarks*, ed. William McNeill (Cambridge, UK: Cambridge University Press, 1998).

27. Philippe Lacoue-Labarthe, 'Transcendence Ends in Politics,' in *Typography: Mimesis, Philosophy, Politics,* ed. Christopher Fynsk (Stanford, CA: Stanford University Press, 1998), 300.

28. Among other treatments of the topic of the figure in philosophy we may cite Sarah Kofman's exemplary analysis of how different figures of 'Socrates' have functioned in the Western philosophical canon in *Socrate(s)* (Paris: Éditions Galilée, 1989).

29. In this respect it is possible to develop some points of contrast between Lacoue-Labarthe's approach to the topic of politics and the work of Michel Foucault. Foucault also treats this theme of the formative position of ideas with respect to materiality in modern politics. Unlike Lacoue-Labarthe, however, he does so from the perspective of the analysis of the historico-institutional constitution of knowledges (rather than 'Western metaphysics'). Further, as I will argue here, the perspective Lacoue-Labarthe takes on the topic of presentation makes it possible to see how the role of these ideas is primarily, in respect of their functioning and force as well as in the sense of temporal priority, aesthetic. In some sense, Foucault does also point out the importance of the aesthetic in the relation of the self to truth.

On the other hand, Foucault's analyses are more sensitive to the details of modern institutional operation and it is not clear whether his analysis of modern 'disciplines' has the status of a 'fiction' as Lacoue-Labarthe defines this term. See Foucault's discussion of 'power-knowledge relations' in *Discipline and Punish: The Birth of the Prison,* trans. Alan Sheridan (Harmondsworth: Peregrine, 1979), 27. See also Deleuze's discussion of the double meaning of form in this discussion: 'Form here can have two meanings: it forms or organizes matter; or it forms or finalizes functions and gives them aims. Not only the prison but the hospital, the school, the barracks and the workshop are formed matter. Punishment is a formalized function, as is care, education, training, or enforced work. The fact is that there is a kind of correspondence between them, even though the two forms are irreducible (in fact, care was not the function of the seventeenth-century hospital and the penal law in the eighteenth century does not refer essentially to prison). So how can we explain such a coadaptation? The reason lies in the fact that we can conceive of pure matter and pure functions, abstracting the forms which embody them,' Gilles Deleuze, *Foucault,* trans. and ed. Seán Hand (Minneapolis and London: University of Minnesota Press, 1988), 33. In this account Deleuze draws attention to the lability that follows from the definition of the idea of form in Foucault, and in particular the way that his conception of form allows it to be shaped in its easy movement between and colonization by emerging institutional practices.

30. Lacoue-Labarthe's most recent discussion of Rousseau's conception of history is in his *Poétique de l'histoire* (Paris: Éditions Galilée, 2002).

31. Lacoue-Labarthe and Hallward, 'Stagings of Mimesis,' 59, my emphasis.

32. See Lacoue-Labarthe's discussion in 'The Unpresentable' where he discusses Hegel's aesthetics as anti-aesthetics, which attempt to sustain the classical dualism between truth and sensuousness against the aesthetic alteration of these terms, 153.

33. 'Once the *Daßeit* of the being is in play' and the shift from what-a-being is to that-it-is occurs, 'presentation as figuration becomes secondary.' Philippe Lacoue-Labarthe, 'Sublime Truth,' 96.

34. In his Nietzsche lectures, Heidegger discusses Plato's *Republic* in modern terms because he focuses not on the topic of the mimetic product (*Darstellung*) but on the installer (*Herstellung*) behind it. It is this focus, which Lacoue-Labarthe also finds in Heidegger's slippage from *Darstellung* to *Herstellung* as the vocabulary for the discussion of poiesis in his technology essay (TYP, 73) that 'immediately allows us to understand mimesis as a *fall*' (TYP, 82). Again the key contrast here is between *aletheia* (truth) that is installed or unveiled [*Unverstelltheit*] and mimesis as the movement of dis-installation. Against this contrast Lacoue-Labarthe argues for the analysis of the constitutive, indissociable relation of installation and dis-installation that is prior to truth (TYP, 129). Derrida has a useful discussion of these points in his essay 'Desistance,' 13 ff.

35. Lacoue-Labarthe and Hallward, 'Stagings of Mimesis,' 57; see too Lacoue-Labarthe, *Musica Ficta (Figures of Wagner)*.

36. Lacoue-Labarthe, *Musica Ficta*, 103.

37. See also Derrida's discussion of this topic in *Of Spirit: Heidegger and the Question of Being*, trans. Geoff Bennington and Rachel Bowlby (Chicago: University of Chicago Press, 1989).

38. Lacoue-Labarthe, 'Transcendence Ends in Politics,' 272.

39. This is the only political text that Heidegger did not disavow. Translated by Karsten Harries as 'The Self-Assertion of the German University,' *Review of Metaphysics* 38 (March 1985): 470–80.

40. See Dominique Janicaud, *The Shadow of That Thought: Heidegger and the Question of Politics*, trans. Michael Gendre (Evanston, IL: Northwestern University Press, 1996). Because I wish to focus on the topic of presentation, I have not discussed here the objections that could be made to Lacoue-Labarthe's reading of Heidegger nor the fact that in its approach it follows and expands on elements of Heidegger's own thinking.

41. Martin Heidegger, *Fundamental Concepts of Metaphysics: World, Finitude, Solitude,* trans. William McNeill and Nicholas Walker (Bloomington and Indianapolis: Indiana University Press, 1995), 9. Hereafter cited as FCM.

42. 'Philosophy has a meaning only as a human activity. *Its truth is essentially that of human Dasein,*' FCM, 19, Heidegger's emphasis.

43. 'No concept of the whole without the comprehending of philosophizing existence. Metaphysical thinking is comprehensive thinking in this double sense. It deals with the whole and it grips existence through and through' (FCM, 9).

44. Cf. Martin Heidegger, *Being and Time,* trans. John Macquarrie and Edward Robinson (Oxford, UK: Basil Blackwell, 1962), 294–95: 'As potentiality-for-Being, Dasein cannot outstrip the possibility of death. . . . Its existential possibility is based on the fact that Dasein is essentially disclosed to itself, and disclosed, indeed, as

ahead-of-itself. This item in the structure of care has its most primordial concretion in Being-towards-death. . . . [I]f Dasein exists, it has already been thrown into this possibility. Dasein does not, proximally and for the most part, have any explicit or even any theoretical knowledge of the fact that it has been delivered over to its death, and that death thus belongs to Being-in-the-world. Throwness into death reveals itself to Dasein in a more primordial and impressive manner in that state-of-mind which we have called "anxiety." Anxiety in the face of death is anxiety "in face of " that potentiality-for-Being which is one's ownmost, non-relational, and not to be outstripped. That in the face of which one has this anxiety is Being-in-the-world itself. That about which one has this anxiety is simply Dasein's potentiality-for-Being.'

45. Lacoue-Labarthe, 'Transcendence Ends in Politics,' 284.

46. Cf. Heidegger, *Being and Time,* 307: 'Being-towards-death is the anticipation of a potentiality-for-Being of that entity whose kind of Being is anticipation itself. In the anticipatory revealing of this potentiality-for-Being, Dasein discloses itself to itself as regards its uttermost possibility. But to project itself on its ownmost potentiality-for-Being means to be able to understand itself in the Being of the entity so revealed—namely, to exist. Anticipation turns out to be the possibility of understanding one's ownmost and uttermost potentiality-for-Being—that is to say, the possibility of authentic existence.'

47. Heidegger, *Being and Time,* 309.

48. Lacoue-Labarthe, 'Transcendence Ends in Politics,' 282.

49. Beyond this, we may ask: is not *Dasein* as a 'metaphysical' questioner modelled on the Greek philosopher? The 'Greek philosopher,' because of his historicity, is not reducible to a first figure or original model. He is a 'trace' as a figure.

50. Heidegger, cited in 'Transcendence Ends in Politics,' 281.

51. Ibid., 291.

52. Ibid., 299. Also in both cases, the relation to what is destined is not resignatory but marked by struggle and strife: 'Truth is understood by the Greeks as something stolen, something that must be torn from concealment in a confrontation in which precisely physis strives to conceal itself. Truth is innermost confrontation of the essence of man with the whole of beings themselves. . . . Man as such, insofar as he exists, in the logos tears physis, which strives to conceal itself, from concealment and thus brings beings to their truth.' And 'truth is a fate of the finitude of man.' FCM, 29 and 30.

53. The structure of 'repetition' in *Being and Time* and the way that it defines *Dasein*'s temporality could also be read in support of the plausibility of a mimetic reading of authenticity independently of the idea of historical mimesis. Cf. section 66, 382: 'if the variations of Being are to be Interpreted for everything of which we say, "It *is,*" we need an idea of Being in general, and this idea needs to have been adequately illuminated in advance. So long as this idea is one at which we have not yet arrived, then the temporal analysis of *Dasein,* even if we *repeat* it, will remain incomplete and fraught with obscurities' (Heidegger's emphasis and capitalisation).

54. See Martin Heidegger, *Nietzsche: Volumes I and II, The Will to Power as Art, The Eternal Recurrence of the Same,* trans. David Farrell Krell (San Francisco: Harper and Row, 1979), 104: 'Hölderlin contrasts "the holy pathos" and "the Occidental Junonian sobriety of representational skill" in the essence of the Greeks. The opposition is not to be understood as an indifferent historical finding. Rather, it becomes manifest to direct meditation on the destiny and determination of the German people. Here we must be satisfied with a mere reference, since Hölderlin's way of knowing could receive adequate definition only by means of an interpretation of his work. It is enough if we gather from the reference that the variously named conflict of the Dionysian and the Apollonian, of holy passion and sober representation, is a hidden stylistic law of the historical determination of the German people, and that one day we must find ourselves ready and able to give it shape. The opposition is not a formula with the help of which we should be content to describe "culture." By recognising this antagonism, Hölderlin and Nietzsche early on placed a question mark after the task of the German people to find their essence historically. Will we understand this cipher? One thing is certain: history will wreak vengeance on us if we do not.'

55. On the topic of this virile structure of identification see Lacoue-Labarthe's analysis of Heidegger's Nietzschean dislike of the passive, spectatorial 'feminine' in relation to his comments on orchestral music, *Musica Ficta (Figures of Wagner),* 105. Nietzsche describes the music of Rossini and Bizet as 'lightness, energy, the intensification of life, joy and the pride of standing-up-straight,' 'striding and dancing.' Wagner's music, in contrast, is unable to be converted to virile forming: it is, in Nietzsche's words, 'enervation, sleepiness and torpor, submission, being-penetrated,' *Musica Ficta (Figures of Wagner),* 111. Lacoue-Labarthe asks whether this 'very old, very profound, and very solid equivalence' between femininity and passive affect is perhaps also an 'indestructible equivalence.' In the same text Lacoue-Labarthe discusses the way that Heidegger's preference for virile styling is tied to the political project of bringing into form an 'authentic' political figure, 85–117.

56. Heidegger, *Nietzsche,* 79.

57. There is a discussion of *défaillance* in Lacoue-Labarthe's 'Il Faut' in *Modern Language Notes* 107 (1992): 421–40.

58. We may also cite Lacoue-Labarthe's short essay on Pasolini, *Pasolini, une improvisation: 'd'une sainteté* (Bordeaux: Pharmacie de Platon: W. Blake, 1995) and his book *Retrait de l'artiste, en deux personnes* (Lyon: MEM/Arte Facts: Frac Rhône-Alpes, 1985), both of which place the same emphasis on technique.

CHAPTER 6

1. Jean-Luc Nancy, 'Of Being Singular Plural.' In *Being Singular Plural,* trans. Robert D. Richardson and Anne E. O'Byrne (Stanford, CA: Stanford University Press, 2000), 93. Hereafter cited as BSP.

2. Cf. Lacoue-Labarthe and Nancy's discussion in 'The Nazi Myth,' *Critical Inquiry* (Winter 1990): 291–312, and BSP 21–22, 71–73.

3. I will come back to some of these points insofar as they are relevant for my own concerns in this chapter.

4. We might add that Nancy casts the very topic of meaning in aesthetic terms. Consider in this regard the way that Nancy describes the 'excess' of meaning as a question of the 'performance' that 'makes up . . . proper meaning.' The question of meaning, he thinks, needs to be approached in the terms of the 'theatrical' or 'musical' senses of the word '*interprétation*' 'as in playing or interpreting a role, or a sonata.' Jean-Luc Nancy, ' "Our World": An Interview with Peter Hallward,' *Angelaki: Journal of the Theoretical Humanities* 8, no. 2 (August 2003): 46.

5. Jean-Luc Nancy, *The Sense of the World,* trans. Jeffrey S. Librett (Minneapolis: University of Minnesota Press, 1997), 135. Hereafter cited as SW.

6. Jean-Luc Nancy, *The Gravity of Thought,* trans. François Raffoul and Gregory Recco (Atlantic Highlands, NJ: Humanities Press, 1997), 67. Hereafter cited as G.

7. Philippe Lacoue-Labarthe and Jean-Luc Nancy, *The Title of the Letter: A Reading of Lacan,* trans. François Raffoul and David Pettigrew (Albany: State University of New York Press, 1992), 126–27.

8. Literature that is capable of engendering itself (LA, 91). *The Literary Absolute* is an enormously influential work in studies on German Romanticism, but what should claim our attention in this work in the present context are the broader narratives that inform it: the history of modern philosophy as a suppression of the problem of presentation (Nancy and Heidegger), the critique of *poiesis* as the fashioning of a product that motivates Lacoue-Labarthe's later critique of Heidegger's politics, and Nancy's attempt to articulate against the romantic emphasis on *poiesis* the *praxis* of sense making as the key philosophical task of our times.

9. It would be interesting to compare the orientation of this critique of the Romantics with the analysis Helmut Müller-Sievers gives of the genealogy and function of epigenesis at the turn of the nineteenth century. See his *Self-Generation: Biology, Philosophy, and Literature Around 1800* (Stanford, CA: Stanford University Press, 1997).

10. In works such as *The Muses,* trans. Peggy Kamuf (Stanford, CA: Stanford University Press, 1996), hereafter cited as TM; *The Gravity of Thought,* trans. François Raffoul and Gregory Recco (Atlantic Highlands, NJ: Humanities Press, 1997), and *Sans commune mésure: image et texte dans l'art actuel* (Paris: Editions Lèo Scheer, 2002).

11. Jean-Luc Nancy, *The Experience of Freedom,* trans. Bridget McDonald (Stanford, CA: Stanford University Press, 1993), 9. Hereafter cited as EF.

12. Among the many works that advocate such a position, see Luc Ferry and Alain Renaut's essay 'Kant and Fichte' in *New French Thought: Political Philosophy,* trans. Franklin Philip, ed. Mark Lilla (Princeton, NJ: Princeton University Press, 1994), 74–81. See also François Raffoul's account of the motif of 'return' as Nancy deploys it in this work in his introduction to the English translation of *The Gravity of Thought.* Nancy makes this point in a number of early works including his 'Preface' to *Of the Sublime: Presence in Question,* essays by Jean-François Courtine et al., trans. Jeffrey S. Librett (Albany: State University of New York Press, 1993), and his introduction to *Who Comes after the Subject? Essays by Jean-Luc Nancy et. al.,* ed. Eduardo Cadava, Peter Connor, and Jean-Luc Nancy (New York: Routledge, 1991).

13. In 'Building Dwelling Thinking,' Heidegger describes and develops the Greek sense of limit *(peras)* 'not [as] that at which something stops but . . . that from which something *begins its presencing'* [*Wesen*]. In Martin Heidegger, *Poetry, Language, Thought,* trans. Albert Hofstadter (New York: Harper and Row, 1971): 154, his emphasis.

14. (G, 67, 81). '[O]ne cannot settle down on the limit, one cannot hold on there as one could hold to a system or order of signification. One must always let the limit present itself anew, and it always presents itself as new' (G, 67). We can contrast here Heidegger's use of *Gelassenheit* in the context of his view that metaphysics culminates in the 'will to will' with Nancy's use of this term in the context of his description of modern metaphysics as the 'will to presentation.'

15. (G, 23–24). Cf. 'The Sublime Offering' in *Of the Sublime: Presence in Question,* 25–53, which gives an earlier treatment of this topic from the specific perspective of the sublime.

16. See Jean-Christophe Bailly and Jean-Luc Nancy, *La comparution: politique à venir.* Paris: Bourgois, 1991, 53.

17. See BSP, *'not only must being-with-one-another not be understood starting from the presupposition of being-one, but on the contrary, being-one . . . can only be understood by starting from being-with-one-another.* That question which we still call a "question of social Being" must, in fact, constitute *the* ontological question' (BSP, 56–57; Nancy's italics).

18. Nancy's Introduction to *Who Comes after the Subject?* 1–8.

19. Nancy claims that 'there is no society without the spectacle because society is the spectacle of itself' (BSP, 67).

20. See also SW, 101–2, 109; BSP, 45–57.

21. Just as the 'idea of nature retains within itself the dominant theme of self-sufficiency, of self-organization, and of a process oriented toward an end state' (BSP, 53), so too ethnic, religious, and civic identities that pretend to a pure identity (whether as a past to be reclaimed or a future to be installed) exclude the dimension of co-appearance: 'A single being is a contradiction in terms. Such a being, which

would be its own foundation, origin, and intimacy, would be incapable of *Being*, in every sense that this expression can have here' (BSP, 12). Nonetheless the suppression of the shared nature of being, not as a given 'togetherness' but as 'being-together,' is the current geopolitical state of 'autistic multiplicity' for which 'Sarajevo' is the 'martyr-name' (BSP, xiii). See also Lacoue-Labarthe and Nancy's 'The "Retreat" of the Political' in *Retreating the Political,* ed. Simon Sparks (London: Routledge, 1997) in which political projects of identity are treated as ontological questions.

22. In contrast to the proliferation of identity politics, the operations of capital seem to confirm the precepts of Nancy's own ontology and its quasi-historical basis: with capital the grounding signification of the earlier systems of sense in the world has been fully lost, and its operations also demonstrate that there is no possible reappropriation of these past meanings. But Nancy argues that capital also violates 'what it exposes' because it reduces its exposure of co-appearance, or being-together to 'being-of-market-value' (BSP, 74). This violation can be understood in relation to its suppression of the core thesis of Nancy's ontology: according to Nancy, co-appearing, the singular coming-to-presence of plural singularities, is the 'being-singular-plural.' Being-singular-plural can be put in terms of Nancy's critique of Heidegger's order of ontological exposition: beings always come to presence in relation, but each constellation of coming to presence is unexchangeable, or singular. Thus, the originary feature of 'relationality' is plurality, and the coming to presence of sense in relation is always singular. According to the operations of capital, however, what is displayed is 'nothing other than the simultaneity of the singular (but the singular posing as the indifferent and interchangeable particularity of the unit of production) and the plural (itself posing as the system of commodity circulation). The "extortion of surplus-value" presupposes this concomitance between the "atomisation" of producers (of "subjects" reduced to being-productive) and a "reticulation" of profit (not as an equal redistribution, but as a concentration that is itself more and more complex and delocalised)' (BSP, 73).

Capital exposes the being-in-common that is without a prior or final value and the 'with' as the indissoluble link between singular-plural, but it turns against these opportunities for insight: capital resurrects in its model of production and exchange a false equivalence of 'singulars' (as commodity units are submitted to the false 'measure' of capital and subjects are reduced to producers measured in relation 'to being-productive') and a distribution of commodity circulation that takes the place of the common or shared feature of being. The operations of capital are the double sided, Janus-head of the ontology of co-appearance: the singular origins of being are revealed but in such a way that they become exchangeable and are stripped of their singularity, and the plural web of communication in which essence is disappropriated, is reappropriated by capital into the concentrated and delocalised reticulation of profit. Cf. Nancy's Introduction to *Who Comes after the Subject?* 6.

23. Cf. Maurice Merleau-Ponty's account of 'the flesh' in *The Visible and the Invisible,* trans. Alphonso Lingis, ed. Claude Lefort (Evanston, IL: Northwestern University Press, 1968), especially Chapter 4, 'The Intertwining—The Chiasm,' 130–55. See also Derrida's book *Le toucher, Jean-Luc Nancy* (Paris: Éditions Galilée, 2000) for an account of the deconstructive work of 'touch' in Nancy. A short, early version of part of this book was published as '*Le Toucher:* Touch/to touch him,' trans. Peggy Kamuf, in *Paragraph* 16, no. 2 (1993): 122–57; see especially 143–45. See also Nancy's 'The Sublime Offering' in *Courtine,* trans. Librett, *Of the Sublime: Presence in Question,* 25–53 for an early formulation of the theme of 'touch' in relation to the topic of presentation in the systematisation of the sublime in philosophical aesthetics.

24. Heidegger is criticised for understanding the stone in 'abstract' terms; for Nancy 'the very compactness of its impenetrable hardness,' that is, its materiality, is what touches sense. See also the criticisms of Heidegger's references to the 'animal' by Derrida and Nancy in Nancy's interview with Derrida: 'Eating Well: Or the Calculation of the Subject,' in Nancy et. al., *Who Comes after the Subject?,* 111–12.

25. Nancy's ontology tries to sustain the role of philosophy to talk about beings in general without relying on the traditional vocabulary of depth and surface. As we have seen, his ontology looks at the contemporaneity of the relation of things, and suggests that sense as such does not emerge as the expression of an interior, but comes *to* presence from a sensible body. In keeping with the quasi-historical context he gives to his ontology, it is not surprising that Nancy turns to art as a paradigmatic form of a sense making that emerges from and at a material locus.

26. 'What counts in art, what makes art art . . . is access to the scattered origin in its very scattering; it is the plural touching of the singular origin. This is what "the imitation of nature" has always meant. Art always has to do with cosmogony, but it exposes cosmogony for what it is: necessarily plural, diffracted, discreet, a touch of color or tone, an agile turn of phrase or folded mass, a radiance, a scent, a song, or a suspended movement, exactly because it is the birth of a *world* (and not the construction of a system). A world is always as many worlds as it takes to make a world' (BSP, 14–15). Cf. Heidegger's history of the world concept in Heidegger, 'On the Essence of Ground,' *Pathmarks,* ed. William McNeill (Cambridge, UK: Cambridge University Press, 1998), 97–136.

27. This is a theme in early works like *The Experience of Freedom:* 'existence is actually in the world. What remains "to be done" is not situated on the register of *poiesis,* like a work whose schema would be given, but on the register of *praxis,* which "produces" only its own agent or actor and which would therefore more closely resemble the action of a schematization considered for itself' (EF, 31). However, the originary status he gives to affectability means that in some contexts

he tries to define sense making as 'another kind of "doing" altogether' to either *poiesis* or *praxis* (SW, 134). Such remarks need to be seen in the context of his reservations about the use of 'art' as a category within philosophy. I will discuss these reservations later in this chapter.

28. The art of today 'has finished being religious or philosophical art, as it has finished being (theologico) political art' (SW, 139). Instead of serving these latter ends 'art is open to [the] . . . fragmentation of sense that existence *is*' (SW, 139).

29. Art is 'a completion that limits itself to what it is, but that, to achieve that very thing, opens the possibility of another completion' (TM, 87). It is the paradox of a complete perfection that is structurally incomplete.

30. 'Art is a fragment: it is not the presentation of being, and thus it is not related to truth in the sense that philosophy would have liked' (SW, 137–38).

31. ' "Art" is merely that which takes as its theme and place the opening [*frayage*] of sense as such along sensuous surfaces' (SW, 135).

32. The French edition of this text includes photos taken by Nancy of someone identified as 'Georges.' The English edition, published under the title *The Gravity of Thought*, collects the text without the photos with a translation of Nancy's polemical text: 'The Forgetting of Philosophy' in *The Gravity of Thought*, first published as *L'oubli de la philosophie* (Paris: Éditions Galilée, 1986).

33. See also EF, 67: '*Mitsein*, being-with, is rigorously contemporaneous with *Dasein* and inscribed in it.'

34. François Raffoul, 'The Logic of the With: On Nancy's *Être Singulier Pluriel*,' *Studies in Practical Philosophy* 1, no. 1 (1999): 39.

35. Ibid., 40; see also Raffoul's 'On Otherness and Individuation in Heidegger,' *Man and World* 28 (1995): 341–58, where Raffoul reinterprets the place of the '*Mitsein*' in Heidegger.

36. Howard Caygill, 'The Shared World: Philosophy, Violence, Freedom,' in *The Sense of Philosophy: On Jean-Luc Nancy*, ed. Darren Sheppard, Simon Sparks, and Colin Thomas (London and New York: Routledge, 1997), 22.

37. Heidegger, OWA, 54.

38. This definition aims to straddle the classical opposition in philosophy of art between *poiesis* and reception in so far as *praxis* denotes affectability. Nancy describes figurative arts such as photography not in the vocabulary of images, but in terms of offering 'an access' (BSP, 14; see also the 'Weight of Thought' in *Gravity* and for a discussion of 'offering,' see the essay 'Sublime Offering' in *Of the Sublime: Presence in Question*). This access is an access to sense through affectability.

39. See Nancy's essay in *Sans commune mésure* and the following quote from *The Muses*: '*each time* it offers *perfection,* completion. Not perfection as final goal and term toward which one advances, but the perfection that has to do with the coming and the presentation of a single thing inasmuch as it is formed, inasmuch as it is completely conformed *entelechy,* to use a term from Aristotle that means "a

being completed in its end, perfect." Thus it is a perfection that is always *in progress,* but that admits no progression from one entelechy to another' (TM, 87).

CONCLUSION

1. See Peter Sloterdijk's discussion of 'ideologies of revitalization' and how they displace the 'thirst for religion,' in his *Critique of Cynical Reason,* trans. Michael Eldred, (Minneapolis and London: University of Minnesota Press, 1987), 285.

2. In critical theory, 'art' is often used to bestow meaning, in the emphatic sense of this term, on social life, perspectives, and practices. In general, the significance of art relates to the role art is given as a vehicle of insight into prevailing social relations. The 'referential ideality' of artworks here meets a pressing need of social criticism that would not otherwise be had. To cite only one influential example, Deleuze's definition of works of art as sensible aggregates and his attempt, particularly in his writing on literature, to de-sacralise this category by functional definitions of the material operations of literary language still, I think, move towards a Romantic conception of presentation as the sensuous embodiment of meaning. See for critical discussions of the use of art to puncture habit-bound schemas of experience in Deleuze's thought, Jacques Rancière's *The Flesh of Words: The Politics of Writing,* trans. Charlotte Mandell (Stanford, CA: Stanford University Press, 2004), 146–65, and 'Is There a Deleuzian Aesthetics?' *Qui Parle,* 14, no. 2: 1–14; and for a very brief account of Deleuze's approach to art as Romantic, Alain Badiou, *Handbook of Inaesthetics,* trans. Alberto Toscano (Stanford, CA: Stanford University Press, 2005), 11. It is in art that Deleuze finds the exemplary mode and practice of reorientation of habit-bound schemas and thus also a constellation of meaning in excess of prevailing material conditions. This use of art is intimately tied to his attempt to renew the semantic force of the category of 'art.' A succinct account of his definition of art can be found in Gilles Deleuze and Félix Guattari, *What Is Philosophy?,* trans. Hugh Tomlinson and Graham Burchell (New York: Columbia University Press, 1994) and of his approach to literary language in another book with Guattari, *Kafka: Toward a Minor Literature,* trans. Dana Polan (Minneapolis and London: University of Minnesota Press, 1986).

3. I take this term from Claus Offe's use of it in a quite different context in 'Bindings, Shackles, Brakes: On Self-Limitation Strategies,' in *Cultural-Political Interventions in the Unfinished Project of Enlightenment,* ed. Axel Honneth et al., trans. Barbara Fultner (Cambridge, MA: MIT Press, 1992), 88.

# Bibliography

Adorno, Theodor. *Aesthetic Theory*. Translated by R. Hullot-Kentor. Minneapolis: University of Minnesota Press, 1997.

Agamben, Giorgio. *The Man Without Content*. Translated by Georgia Albert. Stanford, CA: Stanford University Press, 1999.

Badiou, Alain. *Handbook of Inaesthetics*. Translated by Alberto Toscano. Stanford, CA: Stanford University Press, 2005.

Bailly, Jean-Christophe, and Jean-Luc Nancy. *La Comparution: politique à venir*. Paris: Bourgois, 1991.

Beistegui, Miguel de. *Thinking with Heidegger: Displacements*. Bloomington and Indianapolis: Indiana University Press, 2003.

Benjamin, Andrew. *Disclosing Spaces: On Painting*. Manchester, UK: Clinamen Press, 2004.

Bernasconi, Robert. *Heidegger in Question: The Art of Existing*. Atlantic Highlands, NJ: Humanities Press, 1993.

Bernstein, Jay. *The Fate of Art: Aesthetic Alienation from Kant to Derrida and Adorno*. Cambridge, UK: Polity Press, 1992.

Blumenberg, Hans. *The Legitimacy of the Modern Age*. Translated by Robert M. Wallace. Cambridge, MA: MIT Press, 1993.

———. *Work on Myth*. Translated by Robert Wallace. Cambridge, MA: MIT Press, 1990.

Böhrer, Karl Heinz. *Suddenness: On the Moment of Aesthetic Appearance*. Translated by Ruth Crowley. New York: Columbia University Press, 1994.

Bourdieu, Pierre. *Distinction: A Social Critique of Pure Taste*. Translated by Richard Nice. Cambridge, MA: Harvard University Press, 1984.

Bourgeois, Bernard. *Philosophie et droits de l'homme: de Kant à Marx*. Paris: PUF, 1990.

Brandt, Joan. *Geopoetics: The Politics of Mimesis in Poststructuralist French Poetry and Theory*. Stanford, CA: Stanford University Press, 1997.

Braudel, Fernand. *On History*. Translated by Sarah Matthews. Chicago: University of Chicago Press, 1980.

Caygill, Howard. *A Kant Dictionary.* Oxford, UK and Malden, MA: Blackwell, 1995.

————. 'The Shared World: Philosophy, Violence, Freedom.' In *The Sense of Philosophy: On Jean-Luc Nancy.* Edited by Darren Sheppard, Simon Sparks, and Colin Thomas. London and New York: Routledge, 1997.

Chalier, Catherine. *What Ought I to Do? Morality in Kant and Levinas.'* Translated by Jane Marie Todd. Ithaca, NY and London: Cornell University Press, 2002.

Cohen, Ted, and Paul Guyer, eds. *Essays in Kant's Aesthetics.* Chicago and London: University of Chicago Press, 1982.

Courtine, Jean-François. *Of the Sublime: Presence in Question,* essays by Jean-François Courtine et al. Translated by Jeffrey S. Librett. Albany: State University of New York Press, 1993.

Critchley, Simon. *The Ethics of Deconstruction: Derrida and Levinas.* Oxford, UK: Blackwell, 1992.

David-Ménard, Monique. *La folie dans la raison pure: Kant, lecteur de Swedenburg.* Paris: Librairie Philosophique J. Vrin, 1990.

————. 'Kant's "An Essay on the Maladies of the Mind" and Observations on the Feeling of the Beautiful and the Sublime.' Translated by Alison Ross, edited by Penelope Deutscher. *Hypatia* 15, no. 4 (Fall 2000): 82–98.

Debord, Guy. *Society of the Spectacle.* New York: Zone Books, 1994.

Deleuze, Gilles. 'Economimesis.' Translated by Richard Klein. *Diacritics* 11 (1981): 3–25.

————. *Essays Critical and Clinical.* Translated by Daniel W. Smith and Michael A. Greco. Minneapolis: University of Minnesota Press, 1997.

————. *Foucault.* Translated and edited by Seán Hand. Minneapolis and London: University of Minnesota Press, 1988.

————. *Kant's Critical Philosophy: The Doctrine of the Faculties.* Translated by Hugh Tomlinson and Barbara Habberjam. Minneapolis: University of Minnesota Press, 1990.

————. *The Logic of Sense.* Translated by Mark Lester with Charles Stivale. Edited by Constantin V. Boundas. New York: Columbia University Press, 1990.

Deleuze, Gilles, and Félix Guattari. *Kafka: Toward a Minor Literature.* Translated by Dana Polan. Minneapolis and London: University of Minnesota Press, 1986.

Derrida, Jacques. *Acts of Literature.* Edited by Derek Attridge. New York and London: Routledge, 1992: 38.

————. *Of Spirit: Heidegger and the Question of Being.* Translated by Geoff Bennington and Rachel Bowlby. Chicago: University of Chicago Press, 1989.

————. '"To Do Justice to Freud:" The History of Madness in the Age of Pyschoanalysis.' In *Foucault and His Interlocutors,* edited by Arnold I. Davidson. Chicago and London: University of Chicago Press, 1997: 57–97.

————. *Le Toucher, Jean-Luc Nancy.* Paris: Éditions, Galilée, 2000.

————. '*Le Toucher* Touch/to touch him.' Translated by Peggy Kamuf, in *Paragraph* 16, no. 2 (1993): 122–57.

————. *The Truth in Painting.* Translated by Geoffrey Bennington and Ian McLeod. Chicago and London: Chicago University Press, 1987.

————. *What Is Philosophy?* Translated by Hugh Tomlinson and Graham Burchell. New York: Columbia University Press, 1994.

Fenves, Peter. *Late Kant: Towards Another Law of the Earth.* New York and London: Routledge, 2003.

Ferry, Luc. *Political Philosophy, Vol. 2, The System of Philosophies of History.* Translated by Franklin Philip. Chicago and London: University of Chicago Press, 1992.

Ferry, Luc, and Alain Renaut. 'Kant and Fichte.' In *New French Thought: Political Philosophy.* Edited by Mark Lilla. Translated by Franklin Philip. Princeton, NJ: Princeton University Press, 1994.

Förster, Eckart. *Kant's Transcendental Deductions: The Three Critiques and the Opus Postumum.* Stanford, CA: Stanford University Press, 1989.

Foucault, Michel. *Discipline and Punish: The Birth of the Prison.* Translated by Alan Sheridan. Harmondsworth: Peregrine, 1979.

————. 'On the Archaeology of the Sciences: Response to the Epistemology Circle.' In *Aesthetics, Method and Epistemology: Essential Works of Foucault 1954–1984.* Vol. 2. Edited by James D. Faubion. Translated by Robert Hurley. New York: The New Press, 1998: 297–333.

Fynsk, Christopher. *Heidegger: Thought and Historicity.* Ithaca, NY and London: Cornell University Press, 1986.

Gasché, Rodolphe. *The Idea of Form: Rethinking Kant's Aesthetics.* Stanford, CA: Stanford University Press, 2003.

Grondin, Jean. *Kant and the Claims of Taste.* Cambridge, UK and London: Harvard University Press, 1989.

————. 'Prolegomena to an Understanding of Heidegger's Turn.' Translated by Gail Soffer. *Heidegger and the Political,* Graduate Faculty Philosophy Journal, New School for Social Research 14, no. 1–15 (1991): 85–109.

————. *Le tournant dans la pensée de Martin Heidegger.* Paris: PUF, 1987.

Guyer, Paul, ed. *The Cambridge Companion to Kant.* Cambridge, UK: Cambridge University Press, 1992.

Haar, Michel. *The Song of the Earth: Heidegger and the Grounds of the History of Being.* Translated by Reginald Lilly. Bloomington and Indianapolis: Indiana University Press, 1993.

Habermas, Jürgen. *Between Facts and Norms: Contributions to a Discourse Theory of Law and Democracy.* Translated by W. Rehg. Cambridge, MA: MIT Press, 1996.

Han, Béatrice. *Foucault's Critical Project: Between the Transcendental and the Historical.* Translated by Edward Pile. Stanford, CA: Stanford University Press, 2002.

Hassner, Pierre. *History of Political Philosophy.* 3rd ed. Edited by Leo Strauss and Joseph Cropsey. Chicago and London: Chicago University Press, 1987.

Hassner, Pierre, and G. W. F Hegel. *Phenomenology of Spirit.* Translated by A. V. Miller. Oxford, UK: Oxford University Press, 1977.

Hegel, G. W. F. *Aesthetics: Lectures on Fine Art.* Vol. 1. Translated by T. M. Knox. Oxford, UK: Clarendon Press, 1998.

Heidegger, Martin. *Being and Time.* Translated by John Macquarrie and Edward Robinson. Oxford, UK: Basil Blackwell, 1962.

———. *Discourse on Thinking: A Translation of Gelassenheit.* Translated by John M. Anderson and E. Hans Freund. San Francisco: Harper and Row, 1966.

———. *The End of Philosophy.* Translated by Joan Stambaugh. London: Souvenir Press, 1975.

———. *The Fundamental Concepts of Metaphysics: World, Finitude, Solitude.* Translated by William McNeill and N. Walker. Bloomington and Indianapolis: Indiana University Press, 1995. Cited as FCM.

———. *Identity and Difference.* Translated by Joan Stambaugh. New York: Harper and Row, 1969.

———. *An Introduction to Metaphysics.* Translated by R. Manheim. New Haven, CT: Yale University Press, 1959. Cited as IM.

———. *Kant and the Problem of Metaphysics.* 5th ed. Translated by Richard Taft. Bloomington and Indianapolis: Indiana University Press, 1997. Cited as KB.

———. *Nietzsche: Volumes I and II, The Will to Power as Art, The Eternal Recurrence of the Same.* Translated by David Farrell Krell. San Francisco: Harper and Row, 1979.

———. *On Time and Being.* Translated by Joan Stambaugh. New York: Harper and Row, 1972. Cited as OT&B.

———. *Pathmarks.* Edited by William McNeill. Cambridge, UK: Cambridge University Press, 1998.

———. *Poetry, Language, Thought.* Translated by Albert Hofstadter. New York: Harper and Row, 1971.

———. *The Question Concerning Technology and Other Essays.* Translated by W. Lovitt. New York: Harper and Row, 1977: 3–35. Cited as QCT.

———. *Schelling's Treatise on the Essence of Human Freedom.* Translated by Joan Stambaugh. Athens: Ohio University Press, 1985. Cited as SB.

———. 'The Self-Assertion of the German University." Translated by Karsten Harries. *Review of Metaphysics* 38 (March 1985): 470–80.

———. 'Technik und Kunst–Ge-stell.' In *Kunst und Technik.* Edited by Walter Bienel and Fredrich-Wilhelm von Herrmann. Frankfurt: Klostermann, 1989.

———. 'The Way to Language." In *On the Way to Language.* Translated by Joan Stambaugh. San Francisco: Harper and Row, 1982.

———. *What Is Called Thinking?* Translated by J. Glenn Gray. New York: Harper and Row, 1968. Cited as WIT.

Helfer, Martha B. *The Retreat of Representation: The Concept of Darstellung in German Critical Discourse.* Albany: State University of New York Press, 1996.

Henrich, Dieter. *Aesthetic Judgment and the Moral Image of the World.* Stanford, CA: Stanford University Press, 1992.

Höffe, Otfried. *Immanuel Kant.* Translated by Marshall Farrier. Albany: State University of New York Press, 1994.

———. 'Kant, morale et anthropologie.' In *Philosophie politique: revue internationale de philosophie politique.* Vol. 2, *Kant.* Paris: Presses Universitaires de France, 1992: 143–59.

Horstmann, R. 'Why Must There Be a Transcendental Deduction in Kant's *Critique of Judgment.*' In *Kant's Transcendental Deductions: The Three Critiques and the Opus Postumum,* edited by Eckart Forster. Stanford, CA: Stanford University Press, 1989: 157–76.

Janicaud, Dominique. *Powers of the Rational: Science, Technology and the Future of Thought.* Translated by Peg Birmingham and Elizabeth Birmingham. Bloomington and Indianapolis: Indiana University Press, 1994.

———. *The Shadow of That Thought: Heidegger and the Question of Politics.* Translated by Michael Gendre. Evanston, IL: Northwestern University Press, 1996.

Janicaud, Dominique, and Jean-François Mattéi. *Heidegger from Metaphysics to Thought.* Translated by Michael Gendre. Albany: State University of New York Press, 1995.

Jauss, Hans Robert. 'The Idealist Embarrassment: Observations on Marxist Aesthetics.' In *New Literary History,* Vol. 7 (1975–1976).

Kant, Immanuel. *Anthropology from a Pragmatic Point of View.* Translated by Victor Lyle Dowdell. Carbondale and Edwardsville: Southern Illinois University Press, 1978.

———. *Critique of Judgment.* Translated by Werner S. Pluhar. Indianapolis: Hackett, 1987. Cited as CJ.

———. *Critique of Practical Reason.* 3rd ed. Translated by Lewis White Beck. New York: Macmillan, 1993. Cited as CPrR.

———. *Critique of Pure Reason.* Translated by Werner S. Pluhar. Indianapolis: Hackett, 1996.

———. *The Metaphysics of Morals.* Edited and translated by Mary Gregor. Cambridge, UK: Cambridge University Press, 1996.

———. *Observations on the Feeling of the Beautiful and the Sublime.* Translated by J. T. Goldthwait. Berkeley: University of California Press, 1960.

———. *Perpetual Peace and Other Essays on Politics, History and Morals.* Translated by Ted Humphrey. Indianapolis: Hackett, 1983.

———. *The Prologomena.* Translated by P. Carus and J. W. Ellington. Indianapolis: Hackett, 1985.

———. *What Real Progress Has Metaphysics Made in Germany since the Time of Leibniz and Wolff?* Translated by Ted Humphrey. New York: Abaris Books, 1983.

Kofman, Sarah. 'The Economy of Respect: Kant and Respect for Women.' Translated by Nicola Fischer. In *Feminist Interpretations of Immanuel Kant,* edited by Robin May Schott. University Park: Pennyslvania State University Press, 1997.

———. *Socrate(s).* Paris: Éditions Galilée, 1989.

Krell, David Farrell. *Intimations of Mortality: Time, Truth, and Finitude in Heidegger's Thinking of Being.* University Park and London: Pennsylvania State University Press, 1986.

Lacoue-Labarthe, Philippe. *La fiction du politique: Heidegger, l'art et la politique.* Paris: C. Bourgois, 1987.

———. *Heidegger, Art and Politics: The Fiction of the Political.* Translated by Chris Turner. Oxford, UK and Cambridge, MA: Blackwell, 1990.

———. *Heidegger–la politique du poème.* Paris: Éditions Galilée, 2002.

———. 'Il Faut.' *Modern Language Notes* 107 (1992): 421–40.

———. *Musica Ficta (Figures of Wagner).* Translated by Felicia McCarren. Stanford, CA: Stanford University Press, 1994.

———. 'Oedipus as Figure.' *Radical Philosophy* 118 (March/April 2003): 7–17.

———. *Pasolini, une improvisation: d'une sainteté.* Bordeaux, Pharmacie de Platon: W. Blake, 1995.

———. *Poetique de l'histoire,* Paris: Éditions Galilée, 2002.

———. *Poetry as Experience.* Translated by Andrea Tarnowski. Stanford, CA: Stanford University Press, 1999. Cited as PEX.

———. *Rejouer le politique.* Paris: Galilée, 1981.

———. *Retrait de l'artiste, en deux personnes.* Lyon: MEM/Arte Facts: Frac Rhône-Alpes, 1985.

———. *Le retrait du politique.* Paris: Éditions Galilée, 1982.

———. *Typography: Mimesis, Philosophy, Politics.* Edited by Christopher Fynsk. Stanford, CA: Stanford University Press, 1998. Cited as TYP.

———. 'The Unpresentable.' In *The Subject of Philosophy.* Edited and translated by Thomas Tresize. Minneapolis: University of Minnesota Press, 1993: 116–59.

Lacoue-Labarthe, Philippe, and Peter Hallward. 'Stagings of Mimesis: An Interview.' *Angelaki: Journal of the Theoretical Humanities* 8, no. 2 (August 2003): 57–72.

Lacoue-Labarthe, Philippe, and Jean-Luc Nancy. *The Literary Absolute: The Theory of Literature in German Romanticism.* Translated by Phillip Barnard and Cheryl Lester. Albany: State University of New York Press, 1988. Cited as LA.

———. 'The Nazi Myth.' *Critical Inquiry* (Winter 1990): 291–312.

———. *Retreating the Political.* Edited by Simon Sparks. London and New York: Routledge, 1997.

———. 'Scène.' *Nouvelle revue de psychanalyse* 17 (1992): 73–98.

———. *The Title of the Letter: A Reading of Lacan.* Translated by François

Raffoul and David Pettigrew. Albany: State University of New York Press, 1992.

Le Doeuff, Michèle. *The Philosophical Imaginary.* Translated by Colin Gordon. Stanford, CA: Stanford University Press, 1989.

Longuenesse, Béatrice. *Kant and the Capacity to Judge: Sensibility and Discursivity in the Transcendental Analytic of the 'Critique of Pure Reason.'* Translated by Charles T. Wolfe. Princeton, NJ: Princeton University Press, 1998.

Luhmann, Niklas. *The Reality of the Mass Media.* Translated by Kathleen Cross. Stanford, CA: Stanford University Press: 1996.

Lyotard, Jean-François. *Discours, figure.* Paris: Klincksieck, 1971.

———. *Heidegger and 'the jews.'* Translated by Andreas Michel and Mark Roberts. Minneapolis and London: University of Minnesota Press, 1997.

———. *Lessons on the Analytic of the Sublime.* Stanford, CA: Stanford University Press, 1994.

———. 'The Sublime and the Avant-Garde.' In *The Lyotard Reader.* Edited by Andrew Benjamin. Cambridge, MA, and Oxford, UK: Basil Blackwell, 1989.

Markus, György. 'Changing Images of Science.' *Thesis 11*, no. 33 (1992): 1–56.

———. 'Culture: The Making and the Make-Up of a Concept (An Essay in Historical Semantics).' *Dialectical Anthropology* 18 (1993): 3–29.

Maus, Ingeborg. 'Liberties and Popular Sovereignty: On Jürgen Habermas's Reconstruction of the System of Rights.' *Cardozo Law Review* 17 (1996): 825–82.

McCloskey, Mary. *Kant's Aesthetic.* Albany: State University of New York Press, 1987.

McFarland, J. *Kant's Concept of Teleology.* Edinburgh: Edinburgh University Press, 1970.

Meld-Shell, Susan. *The Embodiment of Reason: Kant on Spirit, Generation and Community.* Chicago: University of Chicago Press, 1996.

Menninghaus, Winfried. *In Praise of Nonsense: Kant and Bluebeard.* Translated by Henry Pickford. Stanford, CA: Stanford University Press, 1999.

Merleau-Ponty, Maurice. *The Visible and the Invisible.* Translated by Alphonso Lingis, edited by Claude Lefort. Evanston, IL: Northwestern University Press, 1968.

Muglioni, Jean-Michel. *La philosophie de l'histoire de Kant: qu'est-ce que l'homme?* Paris: Presses Universitaires de France, 1993.

Müller-Sievers, Helmut. *Self-Generation: Biology, Philosophy, and Literature Around 1800.* Stanford, CA: Stanford University Press, 1997.

Nancy, Jean-Luc. *The Experience of Freedom.* Translated by Bridget McDonald. Stanford, CA: Stanford University Press, 1993. Cited as EF.

———. *The Gravity of Thought.* Translated by François Raffoul and Gregory Recco. Atlantic Highlands, NJ: Humanities Press, 1997. Cited as G.

———. *The Muses.* Translated by Peggy Kamuf. Stanford, CA: Stanford University Press, 1996. Cited as TM.

———. 'Of Being Singular Plural.' In *Being Singular Plural.* Translated by Robert

D. Richardson and Anne E. O'Byrne. Stanford, CA: Stanford University Press, 2000. Cited as BSP.

———. 'Our World: An Interview with Peter Hallward.' *Angelaki: Journal of the Theoretical Humanities* 8, no. 2 (August 2003): 43–54.

———. *Sans commune mésure: image et texte dans l'art actuel.* Paris: Editions Lèo Scheer, 2002.

———. *The Sense of the World.* Translated by Jeffrey S. Librett. Minneapolis: University of Minnesota Press, 1997. Cited as SW.

———. *Who Comes after the Subject? Essays by Jean-Luc Nancy et. al.* Edited by Eduardo Cadava, Peter Connor and Jean-Luc Nancy. New York: Routledge, 1991.

Nietzsche, Friedrich. *On the Genealogy of Morals.* Translated by Walter Kaufmann. New York: Random House, 1969.

———. *Twilight of the Idols.* In *The Portable Nietzsche.* Translated by Walter Kaufmann. New York: Penguin Books, 1976.

Offe, Claus. 'Bindings, Shackles, Brakes: On Self-Limitation Strategies.' In *Cultural-Political Interventions in the Unfinished Project of Enlightenment.* Edited by Axel Honneth et al., translated by Barbara Fultner. Cambridge, MA: MIT Press, 1992, 63–95.

Pickstone, John V. *Ways of Knowing: A New History of Science, Technology and Medicine.* Chicago: Chicago University Press, 2000.

Pöggeler, Otto. *Martin Heidegger's Path of Thinking.* Translated by Daniel Magurshak and Sigmund Barber. Atlantic Highlands, NJ: Humanities Press International, 1987.

———. *The Paths of Heidegger's Life and Thought.* Translated by John Bailiff. Atlantic Highlands, NJ: Humanities Press, 1997.

Raffoul, François. 'The Logic of the With: On Nancy's *Être Singulier Pluriel.*' *Studies in Practical Philosophy* 1, no. 1 (1999): 36–52.

———. 'On Otherness and Individuation in Heidegger.' *Man and World* 28 (1995): 341–58.

Rancière, Jacques. 'The Aesthetic Revolution and Its Outcomes: Emplotments of Autonomy and Heteronomy.' *New Left Review* 14 (March/April 2002): 133–51.

———. *The Flesh of Words: The Politics of Writing.* Translated by Charlotte Mandell. Stanford, CA: Stanford University Press, 2004.

———. 'Is There a Deleuzian Aesthetics?' *Qui Parle* 14, no. 2 (Spring/Summer, 2004): 1–14.

———. *The Politics of Aesthetics.* Translated by Gabriel Rockhill. London and New York: Continuum, 2004.

Reich, Klaus. *The Completeness of Kant's Table of Judgments.* Translated by Jane Kneller and Michael Losonsky. Stanford, CA: Stanford University Press, 1992.

Ross, Alison. 'Errant Beauty: Derrida and Kant on Aesthetic Presentation,' *International Studies in Philosophy* 33, no. 1 (2001): 87–104.

———. 'Historical Undecidability: The Kantian Background to Derrida's Politics.' *International Journal of Philosophical Studies* 12, no. 4 (December 2004): 375–93.

———. 'Introduction to Monique David-Ménard on Kant and Madness.' *Hypatia* 15, no. 4 (Fall 2000): 77–82.

———. 'Lyotard and the Politics of the Avant-Garde.' *Philosophy Today* 49, no. 2, (2005): 34–47.

Rousseau, Jean-Jacques. *The Social Contract.* Translated by Maurice Cranston. Harmondsworth: Penguin Books, 1987.

Schaeffer, Jean-Marie. *Art of the Modern Age: Philosophy of Art from Kant to Heidegger.* Translated by Steven Rendall. Princeton, NJ: Princeton University Press, 2000.

Schürmann, Reiner. *Heidegger on Being and Acting: From Principles to Anarchy.* Translated by Christine-Marie Gros. Bloomington and Indianapolis: Indiana University Press, 1987.

Seyhan, Azade. *Representation and Its Discontents: The Critical Legacy of German Romanticism.* Berkeley and Los Angeles: University of California Press, 1992.

Simon, Josef. 'Teleological Reflection and Causal Determination.' In *Contemporary German Philosophy.* Vol. 3. London: Pennyslvania State University Press, 1983, 121–40.

Sloterdijk, Peter. *Critique of Cynical Reason.* Translated by Michael Eldred. Minneapolis and London: University of Minnesota Press, 1987.

Stiegler, Bernard. *Technics and Time, 1: The Fault of Epimetheus.* Translated by Richard Beardsworth and George Collins. Stanford, CA: Stanford University Press, 1998.

Taminiaux, Jacques. *Heidegger and the Project of Fundamental Ontology.* Translated by Michael Gendre. Albany: State University of New York Press, 1991.

———. *Poetics, Speculation and Judgment: The Shadow of the Work of Art from Kant to Phenomenology.* Translated and edited by Michael Gendre. Albany: State University of New York Press, 1993.

Todorov, Tzvetan. *Theories of the Symbol.* Translated by Catherine Porter. Ithaca, NY: Cornell University Press, 1982.

Van de Pitte, Frederick P. 'Introduction.' *Anthropology from a Pragmatic Point of View.* Carbondale and Edwardsville: Southern Illinois University Press, 1978.

Vattimo, Gianni. *The End of Modernity: Nihilism and Hermeneutics in Post-modern Culture.* Translated by Jon R. Snyder. Cambridge, UK: Polity Press, 1988.

Wright, Kathleen. 'The Place of the Work of Art in the Age of Technology.' *Southern Journal of Philosophy* 22, no. 1 (Spring 1984): 565–82.

Yovel, Yiarmiahu. *Kant and the Philosophy of History.* Princeton, NJ: Princeton University Press, 1980.

Zammito, John. *The Genesis of Kant's Critique of Judgment.* Chicago and London: University of Chicago Press, 1992.

Zanetti, Véronique. 'Teleology and the Freedom of the Self.' In *The Modern*

*Subject: Conceptions of the Self in Classical German Philosophy.* Edited by Karl Ameriks and Dieter Sturma. Albany: State University of New York Press, 1995.

Ziarek, Krzysztof. 'After Aesthetics: Heidegger and Benjamin on Art and Experience.' *Philosophy Today.* 41, no. 1 (Spring 1997): 199–208.

———. *The Force of Art.* Stanford, CA: Stanford University Press, 2004.

———. *The Historicity of Experience: Modernity, the Avant-Garde and the Event.* Evanston, IL: Northwestern University Press, 2001.

———. 'Powers to Be: Art and Technology in Heidegger and Foucault.' *Research in Phenomenology* 28 (1998): 162–94.

# Index

absolute, the, 78; literary, 78, 82, 84, 88, 112

Adorno, Theodor W., 6

aesthetic attitude, 1, 4, 15; analogical mechanism of, 15; structure of, 16

aesthetic experience, 61, 87

aesthetic image, 42

aesthetic judgment: detachment of, 15; and determinative judgment, 21; and logical reflective judgment, 21

aesthetic moment, 122

aesthetics, 101, 122, 128–29; modern philosophical, 91, 97–98; philosophical, 134

affect, 149, 152

affectability, 149–51, 156, 159; of the senses, 137, 143

Agamben, G., 195n16

*aletheia*, 96. *See also* truth

analogy, 28–29

anthropology, 38; pragmatic (in Kant), 39, 51, 53

*Anthropology from a Pragmatic Point of View*, 177–78nn2,3

anxiety: toward death, 124–25

aporia, 139; of epochal thinking, 189n16

appearance, 113, 142, 146

appropriation (in Heidegger), 91, 94. *See also* event, the/*Ereignis*

art, 27, 44, 67–68, 90–92, 98, 103, 105, 136–37, 151–57, 160, 200n45; distinction between nature and, 31; synthetic category of, 39; and technology, 63, 101; aesthetic subjectivisation of, 67; post-aesthetic, 93; as counter-image to technology, 102; modern, 103–4; theatrical, 121; essence of, 128. *See also techne*

arts, the, 154, 157

artwork, the, 94, 96–97, 103, 105, 137, 153, 158–59; the work of, 98; critique of the status of, 197n25. *See also specific works*

Bachelard, G., 100

beautiful, the (in Kant), 100, 119; the shining of, 97; significance of, 131

beauty (in Kant), 25; and the moral idea, 23; and teleological judgment, 23; natural, 29, 176n25

beginning (in Heidegger), 126; another, 196n19. *See also* step back, the (in Heidegger)

being, 63, 105, 143; historicality of, 62; experience of, 64, 68, 75; oblivion of 64, 86; saying of, 64–65; forgetting of, 65; meaning of, 66, 86–87; occurrence of, 66, 73; refusal of, 72, 96; the Greek conception of, as presencing, 74; history of, 75; as representation, 75; as a valorising will, 81; jointure of, 82; as an occurrence in philosophy, 85; thinking of, 85; as disclosive questioning, 88; forgetfulness of, 88; relation to, 94; epochal understanding of, 100, 104, 107; truth of, 100; call of,

107; of beings, 125; primordial disclosure of, 126. *See also* question of being, the
*Being and Time*, 62, 64, 66, 69, 86, 155
being-in-common (in Nancy), 135, 142–43, 213n22
Beistegui, M. de, 93, 195n17
Bernstein, J., 171n3, 194n1, 200n45
*Bildung*, 117
Blumenberg, H., 169n3, 180n13
body, the: erotics of 150
Böhrer, K. H., 7

calculative thinking, 76, 105
capital, 144–48, 162, 213n22
Caygill, H., 155
Celan, P., 119, 130–32
Chalier, C., 179n9
charm, 33–34
civilization, 33; and culture, 176n27
clearing (in Heidegger), 72, 97; double, of truth, 96
co-appearing (in Nancy): presentation as, 137; network of, 143; ontology of, 143; relations of, 144. *See also* social being (in Nancy)
co-belonging, 150
coming to presence (in Nancy), 141, 146, 152, 159–60, 213n22; ontological relations of, 147; social ontology of, 149; fractal, 161
community, 148
concealment: of being, 73, 85
constitutional republic, 47–48, 182n21
critical theory, 147–48
*Critique of Judgment*, 1–5, 16–17, 26–27, 79, 81, 171n5; the importance of, in recent French philosophy, 172n6; in Kant's philosophical system, 174–75n17
*Critique of Pure Reason*, 70, 84; the B version of, 71
culture, 33–36; moral conception of, 40; of skill and discipline, 46; moral 51

*Dasein*, 66, 124–25, 155; historical destiny of, 126
Debord, G., 145
Deleuze, G., 23, 204n18, 216n2
Derrida, J., 6, 34–35, 38, 109–11, 170n12, 175n20, 178n6, 189n16, 206n22
Descartes, R., 69, 75, 77–78
destining (in Heidegger), 86; of being 65, 76, 88; of the oblivion of being, 89
disappropriation (in Lacoue-Labarthe), 115, 147; and theatricality, 123; mimetological, 128; of identity, 147
double concealing (in Heidegger), 65
dualism, 86

earth, the (in Heidegger), 96–97
education: moral, 56
essence, 139, 142
ethico-teleology (in Kant), 45
event, the/*Ereignis*, 75, 91, 199n35
everyday, the, 136
examples: the role of, 55–58
exception, the, 159
existence, 152; as transcendence, 72; philosophizing, 124
experience, 64, 119; of being, 89, 115; of strife, 96; of the call of being, 107; of meaning, 131–33, 149, 165–67

fanaticism, 57
fiction, 114, 127; of subjectivity, 115; of origins, 117; proximity of truth and, in philosophy, 204–5n19; good and bad, 205n19
figuration, 127; exigency of, 154
figure, 115–16, 120, 123; aesthetic, 42, 128; and identity, 114
fine arts, the, 29
finitude, 71, 83; of the subject, 70
forgetfulness (in Heidegger), 101
Foucault. M., 183n25, 207n29
fractality, 157
Fynsk, C., 190n26

*Gelassenheit*, 140–41
*Gestell*, 68, 86, 100–105, 135; epoch of, 90–94, 137, 144, 156, 161–62, 198nn34,35; ordering of, 99
Greeks, the, 65, 74–75, 115, 127, 135
Grondin, J., 64, 190n28

Habermas, J., 7
happiness, 35
Hegel, G., 88, 121–22
Heidegger, M., 3, 8, 16, 38, 61–107, 113–15, 117, 119, 121–22, 124, 135, 140, 151–52, 156–59, 191n39, 192n47
historicisation: of human being, 66; of human persons, 72; of the way things are, 103; of constitutive relations, 107; of the question of meaning of being, 201n51
history, 49, 65; historiality of, 138
history of philosophy, 63, 65, 73, 76, 84–85, 101, 138, 161

idea of criticism, 113
Idealism: German, 17, 74–78, 80–81, 84
ideas of reason (in Kant), 61–62, 75, 77–81, 84
identification: political, 127–28
identity, 114–15; aporetic structure of, 114; political, 115–16; national, 118
imitation: mythic, 115; logic of, 118
impropriety (in Lacoue-Labarthe): 114, 116; of mimesis, 122; mimetic, 204n15

Janicaud, D., 193n49
judgment, the faculty of, 4

Kant, I., 1–3, 15–60, 68–74, 77–80, 83, 85, 118, 125–27, 141; and authentic philosophizing, 191n33
*Kant and the Problem of Metaphysics*, 66, 73
knowledge, 83; of the ideas, 82; sensuous, 82; absolute, 83–84; historical, 85
Kofman, S., 184n34

Lacan, J., 115–16, 136
Lacoue-Labarthe, Ph., 9, 109–33, 207n29
Language, 129–32
Le Doeuff, M., 185n39, 205n19
literature, 112; auto-production of, 112; Romantics' conception of, 113, 119, 136

Marx, K., 7
materiality, 118; of ideas, 112; of meaning, 132
meaning, 114, 129, 142, 144; experience of, 118–19; originary, 134; withdrawal of, 134, 140; signified, 140; accessibility of, 141; exteriorization of 148; coming of, 150. *See also* sense; signification
Menninghaus, W., 174n15
metaphysics, 64, 124–26; modern, 65, 75, 77, 80–81, 84, 101; as the history of being, 67, 76, 86; ground of, 70–73; history of, 73–74, 138; as representation, 77; essential nature of, 102
mimesis, 109–13; and being, 114; originary, 114–15, 121, 126, 203n15; Heideggerian, 115; in philosophy, 116; topic of, in philosophy, 116; and presentation, 119–20
mimetic act, 125
mimetic identification, 111, 118–19
mimetic logic, 125
mimetic relations, 114
mimetology, 111, 124; political, 121; original, 127
*Mitsein*, 155
modern age, the, 77, 80
modesty, 53
moral action, 40; formal conditions of possibility of, 41
moral character: aesthetic stylization of, 59
moral feeling, 27, 53, 183n28
moral idea, the, 29, 48
moral law, the, 50
moral man, the, 53; as an aesthetic image, 42, 54; the idea of, 42
morality, 35, 179n9
myth, 116

Nancy, J.-L., 10, 134–63
nature: the idea of, as a system of ends,
    39, 46; and history, 40; mechanistic
    and teleological explanations of, 44;
    the ultimate purpose of, 50; and art in
    Kant, 180–81n16
Nietzsche, F., 16, 75, 80–81, 113–14, 139
nihilism, 149

object, 82–83
ontology, 127, 134–35, 137–39, 142, 144,
    146, 153, 157, 161; destruction of, 69;
    fundamental, 73, 124; of sense, 136
ordinary, the, 159–62
organic order, 26
origin(s), 117, 142
*Origin of the Work of Art*, 67, 91, 95
outside: relation to, 83

phenomenology, 69, 135, 141
philosophy, 63, 84, 87, 112; thinking of
    being in, 74; Cartesian, 77; modern,
    77, 137; Hegelian, 116; Greek, 125; and
    philosophizing, 125; classical political,
    146
physico-teleology (in Kant), 45
Plato, 76–77
*Plato's Doctrine of Truth*, 2, 191n39
pleasure: feeling of, 21; aesthetic, 22, 33;
    source of aesthetic, 30; and our power
    of judgment, 36; ontological rehabili-
    tation of, 152
poetic experience of yearning, 120,
    130–33
poetic writing, 112, 119
Pöggler, O., 64, 190n28
*poiesis*, 92, 100–101, 198n34
political, the, 118–20
politics, 49, 123, 207n29; modern, 119;
    and literature, 120
Postulates, the (in Kant), 43, 50; and sen-
    sible forms, 49
praxis: of sense-making, 136–37, 156, 159,
    161; ethics of, 139; of sense, 152
prepositions, 142

presentation, 1, 61, 78, 87, 94, 113, 118,
    165–66; distinction between repre-
    sentation and, 3; problem of, 4, 8–9,
    70, 81–83, 85, 151; aesthetic, 5, 26, 32,
    121; of reason's ideas, 5, 17, 23;
    schematic and symbolic, 24; analogi-
    cal, 28, 79; aesthetic, of beauty, 29;
    in *Critique of Teleological Judgment*,
    39; aesthetic, of ideas, 40; of the idea
    of progress, 49; question of, 76, 134;
    questioning relation to, 88; the work
    of, 97; relations of, 98–100, 103–5,
    107; and mimesis, 112; sensuous, 122;
    of identity, 127; originary mimetic,
    128; and poetic experience of yearn-
    ing, 130–31; presentation of, 136, 153;
    as a question, 140; of meaning, 141;
    of the genesis of meaning, 158; and
    characterization (in Kant), 176n24;
    moral problematic of aesthetic,
    187n47
purposiveness, 5, 44–45; formal, 24;
    contingent, of nature, 31; intrinsic,
    181n16

*Question Concerning Technology*, 90–92,
    99
question of being, the, 72, 76, 86, 91, 94,
    104, 117, 122, 126, 134. *See also* being
questioning: disclosive, 65, 74, 88

Raffoul, F., 155
reason: and taste, 35; interest of, 36; syn-
    thesizing interests of theoretical, 45;
    Kantian conception of, 79; representa-
    tions of, 82; Kant's faith in, 192n47
referential ideality (in Nancy), 136, 141,
    144
reflective judgment, 45
representation, 98; for a subject, 76; as
    subject, 145. *See also* presentation
revealing (in Heidegger), 99, 101
Romanticism, 17, 42, 74–75, 119, 157
Romantics: Jena, 112; literature in, 121
Rousseau, J.-J., 118, 121, 145

saying, the (in Heidegger), 64–65,
86–87, 89; of recollective thinking, 88;
of being, 91
Schaeffer, J.-M., 171n2
Schelling, F., 74–75
Schematism, the doctrine of (in Kant), 19
Schiller, F., 7
sense: generativity of, 136, 142; *poiesis* of,
136; systems of, 138; ; of the world,
138; source of 148; eroticisation of,
150; origin of, 151–52
sensible figure, 23
sensible forms, 49, 132; aesthetic force of,
118; presentation of ideas in, 120; and
intelligible ideas, 122
*sensus communis*, 20, 34–35; aesthetic,
32–33
signification, 139, 153; systems of, 140,
145; and meaning, 150
sociability, 34
social being (in Nancy), 145–47; question
of 138
social criticism, 146–47; Marxist and
post-Marxist, 145
sociality, 146
spectacle, the, 146; in political philosophy, 145; society of, 146
Spinoza, B., 78
step back, the (in Heidegger), 65, 89,
101–2, 138; to another beginning, 75
Stiegler, B., 195n16
subject, the, 71, 75, 77, 80, 83–84, 115,
117, 128, 149; transcendental, 70; of
representation, 72; representations of,
77; finite, 82; mimetic deconstitution
of, 116, 120
sublime, 25–26, 51, 53, 185n35
supersensible, the, 44
symbolic, the, 153
symbolic hypotyposis, 28
system, 45, 75–77, 79–80, 84; idea of, 78

Taminiaux, J., 171n2
taste, the judgment of, 21, 25, 29,
183–84n29; and cognition, 19–20

*techne*, 92, 119
technology, 86, 90–91, 196n19, 199n36;
and art, 63; epoch of, 68, 93, 138;
essence of, 91–94, 99–100; as mode of
presentation, 95; modern, 101; framework of, 102; as *techne*, 104; as *poiesis*,
147; and classical philosophy of science, 200n47
teleological judgment, 23
teleology, 25–26
theatre, 121, 203n15
theory: and literature, 112
touch, 151
transcendence, 142; finite, 124; structure
of, 126–27
transcendental imagination, the, 67,
70–73, 78
truth, 94, 105, 137, 153; of beings, 96,
98; double concealing of, 96;
Heidegger's combative conception
of, 96; as *aletheia*, 97; scientific,
97
turn, the (in Heidegger), 64, 72

uncanny, the, 97–98
unconcealing, the: of beings, 97, 126
understanding, the (in Kant), 71

van Gogh, V., 67, 96, 98, 103
Vattimo, G., 194n2
violence, 48, 50

what is, 61, 63, 68, 70–72, 85, 99–103,
124; historical semantics of, 66; totality of, 126
will, the, 78; to system, 80; to presentation, 141
willing, 77
work, the (in Heidegger), 96; dual struggle of, 97; of the artwork, 160. *See also*
artwork, the
world, 96–97, 103, 124, 126
Wright, K., 93

Ziarek, K., 92, 194n2

# Cultural Memory in the Present

Alison Ross, *The Aesthetic Paths of Philosophy: Presentation in Kant, Heidegger, Lacoue-Labarthe, and Nancy*

Gerard Richter, *Thought-Images: Frankfurt School Writers Reflection from Damaged Life*

Bella Brodzki, *Can These Bones Live?: Translation, Survival, and Cultural Memory*

Rodolphe Gasché, *The Honor of Thinking: Critique, Theory, Philosophy*

Brigitte Peucker, *The Material Image: Art and the Real in Film*

Natalie Melas, *All the Difference in the World*

Jonathan Culler, *The Literary in Theory*

Jennifer A. Jordan, *Structures of Memory*

Christoph Menke, *Reflections of Equality*

Marlène Zarader, *The Unthought Debt: Heidegger and the Hebraic Heritage*

Jan Assmann, *Religion and Cultural Memory: Ten Studies*

David Scott and Charles Hirschkind, *Powers of the Secular Modern: Talal Asad and his Interlocutors*

Gyanendra Pandey, *Routine Violence: Nations, Fragments, Histories*

James Siegel, *Naming the Witch*

J. M. Bernstein, *Against Voluptuous Bodies: Late Modernism and the Meaning of Painting*

Theodore W. Jennings, Jr., *Reading Derrida / Thinking Paul: On Justice*

Richard Rorty and Eduardo Mendieta, *Take Care of Freedom and Truth Will Take Care of Itself: Interviews with Richard Rorty*

Jacques Derrida, *Paper Machine*

Renaud Barbaras, *Desire and Distance: Introduction to a Phenomenology of Perception*

Jill Bennett, *Empathic Vision: Affect, Trauma, and Contemporary Art*

Ban Wang, *Illuminations from the Past: Trauma, Memory, and History in Modern China*

James Phillips, *Heidegger's Volk: Between National Socialism and Poetry*

Frank Ankersmit, *Sublime Historical Experience*

István Rév, *Retroactive Justice: Prehistory of Post-Communism*

Paola Marrati, *Genesis and Trace: Derrida Reading Husserl and Heidegger*

Krzysztof Ziarek, *The Force of Art*

Marie-José Mondzain, *Image, Icon, Economy: The Byzantine Origins of the Contemporary Imaginary*

Cecilia Sjöholm, *The Antigone Complex: Ethics and the Invention of Feminine Desire*

Jacques Derrida and Elisabeth Roudinesco, *For What Tomorrow . . . : A Dialogue*

Elisabeth Weber, *Questioning Judaism: Interviews by Elisabeth Weber*

Jacques Derrida and Catherine Malabou, *Counterpath: Traveling with Jacques Derrida*

Martin Seel, *Aesthetics of Appearing*

Nanette Salomon, *Shifting Priorities: Gender and Genre in Seventeenth-Century Dutch Painting*

Jacob Taubes, *The Political Theology of Paul*

Jean-Luc Marion, *The Crossing of the Visible*

Eric Michaud, *The Cult of Art in Nazi Germany*

Anne Freadman, *The Machinery of Talk: Charles Peirce and the Sign Hypothesis*

Stanley Cavell, *Emerson's Transcendental Etudes*

Stuart McLean, *The Event and its Terrors: Ireland, Famine, Modernity*

Beate Rössler, ed., *Privacies: Philosophical Evaluations*

Bernard Faure, *Double Exposure: Cutting Across Buddhist and Western Discourses*

Alessia Ricciardi, *The Ends Of Mourning: Psychoanalysis, Literature, Film*

Alain Badiou, *Saint Paul: The Foundation of Universalism*

Gil Anidjar, *The Jew, the Arab: A History of the Enemy*

Jonathan Culler and Kevin Lamb, eds., *Just Being Difficult? Academic Writing in the Public Arena*

Jean-Luc Nancy, *A Finite Thinking*, edited by Simon Sparks

Theodor W. Adorno, *Can One Live after Auschwitz? A Philosophical Reader*, edited by Rolf Tiedemann

Patricia Pisters, *The Matrix of Visual Culture: Working with Deleuze in Film Theory*

Andreas Huyssen, *Present Pasts: Urban Palimpsests and the Politics of Memory*

Talal Asad, *Formations of the Secular: Christianity, Islam, Modernity*

Dorothea von Mücke, *The Rise of the Fantastic Tale*

Marc Redfield, *The Politics of Aesthetics: Nationalism, Gender, Romanticism*

Emmanuel Levinas, *On Escape*

Dan Zahavi, *Husserl's Phenomenology*

Rodolphe Gasché, *The Idea of Form: Rethinking Kant's Aesthetics*

Michael Naas, *Taking on the Tradition: Jacques Derrida and the Legacies of Deconstruction*

Herlinde Pauer-Studer, ed., *Constructions of Practical Reason: Interviews on Moral and Political Philosophy*

Jean-Luc Marion, *Being Given That: Toward a Phenomenology of Givenness*

Theodor W. Adorno and Max Horkheimer, *Dialectic of Enlightenment*

Ian Balfour, *The Rhetoric of Romantic Prophecy*

Martin Stokhof, *World and Life as One: Ethics and Ontology in Wittgenstein's Early Thought*

Gianni Vattimo, *Nietzsche: An Introduction*

Jacques Derrida, *Negotiations: Interventions and Interviews, 1971–1998*, ed. Elizabeth Rottenberg

Brett Levinson, *The Ends of Literature: The Latin American 'Boom" in the Neoliberal Marketplace*

Timothy J. Reiss, *Against Autonomy: Cultural Instruments, Mutualities, and the Fictive Imagination*

Hent de Vries and Samuel Weber, eds., *Religion and Media*

Niklas Luhmann, *Theories of Distinction: Re-Describing the Descriptions of Modernity*, ed. and introd. William Rasch

Johannes Fabian, *Anthropology with an Attitude: Critical Essays*

Michel Henry, *I am the Truth: Toward a Philosophy of Christianity*

Gil Anidjar, *"Our Place in Al-Andalus": Kabbalah, Philosophy, Literature in Arab-Jewish Letters*

Hélène Cixous and Jacques Derrida, *Veils*

F. R. Ankersmit, *Historical Representation*

F. R. Ankersmit, *Political Representation*

Elissa Marder, *Dead Time: Temporal Disorders in the Wake of Modernity (Baudelaire and Flaubert)*

Reinhart Koselleck, *The Practice of Conceptual History: Timing History, Spacing Concepts*

Niklas Luhmann, *The Reality of the Mass Media*

Hubert Damisch, *A Childhood Memory by Piero della Francesca*

Hubert Damisch, *A Theory of /Cloud/: Toward a History of Painting*

Jean-Luc Nancy, *The Speculative Remark: (One of Hegel's bon mots)*

Jean-François Lyotard, *Soundproof Room: Malraux's Anti-Aesthetics*

Jan Patočka, *Plato and Europe*

Hubert Damisch, *Skyline: The Narcissistic City*

Isabel Hoving, *In Praise of New Travelers: Reading Caribbean Migrant Women Writers*

Richard Rand, ed., *Futures: Of Jacques Derrida*

William Rasch, *Niklas Luhmann's Modernity: The Paradoxes of Differentiation*

Jacques Derrida and Anne Dufourmantelle, *Of Hospitality*

Jean-François Lyotard, *The Confession of Augustine*

Kaja Silverman, *World Spectators*

Samuel Weber, *Institution and Interpretation: Expanded Edition*

Jeffrey S. Librett, *The Rhetoric of Cultural Dialogue: Jews and Germans in the Epoch of Emancipation*

Ulrich Baer, *Remnants of Song: Trauma and the Experience of Modernity in Charles Baudelaire and Paul Celan*

Samuel C. Wheeler III, *Deconstruction as Analytic Philosophy*

David S. Ferris, *Silent Urns: Romanticism, Hellenism, Modernity*

Rodolphe Gasché, *Of Minimal Things: Studies on the Notion of Relation*

Sarah Winter, *Freud and the Institution of Psychoanalytic Knowledge*

Samuel Weber, *The Legend of Freud: Expanded Edition*

Aris Fioretos, ed., *The Solid Letter: Readings of Friedrich Hölderlin*

J. Hillis Miller / Manuel Asensi, *Black Holes / J. Hillis Miller; or, Boustrophedonic Reading*

Miryam Sas, *Fault Lines: Cultural Memory and Japanese Surrealism*

Peter Schwenger, *Fantasm and Fiction: On Textual Envisioning*

Didier Maleuvre, *Museum Memories: History, Technology, Art*

Jacques Derrida, *Monolingualism of the Other; or, The Prosthesis of Origin*

Andrew Baruch Wachtel, *Making a Nation, Breaking a Nation: Literature and Cultural Politics in Yugoslavia*

Niklas Luhmann, *Love as Passion: The Codification of Intimacy*

Mieke Bal, ed., *The Practice of Cultural Analysis: Exposing Interdisciplinary Interpretation*

Jacques Derrida and Gianni Vattimo, eds., *Religion*

THE AESTHETIC PATHS OF PHILOSOPHY